The Healthcare Management Handbook

THIRD EDITION

Consultant

Editors:

Keith Holdaway

& Helen Kogan

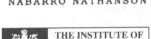

NABARRO NATHANSON

THE INSTITUTE OF
HEALTH SERVICES
MANAGEMENT

Better Management • Better Health

Published in association with The Institute of Health Services Management

**KOGAN
PAGE**

First published in 1995
This (third) edition published in 1998

Kogan Page Ltd
120 Pentonville Road
London N1 9JN

British Library Cataloguing in Publication Data

ISBN 0 7494 25539

Typeset by BookEns Ltd, Royston, Herts.
Printed and bound by Bell and Bain Ltd., Glasgow

Thinking about an Employee Assistance Programme?

Take the next step before he does.

Things don't have to get ***this*** bad before the pressures of modern life have a serious effect on employees and their performance.

All kinds of stress and anxiety can lead to business problems like reduced productivity, increased sickness absence and accidents at work.

BUPA Wellbeing is an Employee Assistance Programme providing confidential counselling and expert advice to your staff and their families – 24 hours a day, 365 days a year.

A little investment on your part can secure a lot of peace of mind for your people – and that could mean significant financial benefits for your business.

The next step is a small one:
call BUPA free on 0800 616 029, or fax us on 0171 656 2716
to find out more about this and other BUPA health care services.

His healthcare claim should be the last thing on his mind.

One call should settle the claim.

If you don't concentrate on your job there's a good chance that you'll make a mistake - like missing out on a Corporate Policy from Norwich Union Healthcare. One thing which makes us different is our Active Claims Management System - a system that allows many of your staff's claims to be authorised within a 15 minute phone call (and without any paperwork). Leaving your staff free to concentrate on more important things. For more information call Norwich Union Healthcare on

NORWICH UNION

0870 9001021

| INSURANCE | INVESTMENTS | No one protects more. | HEALTHCARE | PENSIONS |

Contents

Whether you need emergency care or preventative advice, consult the practice that delivers.

Foreword

Karen Caines

In introducing this edition of *The Healthcare Management Handbook*, it is difficult to know where to start: so much change in so little time! The Government's proposals for the NHS may be less radical than in some other areas of social welfare, at least as far as essential principles are concerned — we will still have an NHS, largely funded out of general taxation, largely free at the point of delivery. But even so, there will still be a huge agenda for change: change in structures, change in partners, change in the shift of focus from healthcare to health. Managers need to understand the proposals for the new NHS if they are to make it modern and dependable. And for those who want to keep a UK wide perspective, understanding the profound differences between the proposed structures in the different nations is no mean feat. I believe *The Healthcare Management Handbook* will be an invaluable guide for getting to grips with the new terminology and organisations.

Managers will greet the new NHS with a range of opinions. Inevitably, there are fears and concerns as well as excitement about the challenges. The existing burden on managers should not be underestimated. The perennial problems of matching resources to needs, of rising waiting lists, and of changing and inadequate priorities remain. On top of this, managers must embrace new ways of collaborative working and make serious inroads on the quality agenda. With mergers, structural reforms and denigration of NHS management looming large, it is not surprising to find insecurity and trepidation at the coalface.

And as we celebrate the fiftieth anniversary of the NHS, it is a good time to look ahead. Today's NHS has access to new tools and technology beyond the imagination of the NHS fifty years ago. How do we make the most of research into clinical and cost effectiveness? How can we apply the new technology, particularly information technology, to best effect? And how do we ensure that we have tackled the ethical issues which go hand in hand with these changes? I hope you find some of the answers, and perhaps other thought-provoking questions, when reading this book.

I have no hesitation recommending this book to you. I hope you find it valuable in coping with the exciting and daunting challenges ahead.

Karen Caines
Director, IHSM

Introduction

Keith Holdaway

I don't normally read introductions myself. The exception is probably when I am leafing through a book wondering what is in it and whether to spend some time or money on it. So that's how I imagine you at this moment, busy, with enough reading matter back at your desk to keep you going for months, yet interested enough in what is going on just to check the book out. It is full of practical advice on how to approach current problems in healthcare management and our readers tell us, they are surprised by how often they refer to it. There is policy analysis to help consider where it's all leading and reference material for addresses and contacts.

We have tried to ensure that the book flows from chapter to chapter to provide a logical structure but we have impressed on all contributors that the book is for 'dipping into' so that each part is self contained, reasonably short and easy to read.

This, third, edition coincides with the NHS's 50th anniversary and with the launch of a series of Green and White Papers by a new government keen to make an impact on health and healthcare throughout the UK. Yet we have resisted the temptation to lead with a batch of self congratulatory prose. Rather, we have invited some working mangers (and yes, a few well known names) to reflect on what it all means for us in the NHS. Brian Edwards sets the historical context of change with a brief (almost headlong) history in **50 Years of the NHS** showing how historical pressures have brought about continuing change and a growing sense of being a 'business' with objectives and obligations to high quality service. Karen Caines surveys the current political position in **The White Paper on the New NHS** whilst a series of contributions look at the Green Papers relating to **Wales, Northern Ireland** and **Scotland**. It is often hard to know just what you've got until you compare it with others and the health service is no exception. Howard Lyon's frequently light hearted look at **Healthcare Management – An International Perspective** shows me some of our strengths and issues a warning not to be complacent nor to be too confident in applying what works in the UK to other countries, with different practices and expectations.

If we expect the medics to have evidence-based medicine we should make sure that, as managers we have **Evidence-based Management**, or so the argument goes. Peter Homa, probably best known for leading work on business process re-engineering at Leicester and now 'waiting list supremo', clearly agrees and provides a framework for ensuring that the necessary systems exist to identify, carry out and learn from management research in NHS organisations. His article is not a collection of whiz-bang examples of how he saved £x million by the application of fourier analysis to waiting lists or 'grant applications made simple'. Instead it is a detailed analysis of process, a challenging but thought-provoking paper. Brian Aird adds to the debate on **Ethical Management** with a discussion on the necessary balance between enacting policy and working within a set of values relevant to healthcare.

Primary Care Partnerships by Robert Sloane takes the pragmatic (and politically fashionable) line that what counts is what works. What works is a case study of such a partnership in Andover. Check out for yourself the improvements to services he describes.

Why Aren't We Waiting? Stephen Day and David Lye give some pointers on how best to spend your share of waiting list initiative money to best effect. How many names have you got stuck in administrative cul-de-sacs?

Roy Lilley has developed a distinctive voice, asking difficult questions (comparatively easy to do) but then proposing answers which are often radical. In this book he turns his attention to **Mergers** arguing that if they don't improve services to patients then forget them, because they are unlikely to deliver anything else of value. For those of you involved in merger mania, Roy has been through it and emerged with credit. Read his observations and you could too. **Risk Assessment** is far more than the process of protecting NHS organisations from being sued. It is central to the well-being of patients by reducing the risk of adverse outcomes, and to NHS staff whose self confidence and professional life are threatened by clinical accidents.

Many managers don't like to admit it but the competitive habit was picked up with striking alacrity in the NHS (as if anyone believed that it was never there) and unlearning the habit may prove a little difficult for some. Suzanne Tyler examines what there is to be gained in her contribution **Learning to Collaborate**, she describes ways to involve individuals and other agencies to provide the patient's perception of th service and what is needed. The revised complaints procedure does not seem to have attracted the kind of bad publicity that some of the merchants of doom were predicting when it was introduced. Some of the deadlines and the resource demands are difficult to live with but in general we seem to be coping. Derek Day explains how to make **Handling Complaints** as painless as possible and, perhaps more importantly, how to obtain the greatest learning from the process. Hazel Brand makes the secret art of spin doctoring and **Press Relations** seem, well, quite straightforward really. Her ideas for getting your retaliation in first and cultivating local, hard pressed, journalists have been taken up by several people who have read them.

Speaking of secret arts the Private Finance Initiative seems here to stay; in **PFI Watch** Richard Meara describes some of the policy which forms the background to the initiative. For those who read Alan Gibb's article in the second edition, the PFI financed energy centre is now half built and the new entrance is open; proof that it can and does work. For those who agree that the PFI is 'clumsy and cumbersome' it was bad news that the Government embraced it so wholeheartedly; the good news is that they have slimmed it down so it should just work. David Anderson goes into the detail of **PFI Procurement; Managing the Legal Process** with a step by step description of what to do and how.

Anne-Toni Rodgers and Maureen Devlin provide an introduction to **Business Planning** which describes both the content of the final product and a route map to produce it. This is not a document for the corporate level planner but for middle managers new to the process (however, corporate planners might just want to sneak a look to see what the rest of us are up to).

Keith Pollard has written what, to me, must be the clearest and most useful guide to the Internet available. In **Can You Afford to Ignore the Internet?** he tells us where to look, what we will find and what use we can make of the material. The direct style and clarity of the title is carried right on through the text to the end. If you can't surf the net (or, like Tony Blair think that the Internet is an Italian football team's target) then this is the place to start; if you can surf I guarantee you will still find useful guidance and advice. To many managers the idea of **Information for Patients** is a little threatening or at least an inconvenience. Bob Gann explains in his article how to get the maximum benefit for patient and for the service from the legislation and best practice. Peter Cochrane indulges in some future watching when he examines how **Healthcare On-line** may transform the working practices of various parts of the health service through widespread application of current technology and the likely improvements we will see in the near future.

My own chapter **New Skills for a New NHS** could be sub-titled

'Give up trying and be happy'. I advance the argument that people are only willing to undertake difficult training when they are convinced it will be of benefit. Since it is not possible to predict the future with any real confidence it requires a strong act of will to undertake training before it is clearly needed. I believe that it is better to concentrate on becoming really good at your current job and being prepared and ready to work to learn new things as they come along. Miranda Coates in **CPD for Managers** gives good advice on how to do just this and how to make things happen so as not to become purely reactive in your career or personal development. Karen Baker takes a gloriously sceptical look at **Family Friendly Organisations** asking if they are myth or reality. Many organisation have framed well meaning and well designed policies on flexible working, career breaks, job sharing, etc only to see them imperfectly implemented or less than enthusiastically taken up. She offers sound and simple advice on why they fail and how to succeed. Valerie Hammond takes the issue of evidence-based management seriously and shows how it can be properly done in her chapter on **Women Managers**.

Tackling Violence at Work has become distressingly necessary in most NHS organisations. Helen Kogan describes how to assess the risks and gives practical advice on doing something about them. This is a good starting place for anyone charged with the important task of safeguarding staff and patients alike. **Risk Assessment** in a large organisation is a daunting task. Gareth Williams likens it to eating an elephant and recommends doing it in small chunks, a process which requires determination and perseverance, but it can be done.

It seems perverse and vaguely absurd to go into a hospital and become ill due to an infection acquired there. **Infection Control Management** is about doing the simple things well. The other source of ill health to NHS nursing staff is back, neck and shoulder injuries caused by repeated heavy lifting or sudden accidents whilst moving or mobilising patients. The particular difficulties of trying to encourage rehabilitation of patients whilst minimising risk to staff are taxing me and many others at the moment. The attitude that 'you aren't a proper nurse unless you have a bad back' is now virtually a thing of the past and staff are actively looking for ways to improve working practices. Moira Tracy's article on **Safer Patient Handling** is not only full of useful advice but acknowledges that changes to patient handling have to be made with regard to service and patient needs.

One of the thrills of editing a book like this is to get first sight of so much really good material. I have already circulated one of the chapters to a few colleagues to help with work we are doing. Dip into a chapter which takes your fancy or relates to work you are involved in; you will find expertise and sound advice based on the experience of having done it for real.

List of Contributors

Brian Aird has worked in health service management since 1971. He is Chief Executive of South Staffordshire Health Authority and a former President of the IHSM. During his term of office he was responsible for the introduction of the Institute's Code of Professional Conduct.

David Anderson is a Partner at Nabarro Nathanson specialising in the health sector, including the Private Finance Initiative. He spent fifteen months on secondment to the Private Finance Unit of the NHS Executive, and on his return to the firm was actively involved in the PFU's review of the PFI process ahead of the general election. David Anderson can be contacted on 0171 518 3147.

Karen Baker is Head of Personnel for Imminus Ltd and a lecturer for the Institute of Personnel and Development. She was formerly Director of Organisational Development at the North Middlesex Hospital Trust.

Hazel Brand trained as an occupational therapist and worked for the NHS and local authority before leaving to pursue a career as a journalist. She is now Communications Manager at the Doncaster Royal Infirmary & Montagu Hospital NHS Trust, and is Secretary of NAHSPRO (National Association of Health Service Public Relations Officers).

Karen Caines is Director of the Institute of Health Services Management.

Miranda Coates runs the Amalfi Partnership, a consultancy specialising in personal and management skills development for individuals and organisations. She is CPD Consultant to IHSM. She has worked previously as a training officer in the NHS, as Management Development Adviser for IHSM, and as Head of Education and Training for the UK Market Research Society.

Peter Cochrane: Further information about the author can be obtained at http://www.labs.bt.com/people/cochrap (also further reading on the subject).

Stephen Day is Regional Director of the NHS Executive West Midlands Regional Office.

Maureen Devlin is part of the Industry and Government Affairs Department of Glaxo Wellcome and joined the Health Services Management Centre as a Honorary Fellow (on a part-time basis) in September 1997. She holds a similar position at the National Primary Care Research and Development Centre in Manchester. She has explored possibilities for synergy in areas such as quality in primary care, primary care development and formation of health policy, and acts as a main contact between HSMC, NPCRDC and Glaxo Wellcome to assist in resource planning.

Jennifer East runs a consultancy with a colleague covering Infection Control and Risk Management for GPs, dentists, nursing homes, community hospitals, NHS trusts, private hospital groups and other healthcare providers.

Brian Edwards, CBE, FHSM, CBIM, Hon FRCPath, Hon DUniv, is Professor of Health Care Development at the University of Sheffield. He has extensive experience of managing health service at all levels, having been Chief Executive for fifteen years, first with Trent and then the West Midlands regions. He has a reputation for innovative change which he combined with an interest in the history of the development of the NHS.

Bob Gann is Director of the Help For Health Trust, a registered charity involved in communication of healthcare information to patients and the public, and also directs the Centre for Health Information Quality. He sits on a number of NHS committees and advisory groups including the Clinical Systems Group and the Standing Advisory Group on Consumer Involvement in NHS R&D.

Valerie J Hammond, Chief Executive of Roffey Park Management Institute, researches and advises on organisational and management issues and is a specialist in women's development. She works regularly with the NHS and is adviser for the Opportunity 2000 initiative.

Keith Holdaway is a staff and organisational development specialist. He divides his time between an acute trust (Mayday University Hospital, Croydon) and Bournewood Trust, a community and mental health trust in Surrey.

Peter Homa is Chief Executive of Leicester Royal Infirmary.

Helen Kogan is a freelance journalist specialising in the health sector.

Institute of Health Services Management (IHSM) promotes and organises NHS management bodies and fosters good practice in the health sector.

Roy Lilley is a frequent broadcaster and writer on health, current affairs and social issues, speaking at conferences and seminars throughout the UK and overseas. Formerly he was chairman of a first wave trust, vice-chairman of West Surrey and North East Hampshire Health Authority and a member of Surrey Heath Borough Council.

David Lye is Regional Director of Purchase Performance Management at the NHS Executive West Midlands Regional Office.

Howard Lyons, MSc, BSc(Econ), FHSM, MIPD, is Managing Director of London International Healthcare. A national graduate trainee in hospital management in 1972, he was House Governor of St Stephen's, Chelsea, after his first ten years in the NHS. Since 1982, he has worked as a healthcare management consultant for governments, aid agencies and private companies in over 50 countries.

Donald McNeill is the Secretary of the Scottish Council of the Institute of Health Services Management. He has almost 40 years' experience in the NHS in England and Scotland being latterly the Chief Executive of the South Ayrshire Hospitals Trust. Appointed by the Secretary of State for Scotland as a part-time member of the Accounts Commission for Scotland he undertakes voluntary work for the MS Society and Heartstart Ayrshire.

Richard Meara worked as a manager in the health services for 20 years, for the last seven as a chief officer. He left his post as District General Manager in North West Surrey in 1989 to undertake an MBA, which he gained in 1990. Since then he has run his own management consultancy, Meara Management Consultancy, which has undertaken assignments for the NHS, RHAs, HAs provider units and the voluntary sector.

Keith Pollard is a director of Acumen Solutions, a web and Internet consultancy that specialises in helping healthcare companies and organisations explore the opportunities of this new technology. Keith has worked in healthcare management in the private sector and in senior marketing roles in the healthcare industries. Acumen has worked closely with the IHSM in developing IHSM Online, and running a hands-on workshop for IHSM members.

Michael Ponton is Chairman of the IHSM's Welsh Division. He has been a member since 1973, and is now a Fellow of the Institute. He is Chief Executive of Health Promotion Wales, which is based in Cardiff, and is also a fellow of the NHS Staff College Wales.

Anne-Toni Rodgers is a pharmacologist employed as a health policy adviser. She advises both Glaxo Wellcome and the NHS on the development and implications of NHS policy and identifies new opportunities for them both. She is a member of Glaxo Wellcome's Regional Management Board and the South Thames IHSM Regional Council.

Robert Sloane is Chief Executive of Andover District Community Health Care NHS Trust, which has become a national focus as a model for change for the 21st century. He joined the NHS in 1964 as a management trainee and progressed through operational posts in general hospitals before moving to London in 1971 to work in a teaching hospital environment. In the late 1970s he headed the planning and commissioning of the first nucleus hospital, later working in private sector consultancy, before returning to the NHS in 1984, managing development projects for Wessex RHA.

Moira Tracy is Health and Safety Adviser for the Victoria Infirmary NHS Trust, Glasgow. She is a member of the RCN's Advisory Panel for Back Pain Nurses.

Suzanne Tyler is Deputy Director of the Institute of Health Services Management.

Gareth Watkins is based in Nabarro Nathanson's Sheffield office, from where he leads the cross-departmental health and safety group, part of one of the most extensive health and safety practices in the UK. He has 20 years' experience of dealing with health and safety issues and employers' liability claims on behalf of employers and insurers, and can be contacted on 0114 279 4163.

PART ONE

OVERVIEW

Fifty Years of the NHS

Brian Edwards, Professor of
Health Care Development,
University of Sheffield

The NHS is now so firmly rooted into the British psyche that for the most part it is taken for granted. It has been a fixed point in a society whose other social structures have undergone dramatic change. For 50 years the political debate has not been about the principle of a service free at the point of need but rather about its level of funding, its organisation and its management. When occasionally the unthinkable was voiced and somebody talked about an insurance-based system they were quickly silenced, even under radical leaders like Margaret Thatcher.

Creation of the NHS and early days

The thinking that led to the creation of the NHS in 1948 had its roots in the patchwork quilt of services that existed before World War II, the experience of managing them as a co-ordinated system during the war and the social solidarity that grew at this time of crisis.

The Beveridge Report, published in 1942 as the tide of war was beginning to shift, gave political expression to these changes in society as it addressed the challenge of reconstruction once the war had ended. Disease was one of five giants that needed to be dealt with. The others were want, ignorance, squalor and idleness.

While the principles gained wide support, the idea that all these services should be welded together in one organisation produced a furious row among those most closely involved. However, the hospital world was in a serious financial mess, so change was inevitable. It took a person of Bevin's stature to battle it through the

3

welter of objections. He is now one of the heroes of the 20th century, but at the time he was seen by many as a villain, particularly by the leaders of the medical profession, the trustees of the voluntary hospitals and almost everybody else in the healthcare world who was going to have to give up their independence. The population, however, loved it and in no time at all 90 per cent had signed up with a general practitioner and joined the queue to receive their free spectacles and dentures.

The service ran into serious financial difficulties almost immediately, but the subsequent Guillebaud Inquiry found that the NHS had been underfunded at the start. This took the steam out of the early crisis but keeping within budgets and cash limits was to remain at the centre of managers' and politicians' agenda for the next 50 years. The NHS budget in 1951 was £499 million which represented 3.4 per cent of the national GDP.

Development of new posts

General practice secured for itself an independent status (a contract of service rather than employment). Their contract holder and paymaster was the local executive council, which also dealt with the pharmacists, opticians and dentists. Despite the relatively high status of the family doctor in the community, professional status was low. Many practised as single-handed doctors often from poor premises. Health centres never really took off. Most GPs practised from home, the hospital specialist ruled the roost and general practice had to wait until the mid-1960s to see change.

The hospital world was organised separately under regional boards and hospital management committees except for the teaching hospitals – these reported directly to the Ministry of Health. One of the legacies of the early financial crisis was very strict financial control. For some years all new posts (doctors, nurses, porters, clerks) had to be approved at either a regional or ministry level. The Secretary to the board or committee, the administrator, was the overall co-ordinator but hospital doctors firmly resisted any hierarchical structure and stoutly defended their personal clinical freedoms. 'Cogwheel', the report which recommended clinical divisions, was not published until 1967 (and even then it took a further five years for significant progress to be made).

Matrons were already powerful in their own domains which at this stage included many housekeeping services. Chief executives were generations away. For the most part the system worked well as the NHS got into its stride and began to grow.

Community health services and public health remained with local government under the leadership of the Medical Officer of Health.

Growth in the 1960s and 1970s

In July 1960 Enoch Powell became Minister of Health and George Godber was appointed Chief Medical Officer. Together with Bruce Frazer, the new Permanent Secretary, they quickly produced the first hospital plan. It envisaged a network of local general hospitals of between 600 and 800 beds, but with a 15 per cent reduction in the overall number of beds. Ninety new hospitals were planned and even more programmed for reconstruction and upgrading. Many hospitals in this period had wards in huts put up during the war. Over the next 20 years new hospitals began to emerge, particularly in the communities that surrounded the major cities. The notion of a general hospital that provided a comprehensive range of services (including geriatrics and acute mental health) grew strongly and many small cottage hospitals and sanatoria began to close. The Bonham Carter report in 1969 pushed the centralisation issue further by arguing for a larger population base (200,000–300,000) and hospitals with over 1,000 beds. By the end of the 1970s this major building programme was running out of steam and community hospitals suddenly came back into their own. Investment in the older city hospitals had been slower than the new builds on greenfield sites and they continued to struggle to cope with new medical science in old dilapidated buildings. Standard design solutions such as nucleus became popular.

Throughout the 1960s concern was growing about the structural separation of the NHS into three arms (four if you included the separation of the teaching hospitals from the rest of the hospital world). A series of plans, ideas and consultative documents was produced for an organisational change that would secure a higher degree of integration.

The result was the 1974 reorganisation which brought the health functions of local government, hospital management committees and executive councils together under 90 area health authorities. The teaching hospitals lost their special relationship with the Department of Health. The preparation for this change was extensive: there was national and regional competition for the most senior managerial jobs (most went to administrators from the hospital world); the administrative arrangements were proscribed in the most amazing detail (the Grey Book) with a new and fashionable idea of multidisciplinary consensus teams (to make a decision valid the whole team had to agree); there was also a separation between the management team at the area health authority which handled policy and the team or teams at district level which carried the responsibility for operational matters (at this level the team of six included a hospital consultant and general practitioner). For many these new teams were a revelation as the individuals learned from each other and began to tackle the practical problems of integration. For others the tensions within the team became intolerable and they and their teams became dysfunctional. To make matters worse many of the teams at area and district level found the distinction between policy and operations difficult and they began to fight for territory. The other crucial change was the emergence of professional and managerial structures for functional services such as engineering, physiotherapy, dietetics, pharmacy, domestic, catering and laundry services. Nursing had been reformed in 1966 when the Salmon Committee introduced a ten-point grading structure and eschewed non-nursing duties. The assistant matron in charge of the nurses home slid quietly away.

More financial trouble and strikes

It was this new and fragile management structure that found itself coping with another bout of strikes and industrial action over pay and private practice. The first really serious breakdown in industrial relations had been in 1972 when ancillary staff went on strike over pay. Militant shop stewards exercised enormous power in some hospitals. By 1976 the recurrent problems about pay were compounded by Barbara Castle's determination to stop private practice in NHS hospitals. The policy backfired badly and provoked an acrimonious row with the consultants while actually stimulating growth in the private hospital sector.

Management costs and the salaries of senior managers had risen sharply as a consequence of the reorganisation and doctors' leaders attacked this new bureaucracy vigorously. The local hospital manager they dealt with was very junior and had been disempowered by the more senior managers and functional heads above him at district and area levels. Decision making became slow and complicated. This reorganisation was judged a failure after only 19 months when Harold Wilson stood up in the House of Commons and announced the creation of a Royal Commission.

A general election intervened but when it reported in 1979 to Patrick Jenkin who was now Secretary of State it concluded that the NHS was essentially fine. 'It was not suffering from a mortal disease susceptible only to heroic surgery ... it just needed to get on with the long slogging job of improving performance.' Its conclusions were well balanced and right but the pressure for more change was inexorable. By 1982 the area health authorities had been put to the sword and replaced by district health authorities. One whole tier in the organisation had been removed. In the process general practitioners re-emerged with their own separate body to hold and manage their service contracts − the family health service authorities.

Meanwhile the mental health services continued down the path towards community care. The large mental and mental handicap hospitals first shrank in size and then closed. Selling the redundant land and buildings became a serious management preoccupation. Acute psychiatric admission units were opening in the district general hospitals (DGHs) and secure treatment facilities were developing very slowly. There were many scandals and inquiries along the way.

In the acute sector clinical science was expanding the range of diagnostic and treatment options and as a result the financial pressures inside the system started to build up. The number of hospital consultants continued to expand. The financial problems in London and the south east were compounded by a determined policy of equalising the levels of investment across the country. In 1978 there was a 25 per cent variation in investment between different parts of the country. Regions such as Trent (which covered the East Midlands) and the North West (centred in Manchester), which had both been historically underfunded, received preferential growth largely at the expense of the Thames regions. Perhaps even more potent was the internal equalisation within each of the fourteen regions which almost always worked against the cities. By 1990 this painful process of financial adjustment had been largely achieved at the regional level with eleven of the fourteen regions being within 3 per cent of each other. Sharp local variations within regions continued particularly in the Home Counties.

A similar process of readjustment was taking place in Scotland, Wales and Northern Ireland whose health services remained tied firmly to a UK model and London-based policy making. Only the Scots managed a modest degree of difference in the shape of their health service but with a much higher level of funding per head of population.

The 1980s

As the tension grew between what medicine could achieve with its new science and the resources available, notions of efficiency and effectiveness grew more powerful. A full-blown accountability process was launched in 1982 with regional teams presenting themselves in front of ministers in London for an annual inquisition, and then in their turn calling the health authorities in their region to account. In some regions these were cosy chats, in others a full-blooded accountability meeting that reviewed performance in the previous year, discussed outstanding problems and agreed targets for the next year.

The values of multidisciplinary working were still strong in the service despite the end of consensus management in 1982, when every health authority had to appoint one member of their senior team as general manager. This policy change resulted from a short but pithy report by Roy Griffiths, the man from Sainsburys, who said 'If Florence Nightingale walked the corridors of the NHS today she would be searching for the person in charge.' There was another merry-go-round of appointments but this time the jobs went to public advertisement and some managers were recruited from industry and the armed forces.

The first NHS Chief Executive, Victor Paige, came from industry but he resigned after only 18 months. Like most of those recruited from outside the NHS he could not stomach the blend of management and politics that is so peculiar to it.

Regionalisation and further crises

The 1970s and 1980s saw the regionalisation of many of the smaller and more expensive clinical specialities and some such as the heart transplant programme was effectively funded and run on a national basis. Others such as neurosurgery were funded and planned at a regional level.

The hurricane of 1987 coincided with another financial crisis. This time it was really serious and Ian Mills, then Director of Finance, told ministers that the NHS was technically bankrupt. Hospitals were closing beds all over the country. Short-term relief was found over the Christmas of 1987, but Margaret Thatcher was fed up with what she saw as the inefficiency in the system and the constant special pleading for more money. She had started to think about change. Ken Clarke took over from John Moore in 1988 and appointed Duncan Nichol as Chief Executive. Together they handled another industrial dispute with the ambulancemen, and Mrs Thatcher announced her review of the NHS on 'Panorama'.

It was conducted in private and led eventually to the decision in 1989 to introduce an internal market in the belief that competition would force the efficiency gains that the NHS needed.

In a bloody public fight reminiscent of 1946 Ken Clarke first elaborated and then implemented the reform package. The separation of purchasers and providers was relatively non-controversial as few understood its potential. Opposition to the formation of NHS trusts was led primarily by the trade unions and professional associations concerned about the demolition of national pay bargaining structures. The Whitley System of pay bargaining had been in place since 1948.

In the early days (even before the Act had been passed by Parliament) it was for the managers of individual hospitals and their senior colleagues to volunteer to move to trust status. Ken Clarke could have created trusts by edict and saved himself a lot of aggravation, but that was not his style. He wanted to pull down the old order and forge something new out of the fire of change. By 1994 all services had been assimilated into one form of NHS trust or another.

In 1996 another restructuring produced a new style NHS Executive, 8 regions instead of 15 and the merger of district health authorities and family health service authorities.

GP fundholding

The so-called wild card in the pack of reforms was GP fundholding. The idea that family doctors should buy services from hospitals with money taken out of the hospital's budget was indeed radical. The BMA strongly opposed the idea but many GPs were instinctively attracted to it. The hospital consultants were deeply sceptical but their eyes were on the creation of independent trusts which many supported.

The fundholding scheme started in 1991 with a limited budget for a small range of non-emergency hospital treatment, diagnostic services and drugs but in subsequent years developed quickly to more ambitious models that included many more services. Total fundholding, whereby the GP(s) received all the funds for the patient list, developed on a pilot basis. These schemes gave GPs real power to improve services for their patients and forced the hospital sector to provide services that they and their patients valued. The opponents (including, it must be said, a significant minority of GPs) acknowledged this, but argued that it was only possible at the expense of somebody else's patient. The patients of fundholders undoubtedly got preferential access to non-emergency care in many hospitals.

The early 1990s

The Patient's Charter arrived in 1991 with its emphasis on service guarantees and patients' rights.

As it turned out, the internal market was heavily constrained by local and national politics and national rules. Health authorities took a long time to forget about managing services and think instead about purchasing them. Trusts were slow to take up the option of local pay bargaining. In some parts of the country, competition was fierce, but for the most part the fireworks were restricted to the innovative fundholders who were prepared to take on their local hospital and transfer their patients somewhere else if they did not get satisfaction. The internal market did produce very sizeable efficiency gains in the acute sector but it also allowed inefficient trusts to continue, sometimes with explicit ministerial approval. Another attempt to sort London out by Bernard Tomlinson got stuck on Barts and Edgware although some changes and mergers did happen.

In general practice GPs poured their 'savings' into improved practice premises and equipment. Waiting lists began to fall sharply, particularly in the Mersey and West Midlands regions, where the chairs and senior management made it a priority for action. But not all regions had performed well, and scandals in Wessex, West Midlands and Yorkshire played a major part in their demise in 1996.

Virginia Bottomley was then Secretary of State, and it was she who took the decision, but many saw the strong hand of Ken Clarke, then Chancellor of the Exchequer, behind it. The role of the regions was subsumed into the Department of Health and eight new regional offices emerged. They were all part of the new empire of Alan Langlands, the new Chief Executive at his office in Leeds. The NHS Executive has always been part of the Civil Service. At this stage the Department of Health underwent it own major reorganisation and downsizing.

It was not until 1991 that anybody took the health of the nation seriously although many in the field of public health had tried to develop local variants of the WHO policy of health for all. Clinical audit which had been part of the Thatcher reform package started as an educational process but fuelled the evidence-based medicine movement.

Throughout the early nineties the NHS was at the forefront of the political agenda. The public did not approve of what it always saw as Margaret Thatcher's NHS reforms. When Labour won power in 1997 it quickly announced the end of the internal market and fundholding.

Co-operation and collaboration were to be the hallmarks of the new and modern NHS which was to be much more concerned with quality and equity. General practitioners would retain a powerful influence over the purchasing decisions in a new partnership with health authorities. NHS trusts would remain but many would merge as a means of securing the targeted reductions in management costs. The annual contract negotiations were to be replaced with three-year agreements.

The present

Fifty years on, the principle of a service free at the point of need is still intact. No serious alternative is on the political agenda. The organisation has undergone frequent and radical change which while painful to those involved may have played a major role in its longevity. Levels of investment at 5.8 per cent of GNP (£43 billion) remain low by comparison with other developed economies but efficiency has stayed on an upward trend line. The rationing debate is, however, getting tougher. Overall quality is reasonable and by international standards excellent. More important the British public still wants its NHS and while this remains the case, its future is secure.

1.2

The White Paper on the New NHS

Karen Caines, Director, IHSM

It is not surprising that the Labour government, coming into power after a long stretch in opposition, should want to lay down its vision and programme for an NHS which has become a major political battlefield over the last few years, despite concern about further upheaval in the NHS.

Accordingly, in December 1997 and January 1998, the government published three White Papers on the future of the NHS in England, Scotland and Wales. Interestingly, in Northern Ireland, the intention is first to issue a consultative document which at time of writing has yet to see the light of day.

The three White Papers themselves demonstrate government willingness to enable the individual countries of the UK to shape their own programmes within the framework of a common vision for the National Health Services and some important common principles. Even the titles are different, reflecting particular emphases:

- *The new NHS: Modern, Dependable (England)* [1]
- *Designed to Care: Renewing the NHS in Scotland* [2]
- *NHS Wales: Putting Patients First* [3]

Renewed commitment to the NHS

A key common pledge is a renewed commitment to the principles of the National Health Service as we have known them: national, universal, comprehensive, based on need, largely funded out of taxes, largely free at the point of delivery. On other social welfare fronts such as pensions, benefits and long-term care, there is much talk of a shift to more self-responsibility and personal financial provision. In terms of principle, there seems little to distinguish health from such areas. But while the government clearly wants individuals to pay more attention to their own health, any question of direct financial contributions (for example, hotel charges or charges for GP visits) is explicitly ruled out. This is a programme for the kind of NHS we have known since its inception.

The government's commitment:

If you are ill or injured there will be a national health service there to help: and access to it will be based on need alone — not on your ability to pay, or on who your GP happens to be or on where you live.[1]

What is new is the stronger emphasis on equity — equity of both access and outcome — a theme pursued in more detail in the consultative Green Paper on public health, *Our Healthier Nation — A Contract for Health.*[4]

Can the NHS survive?

The White Paper takes head on the allegations that the NHS is in financial crisis and is being overwhelmed by three big pressures: growing public expectations, medical advances and demographic changes.

Those who argue that the NHS cannot accommodate these pressures say it will need huge increases in taxation, a move to a charge-based service, or radical restrictions in patient care. The government rejects this analysis.[1]

The government commits itself to increasing spending in the NHS in real terms every year. It also argues that an NHS funded through general taxation is the fairest and most efficient way of providing healthcare for the population at large.

The cost-effectiveness of the NHS helps to reduce the tax burden to well below the European Union average, encouraging investment and strengthening incentives to work and save. The alternatives — rationing or a 'charge-based' system — would dissipate these advantages.[1]

There is an argument that this White Paper, as with the previous government's *A Service with Ambitions*[5] before it, fudges the funding and rationing debates. Some GPs in particular have expressed concern that it denies rationing is needed while devolving responsibility for precisely that away from politicians to GPs. The level of baseline funding for the NHS is likely to remain a critical issue.

Tough choices: quality and efficiency

Even so 'there are tough choices facing the NHS'.[1] The language of the White Paper reverberates with repeated references to performance, efficiency, effectiveness and evidence. This is no starry-eyed version of the NHS. It is a hard-edged manifesto for standardised high performance with clear twin goals of quality and efficiency.

> *There will have to be big gains in quality and big gains in efficiency across the whole NHS.*[1]

It is explicitly designed to rebuild public confidence in the NHS.

The big question remains however: how this is to be achieved. Despite the White Paper's recurrent theme of better systems and processes, there are scant references to managers. The main drivers are doctors, nurses, partnerships. In hospitals and most strikingly in primary care with the establishment of primary care groups and evolution to primary care trusts, there is an explicit shift to a much greater contribution from clinical management.

The third way: partnership and performance

In terms of approach, the government declares no return to the centralised command and control systems of the 1970s, and no continuation of the internal market system of the 1990s.

> *Instead there will be a 'third way' of running the NHS – a system based on partnership and driven by performance.*[1]

It will be interesting to see if a genuinely new approach to the management of a public service emerges from this 'third way'. The White Paper description looks remarkably similar to the model developed incrementally across government over the last decade, with a balance between national specification and oversight, and local delivery. Education, for instance, has seen the development of a tight national definition of curriculum, standards, training and funding, reinforced by national monitoring of performance and publication of results. But delivery is a matter for local responsibility and action. Certainly the NHS White Paper echoes much of that structure with a strong polarisation between national oversight and local delivery.

Six key principles

Six key principles underline the changes:

- to renew the NHS as a **national** service;
- to make delivery a **local** responsibility, driven by local doctors and nurses who know what patients need;

- to get the NHS to work in **partnership**, especially with local authorities;
- to drive **efficiency** through a more rigorous approach to performance and by cutting bureaucracy;
- to shift the focus to quality to guarantee **excellence** to all patients;
- to rebuild **public confidence** in the NHS.

'What counts is what works'

In designing the new start, the government says that it has consciously kept what has worked:

- the separation between the planning of hospital care and its provision (the purchaser/provider split);
- the increasingly important role of primary care;
- decentralising responsibility for operational management, e.g. to trusts.

By the same token, government has discarded what has failed:

- the internal market, including extra-contractual referrals;
- fragmentation which will be replaced by strategic co-ordination through the vehicle of a jointly agreed health improvement programme;
- GP fundholding and two-tierism;
- the purchaser efficiency index which will be replaced by better measures of efficiency and broader performance assessment;
- bureaucracy so that management costs will be capped and commissioning bodies cut from c.3,600 to 500;
- annual contracts which will be replaced by three-year or longer funding agreements to ensure stability;
- secrecy which will be replaced by open trust meetings, publicly available comparative data, and public involvement.

Driving quality in the new NHS

The new NHS will have quality at its heart ... quality measured in terms of prompt access, good relationships and efficient administration.[1]

The quality agenda is fundamental to this new NHS. Quality is not just a vague aspiration: here there are real specifics about national bodies, standards, frameworks, systems, processes, responsibilities, monitoring, reporting and sanctions. And about spreading best practice where traditionally the new NHS has scored less than gloriously.

The White Paper launches the idea of clinical governance to sit alongside corporate governance, with NHS trusts being given a new legal duty to ensure the quality of care. Ultimate responsibility will rest with the chief executive but trust boards should expect monthly reports and there might be a board sub-committee led by a clinician. The government is clearly determined to get a grip on clinical quality. Experience elsewhere suggests that being rigorous about professional quality – but even more important, being public about it – is likely to bring initial discomforts for all involved. The government will need to be brave here.

On quality as a whole they propose three areas for action. At national level there will be:

- new evidence-based national service frameworks for major care areas and disease groups to ensure consistency across the country;
- a new National Institute for Clinical Effectiveness to lead on clinical and cost effectiveness, and draw up guidelines and audits.

Locally there will be:

- teams of local GPs and community nurses working in primary care groups;
- explicit quality standards in local service agreements;
- a new system of clinical governance in NHS trusts and primary care, backed by a new statutory duty of quality in NHS trusts.

A new independent statutory body, the Commission for Health Improvement, will be set up to support and oversee the quality of clinical services at local level, and tackle the shortcomings. It will be able to intervene by invitation or on the Secretary of State's direction, and may also undertake an agreed programme of systematic reviews. There are clear echoes here of OFSTED in the world of education.

Driving efficiency in the new NHS

The White Paper outlines 5 ways to secure more efficient and effective use of resources:

- aligning clinical and financial responsibility, with primary care groups able to take devolved responsibility for a single unified HCHS/GMS budget;

  Funding for all hospital and community services, prescribing and general practice infrastructure will be brought together into a single stream at Health authority and Primary Care Group level – a single cash-limited envelope.[1]

- capping management costs in health authorities and primary care groups and bearing down on those in NHS trusts;

- a national schedule of reference costs for individual treatments, publicly benchmarked against individual trusts' costs;
- incentives to efficiency, with high-performing health authorities eligible for extra cash while high-performing NHS trusts and primary care groups use savings from longer term agreements to improve services for patients;
- sanctions against poor performers, including withdrawal of free-doms from primary care groups or withdrawal of agreements from trust providers if, over time, performance falls below standard.

Of these, the proposal with the potential for driving real change in the pattern of care is the unification of the HCHS/GMS budgets available to health authorities and primary care groups. It will open the opportunity to transfer resources between primary and secondary care, for example by funding expensive prophylactic treatments in primary care and keeping patients away from hospital. This is one of the points in the White Paper where it is hard to foresee where the dynamics will lead.

All these aspects of quality and efficiency will be reflected in a new performance framework measuring performance in the round – health improvement, fairer access to services, better quality and outcome of care, and the views of patients as well as real efficiency gains.

Structural change

Health authorities

Despite Frank Dobson's early words of reassurance to NHS staff about avoiding upheaval, there can be no doubt that the White Paper is genuinely radical and will lead to major structural change.

It is most radical and laudable in the seriousness of its intention to grapple with health and health inequalities as well as healthcare. Health authorities will have an exciting strategic leadership role in this extraordinarily difficult but extraordinarily important task.

It is vital though that they are supported in developing the appropriate skills and protected from undue distraction from mergers.

Fewer authorities covering larger areas will emerge.[1]

They will be leaner, with stronger powers to improve and oversee the effectiveness of the NHS locally. They will act in partnership with local authorities and others and, over time, they will relinquish direct commissioning.

Their key tasks will be to:

- assess the health needs of the local population;
- develop a health improvement programme to meet those needs, in partnership with other key players;

- decide on the range and location of healthcare services for their residents;
- determine local targets and standards for quality and efficiency;
- support the development of primary care groups, allocate their resources and hold them to account;
- participate in a new national survey of patient and user experience.

The first health improvement programmes will be in place by April 1999 and will cover three years. Specialist hospital services (such as bone marrow transplants) will be commissioned by regional offices.

The initiative on health action zones, which was announced in advance of the White Paper, will see NHS and other bodies working closely together on strategies to improve the health of local people. Eleven zones, generally covering an area of at least health authority size, were set up in April 1998.

Primary care

There will be major change in primary care. Subject to legislation, the GP fundholding scheme will be wound up in 1999 and fundholders, total purchasing projects, multifunds and locality commissioning GPs will move on to primary care groups. These groups will bring together all GPs and community nurses in natural communities, typically serving about 100,000 patients.

Their key tasks will be to:

- contribute to the health authority's health improvement programme;
- promote the health of the local population;
- commission health services for their populations;
- monitor performance against service agreements with NHS trusts;
- develop primary care;
- integrate primary and community health services better and work more closely with social services on both planning and delivery of services.

To reflect the different stages of development currently found in primary care, there is a spectrum of different models for primary care groups, from simply advising their health authority through to becoming primary care trusts accountable for commissioning care and providing community services (subject to legislation).

Primary Care Groups will begin at whatever point on the spectrum is appropriate for them. They will be expected to progress along it so that in time all PCGs assume fuller responsibilities.[1]

The new primary care trusts will not be expected to take responsibility for specialised mental health or learning disability services.

Specialist mental health Trusts are likely to be the best mechanism for coordinating service delivery.[1]

These are early days in which to make judgements, and there is much work to be done to develop the concept and pilot the approach. Conceptually locating responsibility with those best placed to assess patients' needs is very sensible. But there may be some questions about whether the primary care structures will bear the weight of what is intended. Can primary care groups of this size be cohesive — and what about members of the primary care team other than doctors and nurses? Will all GPs and nurses want to play ball, not just the enthusiasts? Will they have the skills as well as the inclination? Is this genuinely a model which can apply universally? Who will be prepared to be the accountable officer? What other management infrastructure will there be? How will GPs as independent contractors react to the implications of tighter management?

NHS trusts

Trusts were the focus of major structural change under the 1991 reforms but this time their challenges are less fundamental. Rather, the impetus for structural change is coming outside the White Paper from the round of rampant reconfiguration and mergers now taking place throughout the UK.

In the new NHS, NHS trusts will:

- contribute to strategy and planning in the local health improvement programme;
- involve senior clinicians much more closely in designing service agreements with commissioners and in budgetary responsibilities;
- develop clinical governance arrangements to ensure quality;
- work under new statutory duties of quality and of partnership with other NHS organisations;
- be accountable, more broadly than before, to the relevant NHS executive regional office;
- benchmark costs and performance;
- develop and involve their staff, and tackle some immediate human resource priorities including avoiding accidents and violence, addressing stress, recognising and dealing with racism, developing family-friendly employment policies, ensuring on-call junior doctors have reasonable standards of food and association, and making sure staff can speak out when necessary, without victimisation;
- maintain control of their estate, but health authorities will be responsible for monitoring its utilisation.

To assist these developments, the government will

- work with the professions on principles underpinning effective continuing professional development and the respective roles of the state, the professions and individual practitioners, and on strengthening existing systems of professional self-regulation;
- undertake a national consultation on a strategy for nursing, midwifery and health visiting;
- pursue a longer term objective of national pay;
- establish a task force on improving the involvement of frontline staff in shaping new patterns of healthcare.

Modernising the NHS

In tune with the government's broader theme of modernising Britain, there is a heavy emphasis on modernising the NHS.

The hidden wiring for many of the proposals lies with better technology both to support service delivery and to assist effective management. For the details, we must await the NHS Executive's new information management and technology strategy. But the general message is clear: the NHS has lagged behind other areas of the public and private sector in harnessing technology successfully. Modernising the NHS means a step change, particularly in realising the potential of IT to support frontline staff in delivering benefits for patients.

This White Paper begins a process of modernisation ... For example, a nurse-led helpline to provide advice round the clock. And new technology that links GP surgeries to any specialist centre in the country.[1]

Immediately, there are some specific goals, with all GPs and hospitals on the NHS net by 2002, on-line booking of appointments, quicker test results, access to information and telemedicine support.

Conclusion

Initial reactions to the English White Paper on the new NHS were generally characterised by good will and optimism. This may have had much to do with its tone: its unequivocal support for the NHS and its strong emphasis on integration not fragmentation, on co-operation not competition, on partnership not direction.

Over time, comments became more questioning, without dissenting from the overall vision of a high-quality, modern NHS. The White Paper proposals are wide ranging and complex. Beyond an immediate concern about how the changes are to be achieved lurks a larger, harder issue about where the dynamics will lead.

When the 1991 NHS was framed, there was no thinking then of a 'primary care-led NHS' but the dynamics of the purchaser/provider split and the introduction of GP fundholding led to that vision in a remarkably short time. Where will the new White Paper's proposals for a much more tightly managed system with strategically focused health authorities and powerful primary care groups lead? What will be the impact on service delivery and the role and distribution of hospitals?

None of these caveats need be fatal to the vision, if properly addressed. The White Paper sensibly sets a timescale of ten years for change, so there is scope for experiment and development where new structures and skills are needed. Much on the quality agenda can be set in motion quickly and undoubtedly the government will need a few quick hits.

But success on the broader canvas is for the longer haul. Almost every member of the NHS will need to be engaged. They will need to develop new skills and activities, fostered with support and encouragement. A naming and shaming approach will be counter-productive. At heart the White Paper is about cultural rather than structural change.

And perhaps as Director of the IHSM, I can end on a personal point. If the NHS is to achieve the goals now set for it, effective managers of every background will be crucial and should be valued. In terms of this White Paper, good management is as fundamental to better health as good clinical quality is to better healthcare.

References

1. The Secretary of State for Health (1997) *The New NHS: Modern, Dependable*. Cm 3807, The Stationery Office, London.
2. The Secretary of State for Scotland (1997) *Designed to Care: Renewing the National Health Service in Scotland*. Cm 3811, The Stationery Office, London.
3. The Secretary of State for Wales (1998) *NHS Wales: Putting Patients First*. Cm 3841, The Stationery Office, London.
4. The Secretary of State for Health (1998) *Our Healthier Nation − A Contract for Health*. Cm 3852, The Stationery Office, London.
5. The Secretary of State for Health (1996) *A Service with Ambitions*. Cm 3425, HMSO, London.

All Change for Healthcare in Wales

Michael T J Ponton, Chairman,

IHSM Welsh Division

There is no doubt that Wales will be very much to the forefront of the healthcare scene in 1998, and the IHSM Welsh Division will be playing its part during an exciting and challenging year. A number of important international events are due to take place in the Principality which will be supported and attended by IHSM members, and in addition to its own annual conference in October, the IHSM will be combining with the NHS Confederation to run a joint conference in November.

1998 therefore promises to be an eventful year, and in keeping with this, the Welsh Division of the IHSM has set itself some stretching objectives designed to build upon the progress made in 1997 and to help its members meet the challenges which will be specific to Wales as well as those which arise from a rapidly changing healthcare environment.

Three major issues

There are currently three major issues which will concern healthcare managers in Wales during 1998 and into 1999: first, we are in the middle of an exercise which will reconfigure all the NHS trusts within Wales, and the indications are that the total number of trusts will be reduced by at least a half. A very tight timescale has been placed upon this process, in order that the new trusts will be in place by April 1999, and this is inevitably placing additional demands particularly upon senior managers. However, the effects will be felt by managers at every level, and it is in this situation that the Institute can play a vital role in supporting members who may need advice and help in coping with the inevitable changes which will occur.

In providing this support, an innovation which was introduced by the Welsh Division during 1997 will be invaluable: this is the publication of a Directory of Members' Interests which lists all members of the division along with details of their special professional interests and the areas where they are willing to offer support to fellow members. The directory has been designed to be updated each year, thus providing a very practical resource available only to members of the IHSM in Wales.

The second important area of change concerns, of course, the White Paper on the future of the NHS in Wales *Putting Patients First*, published in January 1998. With its emphasis on the role of primary care and the need for all agencies concerned with healthcare to work more closely together, the White Paper is the subject of much debate on the part of those who will be tasked with putting it into practice. In particular, the introduction of local health groups and the end of fundholding will require careful and skilled handling.

The Institute is closely involved in the discussions arising from the White Paper, and will ensure that the views of managers will be reflected in its comments. The opportunity for managers in primary and secondary care to work more closely together is welcomed, and the IHSM particularly wishes to emphasise its increasing relevance to primary care managers and its ability to offer them support and scope for career development.

In recognition of the importance of this issue, the theme for the Welsh Division's annual conference in October will be the interface between primary and secondary care, which will explore some of the benefits of a closer relationship, and the potential for a more integrated service.

The third area of change and innovation in Wales is the introduction of a Welsh Assembly which will devolve much of the power currently vested in Westminster to the new body, including responsibility for the NHS in Wales. The IHSM has run a series of branch meetings in conjunction with Bevan Ashford to inform members about the structure and powers of the Assembly, as far as they are known at present, and these have been well attended and appreciated by members.

Against the background of all these developments and changes, the IHSM in Wales endeavours to be the voice of professional healthcare managers as well as providing its members with continuing education and career development opportunities. This means working closely with other organisations, such as the NHS Staff College Wales, which is also concerned with the ongoing development of managers from all sectors of the health service.

Research and management practice

The Welsh Division has recently taken a special interest in the area of research into improving management practice and effectiveness in the health service, and during the latter part of 1997 brought together a group of interested organisations to launch an annual event designed to encourage this type of research. The first Research and Effectiveness in Health Services Management conference was held in February 1998 and was a highly successful event. Its particular aim was to encourage practising managers to involve themselves in research projects, rather than seeing this area as the preserve of academics. Having achieved this, the Welsh Division is maintaining the momentum and is working with the Wales Office of Research and Development for Health and Social Care to develop a bursary which will provide support for managers undertaking research projects.

To sum up, the Welsh Division is engaged in a wide variety of activities designed to support and develop its membership, and is fully involved in the current developments within the NHS in Wales. Although much has been achieved, the Division recognises that much still needs to be done to improve the services to managers in primary care, to students and new managers who will need the skills to meet the challenges of the new millennium.

1.4

Northern Ireland – A Different Approach

Patricia Gordon, Chief Executive,

Mater Hospital

Northern Ireland has taken a slightly different approach to the rest of the United Kingdom with regard to the changes to take place in the Health Service. A consultation paper entitled *Fit for the Future* was published on 30 April 1998. The foreword in the document indicates the reasons why a consultation paper is being published at this time. The foreword indicates that the government wishes to examine whether there is the right organisational structure to permit the Health and Personal Social Services (HPSS) to meet their fundamental objective of improving the health and well-being of Northern Ireland. The foreword goes on to say that they 'believe it is very important all those who may be affected by any changes – those who work in the service as well as those who use them – have an opportunity to express their views on how the HPSS should be organised.'

The paper does build on the papers published in England, Scotland and Wales and there are many principles and givens that will direct a restructuring.

- The internal market will be replaced and we will have a system based on co-operation
- GP Fundholding will cease to function from 1 April 2000
- The integrated health and social care arrangements will continue
- There will be primary care centred local commissioning
- It is anticipated £25 million will be saved in administration through examination of the structures, roles and responsibilities
- There will be an end to unfairness and fragmentation

- Longer term funding agreements
- Openness
- Separation of the commissioning and providing functions will remain
- There is an emphasis on value for money and intersectorial co-operation.

The paper indicates that there are three service areas that they wish to focus on.

- Access to specialist cancer services will be improved
- There will be a reduction in hospital waiting lists
- The need to take advantage of IT developments.

To help the debate the paper gives two examples of how the service could be structured. These examples are called Model A and Model B.

Model A involves, to quote the document, 'relatively little change to existing organisations and structure.' The structure envisaged in this model is developed around the existing health and social services boards and trusts, but adds a new dimension with the establishment of primary care centred local commissioning bodies. The Model envisages the Boards taking on a more strategic role and taking on the lead responsibility for improving health and well-being. The local commissioning arrangements will be carried out by primary care groups serving populations of 50,000–100,000, supported by the population share of resources. This model states that over time the primary care groups could become free-standing primary care trusts which could combine with all or part of an existing community trust. This ties in with the thrust to ensure greater involvement at primary care level and may mean that over time the health and social services boards devolve the lead role in commissioning to these local bodies. Indeed, the paper states that as these develop the number and configuration of boards would be kept under review. This model envisages HSS trusts participating in local planning with new quality and efficiency standards. The number and configuration of trusts will be reviewed in this model.

Model B is a more radical approach and seeks to provide a streamlined organisational framework. Within this the main organisational element is a local care agency. This local care agency would replace boards and some or all of the trusts, they would embrace commissioning and providing whilst preserving a clear and distinct separation between the two functions. The local care agency would have two operational elements. On one side, primary care partnerships and on the other, providers who, it is stated, would have significant management autonomy. These local care agencies would serve local populations of around 200,000–300,000. In other words it is envisaged that there would be six to eight local care agencies for Northern Ireland. The primary care partnerships referred to above would serve populations of 25,000–50,000. Indeed, this is one of the main questions asked in the document; the government would like views on the population coverage of primary care partnerships. The provider arm of the local care agency could have three different approaches with regard to provider organisations. There could be, for example, fully integrated provider, hospital and community services, in this model, there would be one per cent local care agency, again six to eight for Northern Ireland. Secondly, there could be seperate acute and community providers. The third variation is that there could be a mixture of providers. Throughout the document there is an indication the there needs to be stonger strategic planning and in Model B it is envisaged that there is a single regional organisation which would be combined with the HSS Executive and be sited within the Department of Health.

Finally the document says 'there is scope for developing separate organisational arrangements in Northern Ireland which have the scope to meet the needs of any new political structures which may emerge.' The consultation approach adopted by the Department has been broadly welcomed by staff within the service who feel that they are being given a real opportunity to take part in a debate which will shape the structure of the service for the next number of years.

Renewing the NHS in Scotland

Donald McNeill, Secretary of the

Scottish Council of IHSM

The sub-title of the Government's White Paper, *Designed to Care* reflects key elements of both the past and the future of the NHS in Scotland. First, it is a National Health Service for Scotland established within a UK framework, based on Bevan's founding principles. It is an NHS free at the point of use, funded through general taxation and available to all on the basis of need. Second, as in 1948, the need to legislate and provide for the distinctive features of the Scottish nation and its health is recognised. This approach to separate legislation is based substantially on the Act of Union of 1707 which guaranteed Scotland its own system of law, education and national church. Interestingly, the NHS and Community Care Act 1990, with its main elements the internal market and the purchaser/provider split, was enacted as UK-wide legislation and never really took root in Scotland where there is an identifiable social, cultural and corporate cohesion. This aspect of Scottish life perhaps demonstrates why after nearly 300 years within the UK, Scotland can justly claim to being a nation if not a sovereign state. In the General Election of May 1997 a Labour UK government was returned with a huge majority in Scotland with no fewer than 56 Labour MPs out of 72 being returned to Westminster; Conservative representation was totally absent. This massive mandate validated their policies on devolution and its reform of the NHS. In September 1997 the overwhelming result in the Devolution Referendum, which supported the establishment of a Scottish Parliament with certain tax raising powers while maintaining the integrity of the UK, signalled major change in the governance of Scotland and its relationship with the rest of the UK. The Scotland Bill with its stirring declaration 'There shall be a Scottish Parliament' now progresses through the legislative process with a parliament scheduled for Edinburgh by the year 2000. So what of the NHS in Scotland?

Scotland and its health community

It is clear that the Scottish Parliament will legislate, scrutinise and be democratically accountable for the £4.5 billion public service funding of the NHS in Scotland. It will have the responsibility of deciding policies and solutions within a UK framework that meets the needs and circumstances of Scotland's health. It will govern the relationship between NHS authorities in Scotland and its 136,000 plus staff.

The scale of the challenge is huge. Scotland spends on average 23 per cent more on its health services than England. Yet in almost every health index its performance is much poorer. Indeed, in European terms Scotland is consistently bottom of the league, below Portugal and Ireland in the major causes of ill health and death – coronary heart disease, strokes and cancer. And this is despite the presence and influence of some of the longest established, pioneering and world famous university medical schools and hospitals in Edinburgh, Glasgow, Aberdeen, Dundee and St. Andrews. The inequalities of health in Scotland are very marked and rooted in poverty, employment, poor housing, diet and lifestyle. These require to be addressed within a new Scottish parliament and not only in a health context. There is a recognition that an opportunity exists to harness the many agencies such as local authorities (with their responsibilities for social work, housing and education) the active and thriving voluntary sector and the national welfare system into this most crucial challenge.

The first indications as heralded in the government's White Paper, *Designed to Care*, are promising and have been well received within the Scottish health community. Significantly, in the 50th anniversary year of the NHS, it states its intention to lay the foundations for a service fit for the next 50 years. It rejects claims that a NHS cannot cope with the current pressures and tensions and commits itself to real ongoing increases in resources. It intends to create a service that is clinically effective and designed from a patient of view. It rejects the concept of the internal market and the purchaser/provider split which it sees as wasteful, leading possibly to a two-tier service and to duplication of services. It estimates that over the lifetime of parliament savings of £100 million can be made through co-operation as opposed to competition, and these monies re-directed into patient care.

However, the replacement of the internal market does not envisage the return to the previous 'command and control' style of management. It recognises the value of retaining and developing the roles of the strategic authorities (management executive and health boards) as opposed to operational bodies such as trusts that deliver services direct to patients. The number of trusts will roughly half from 47 to about 28, with many acute trusts particularly outwith the major cities being amalgamated. The current review of acute services by the Chief Medical Officer, Sir David Carter, will have a major impact on these configurations The new concept of primary care trusts which will bring together primary care and community healthcare services with local healthcare co-operatives of GPs firmly in at their heart has been well received. Significantly, a large majority of GPs support this new initiative which while abolishing fundholding retains the position of GPs as independent contractors.

An alphabet soup of measures has been well received. That is:

- HIPs (strategic health improvement programmes to protect and improve public health);
- TIPs (operational trust improvement plans to implement HIPs at a patient level);
- JIFs (joint investment funds to support clinical improvements and the shift from secondary to primary care).

At a recent conference in Dunblane organised by the Institute of Health Services Management both clinicians and management in the NHS in Scotland supported the overall thrust of the reforms and commended the new initiatives.

The White Paper was quickly followed up with a more reflective and discussionary Green Paper — *Working Together for a Healthier Scotland*. Once again the emphasis is on public health solutions to fit Scottish circumstances. It sets wider targets than its English equivalent reflecting Scotland's poor showing in the key areas of coronary heart disease and strokes, cancer, teenage pregnancies, oral and dental health and accidents. It undoubtedly sets the ambitious way forward which will be needed if Scotland's well-documented poor record in health is to be improved. The principles are agreed so the devil may well be in the detail.

The next few years should be some of the most exciting in the history of the NHS with reform, new initiatives and opportunities on the busy agenda. This is true all over the UK but particularly in Scotland. The Institute in Scotland is both well placed and determined to make its contribution.

Healthcare Management – An International Perspective

Howard Lyons, Managing Director,

London International Healthcare

Introduction

Managing healthcare services in the UK is a tough business. But just imagine for a moment what it would be like to manage a large acute hospital without any running water – not simply because it has been cut off for an hour but because your hospital has never had running water. That is what it is like trying to manage a hospital in many parts of the former Soviet Union where it is estimated that nearly 50 per cent of all hospitals have no running water or integral sewerage.

Or imagine being without soap. I once visited the biggest general hospital in the Gambia where the surgical ward sisters were sharing one bar of soap among 80 patients because they were rationed to one bar of soap per week.

Without drugs? In Cameroon, I have worked with hospitals in remote areas where patients and potential patients bought as many drugs as they could afford from the hospital pharmacy immediately after the harvest to tide them over the expected illnesses of the coming year. As a result, the pharmacy was out of stock for the next six months until the next main delivery. In a large hospital we were managing in Kenya, we discovered that drugs were regularly being smuggled out via the mortuary, in the sewn-up bodies of patients.

Without doctors? In Algeria, after the war of independence in the 1960s, virtually all French doctors fled the country leaving the hospitals bereft of highly trained medical staff. The initial solution proposed by the Ministry for Higher Education was to build seven

1,000-bed hospitals to use as centres for a fast-track programme to train large numbers of medical students. The country had newly realised gas and oil wealth so capital costs were not the usual deterrent but lack of management skills became an overriding consideration which eventually led to the project being scaled down. The government finally conceded that if it could not manage its largest hotel of 600 beds effectively, the country certainly did not have the management skills to run larger, more complex institutions such as teaching hospitals.

Buying in management

Of course, in the considerably wealthier Middle East countries of Saudi Arabia, Oman and United Arab Emirates, healthcare management could be bought in just like everything else and so hospitals sprang up right across the Arabian peninsula. Did I say hospitals? They were more like palaces rising out of the desert heat as if a mirage, a treasure store of all the latest medical equipment and technology that NHS staff only dream of. And to manage these alhambras, the best of British and American hospital administrators were lured at great expense on short-term contracts which required them to train their Arab successors to replace them. Unfortunately, there is neither the word nor the concept of 'career' in Arabic and its culture. Being successful depends on creating relationships with other people of influence. Becoming a hospital manager for well-connected Arabs usually meant starting at the top as chief executive – complete with large desk, enormous office and absolute power. British managers who stayed on to smooth the handover process would spend most of their day trying to undo the damage caused by decisions made by the Saudi CEO in the morning.

Beds no indication of size

The idea of describing the size of a hospital by the number of beds is not the universal phenomenon we have come to accept in the UK. For a start, most Bedouins being treated in Saudi Arabia would never have slept in a bed in their life and would not be comfortable doing so just because they were ill.

In most African countries, bed numbers are used only very loosely to indicate inpatient capacity. Often a ward will be treating at least twice the number of inpatients compared with the beds available and doing a ward round will involve stepping over patients sleeping on the floor as much as examining patients in bed. In Botswana, strenuous efforts were made by our British team of commissioning experts to persuade the local managers to make a fresh start when the new general hospital opened. For months beforehand, nursing staff discussed and agreed new policies and procedures for each ward based on the NHS concept of one patient per bed with proper admission and discharge procedures, patient charts on each bed and such like. Yet within days of opening the new wards, all the six-bed bays were filled with nine or ten patients sharing beds or sleeping on the floor. NHS ideas clearly don't suit everyone.

Getting a wider perspective

There is much to learn from seeing how healthcare is delivered in different parts of the world. Algeria is a case in point. To overcome their shortage of doctors, they became much more flexible in how duties were shared across professional boundaries and instead of having separate hierarchies within each profession, staffing was organised and graded so that in theory (and in practice too) a person could start off as a hospital porter, train as an operating department assistant, get further training to become an anaesthetic nurse in intensive care and then receive further training to carry out duties which in the UK can only be carried out by a medically qualified anaesthetist. This produced a much more flexible labour force on the one hand, and, on the other did a lot to break down interprofessional rivalry which can be so destructive in public sector health services in Britain, especially the antagonism between managers and clinicians.

This is much less of an issue in the private healthcare sector where the goals of managers and doctors are more likely to be shared. NHS managers usually benefit from working in such an environment, whether in the UK or overseas, because they are more likely to be appreciated for the contribution they make to the success of their organisation, even if the key measure is often financial. In the NHS, agreeing criteria to measure successful management performance is still too much of an emotive issue.

Getting a different perspective on the way we manage, whether from the private side or from working overseas, is always refreshing and often enlightening. My imagination was fired by an elective experience in the USA just after completing the National Graduate Training Scheme in hospital management in the 1970s. What impressed me most were the sheer numbers involved in management at all levels compared with the NHS and whatever reservations I had about the US system of healthcare – which made the NHS seem a model of economy and fairness – I became convinced, and have been ever since, that the NHS is seriously undermanaged.

Management and propaganda

Not underadministered however. That was an important distinction to learn from a study visit to hospitals in the People's Republic of China two years later. In China, management was non-existent and bureaucracy rampant, a caricature of our own NHS prior to 1974. Even so, the value of propaganda to change behaviour and improve morbidity and fertility statistics was notable. My recollection of our attempts in Britain to eliminate the unhealthy practice of spitting is limited to discreet signs on the top of double-decker buses in the 1960s. In China, it was a major national campaign with practical implications involving the placing of spittoons in hospital corridors to encourage people not to spit on the floor.

China's economically threatening population growth was tackled by appealing to people's patriotic duty to have only one child per family and enforced vigorously by fearsome neighbourhood health visitors who kept a careful and interventionist watch on fertile mothers in their community. Any woman found to be pregnant with a second child was hauled off for an abortion and given strict supervision on contraception thereafter.

In less vigilant and more liberal societies, infant and maternal mortality is still a major problem, especially in Africa, and needs an understanding of the culture before trying to apply management solutions. In the absence of western-trained midwives outside the main urban areas, most babies are delivered by so-called traditional birth attendants (TBAs), women with high standing in the village who apply time-honoured potions and remedies to various ailments including cutting the umbilical cord with a broken pot shard dipped in cow's dung. Improving the chances of survival of African women and babies usually involves a long process of on-the-job training for these TBAs rather than attempting to replace them with more highly educated midwives who have been fortunate enough to receive a British Council bursary to come and train at St Thomas's.

Management and culture

Trying to understand and take account of the effect of culture on the organisation and delivery of healthcare became the main reason why I eventually decided to leave the NHS in 1982. Expecting to work mainly in developing countries as a consultant, it came as a shock to be given a first assignment in Ireland planning a new private hospital but, in the end, the same principles applied. Healthcare in Ireland, unlike the UK, was funded through the mechanism of voluntary health insurance (VHI), which, despite its name, was virtually compulsory for all workers. Most hospitals were run by religious orders of nuns who received little or no salary thus keeping staff costs very low. VHI reimbursement rates were correspondingly small and left little scope for any new investors entering the market to provide high-quality healthcare to the insured population. People in Dublin were, however, prepared to top up VHI rates from their own pockets to obtain treatment in certain circumstances. The challenge was to quantify and analyse this activity in order to produce a case to the VHI Board that they should introduce a new gold insurance band which workers could subscribe to – and then to provide facilities which would meet the demand for better services.

The advantage of doing a first assignment in Ireland was that the additional problems of working in a foreign language were avoided. This unfortunately did not apply to the second assignment, in Algeria, where few people spoke English and consultants were expected to conduct business in French. Algeria was a challenge in other ways as well. Its culture was a rich mixture of post-colonial French, Berber North African, Arabic Moslem and its own unique brand of non-aligned socialism. Government was highly centralised with power concentrated in one or two ministries, not including the Ministry of Health.

The Ministries of Planning and Higher Education had decided that Algeria should have seven 1,000-bed hospitals to train its doctors of the future and, in keeping with the country's policy of non-alignment, they had commissioned top hospital architects in seven different countries to plan the new facilities. With only a simple brief of two pages, the architects from Japan, France, Sweden, UK, Germany, USA and Denmark had had a field day. Our job was to analyse their output and project manage the implementation. With the same brief, the diversity ranged from 36 operating theatres in one design down to only 8 in another; from 6 to 30 X-ray rooms, and space ratios per bed ranging from 90 metres up to 280. Nobody had consulted the Ministry of Health about their requirements. All they wanted was funding for a series of nucleus-style 240-bed DGHs to meet the main secondary care needs of the population. In the end, a serious downturn in the economy gave victory by default to the Ministry of Health.

Developing a management culture

One of the turning points in the project was the realisation by the government that they did not have a management culture capable of providing the people to run such large institutions. In many countries, not only is healthcare management not recognised as a competence but in some cases management itself is not seen as a professional skill that can be acquired through training and education. Often a hospital is administered by the most senior doctor who continues his or her clinical practice and regards management as a tiresome duty rather than an opportunity to improve things. Not that there is much freedom to change things. Working in Mexico recently, we found that medical directors of large acute hospitals had no powers of hire-and-fire, no right to discipline staff, no freedom to negotiate wages, no authority to purchase equipment, no real budgetary responsibilities and no involvement in capital planning projects. And this is not unusual.

But maybe not for much longer. There is a wind of change blowing through the organisation of healthcare services, especially in developing countries. Healthcare reform is high on the agenda and many Commonwealth nations still look to the UK for a lead. Autonomous hospitals, public-private partnerships, purchaser–provider splits and market testing are all topics of interest; and the pressing need is for skilled managers to help developing countries to improve the quality of healthcare for whole communities with limited resources using proven management techniques in a culturally sensitive manner.

Managing healthcare in the UK *is* tough and complex which is why British health service managers are better equipped than most to help other countries succeed. The opportunities are there for this generation of managers to make a difference on a much larger scale.

PART TWO

MANAGING IN THE NHS

2.1

The Obligation of Evidence-based Management

Peter Homa, Chief Executive,

Leicester Royal Infirmary

Evidence-based management uses reliable information, based on research, as the foundation for management and policy formulation at all levels (Ham, Hunter and Robinson, 1995). This requires management and policy decisions to be based on good-quality information gained from a combination of sources including comparable organisations as well as skilful analysis and diagnosis. The objective is improved patient care through more effective management. The two are inseparable; good care badly delivered is always diminished.

Some questions that one might expect a management team adopting an evidence-based management approach to ask when considering an issue include:

- What is the problem that we are trying to solve?
- Why are we trying to solve it?
- Is it the right problem on available evidence?
- Where is the evidence to support this?
- What is the quality of the evidence and what does it tell us about what we should do?
- Is the evidence generalisable to our situation or is it specific to another setting?
- Has this been attempted elsewhere and, if so, what was the outcome?
- If we proceed with this proposal, how can we extract maximum learning and share this with colleagues attempting to address the same problem?

- What evidence will we use to measure success and over what period of time?
- Is this more important than the least important management initiative underway and should the two be substitutes?

Stay 'on the problem side'

It is helpful to stay 'on the problem side' for as long as possible before permitting solutions to be offered. In the frenetic race 'to get things done', managers can too readily impose a solution without really understanding the problem. The means, therefore, unintentionally become the ends. There is more to good management than increasing its speed. Some of the discussions about healthcare provider mergers appear to start from the predisposition that merger is the answer without fully understanding the nature of the problems to be solved. In such cases, the task of merging two or more organisations becomes the major managerial objective taking several years before evidence can be adduced as to whether or not this manoeuvre resolved the original problem.

It is an ethical and professional obligation for those engaged in healthcare to practise evidence-based management. The prize for successful evidence-based management is improved patient care. Failure to practice evidence-based management obstructs improvements in patient care and should be seen in this light. Evidence-based healthcare management is no longer an optional extra or professionally exotic. Managers whose managerial practice fails to satisfy the test of being evidence based will be regarded as professionally idiosyncratic and breaking faith with those who need healthcare. Managers have the same duty as clinicians to act according to the evidence provided by reliable information, based on good quality research (Sackett *et al.*, 1996). This duty is based on the obligations that healthcare managers have to patients, the taxpayer (in the case of the National Health Service), their organisations, their staff and themselves. Managerial decisions that are not evidence based are at greater risk of leading to inappropriate use of resources with consequential diminution of patient care.

This is not an appeal for a return to Taylor's scientific management or some sort of formulaic management. It is, however, a call for healthcare managers to take every reasonable action to ground their decisions in reliable, research-based information – as Drucker advises, to do the right thing right. Organisational politics are often finely woven into managerial decision taking. The effect of organisational politics may result in a decision contrary to one based exclusively on the evidence. This is *Realpolitik*. The crucial point here is not to attempt to beguile oneself or others that such decisions are exclusively based on rational evidence through reconstructing the decision-making process.

Managerial decision making of this nature is difficult not least because there are often powerful baronies vying to secure their position. In such situations, managers are at risk of becoming dominated by the politics of the situation rather than its effective resolution. It is precisely in such situations (which occur more frequently than most of us would like to admit) that it is useful to refocus upon the problem and why are we attempting to solve it. 'What is right may not be popular and what is popular may not be right' applies in this instance.

This approach helps to free those concerned with management, including those who bear the consequences, from the tyranny of prejudicial management. This does not deny the importance of intuition to the manager's craft but avoids enteric management (or gut feeling) being the only club in the manager's bag.

The objective of evidence-based management is that managers should simultaneously and optimally manage today, learn from yesterday in order to create a better future. Management decisions may be plotted along a continuum indicating the extent to which research based information is used (see Figure 2.1.1). Applying this test to management decisions, including, for example, reorganisations or judgements on individual and organisational performance, is a useful element of the decision making process. Some managers, of course, will prefer not to allow evidence to challenge well-formed prejudice matured over an extended period. The uncomfortable realisation that some long-standing view may be wrong or outdated is captured by a rhetorical question ascribed to John Maynard Keynes: 'When the facts change, I change my mind. What do you do?' A valuable management mantra is: 'There will always be a better way' and the challenge is its perpetual discovery and skilful implementation.

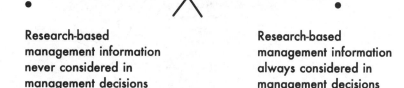

Figure 2.1.1 Evidence-based management continuum

The frequent requirement for urgent management decision making is, of course, recognised. Fast, intuitive management responses are often essential. This is not challenged. However, there are management issues, often long-term initiatives, that can benefit from strengthened evidence-based consideration. Designing evidence-based management into a project plan, at an early stage, enables inclusion often without the overhead of additional time. Taking the right decision ultimately saves time and management effort because it avoids the need to rework the problem or repair damage. An evidence-based management approach will also help to ensure that the right, well-defined problem is addressed through effective analysis, implementation and evaluation.

Where is the evidence in evidence-based management?

Evidence-based management is at an earlier evolutionary stage than evidence-based clinical practice. The evidence-based management cycle is iterative (see Figure 2.1.2).

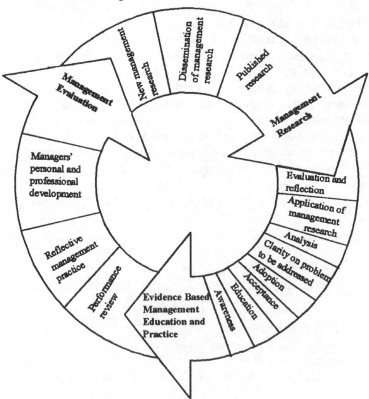

Figure 2.1.2 Evidence-based management cycle

Many sources of research exist to inform management decision making. The problem is distilling management research findings to the most high-quality, relevant and pithy. This is a skill itself. There are many high-quality, peer reviewed journals that publish accessible management research of relevance to the practising manager. Care needs to be exercised when reading research papers to ensure that they satisfy quality assurance criteria. There may be opportunities for action research using resources within the organisation, perhaps associated with management development activities. Local university departments and libraries can provide guidance on published research and support. Well-framed benchmarking exercises provide pertinent information. Secondments can be constructed for managers undertaking focused research, with appropriate supervision, on particular issues. The secondment project should include the requirement critically to synthesise available research and describe the implications for the question under examination.

Managers often undertake undergraduate and postgraduate courses that include management research. The emphasis suggested is that such research should not be seen as disconnected to the management mainstream. Properly focused and conducted, it *is* the management mainstream. The focus should be upon the why, what and how of effective management intervention. It is important to create time for managers to be trained in research techniques and encouragement for their application to contemporary management problems. Opportunities can also be designed into management teamwork and decision taking for reflection and evaluation about the quality of the content and process of the group's work. While this is not research-based evidence, it contributes to an evaluative climate in which constructive challenge is positively encouraged. For some organisations this will be more radical than it sounds.

Information grounded in research can be generated from well-designed management pilot projects. This applies to the recently announced first wave of health action zones. Considerable learning may be derived from such work providing this objective is designed into the exercise and appropriate plans are made for effective dissemination (Dawson, 1995).

Organisational transformation requires individual transformation

Organisational transformation is an increasingly common corporate objective in today's turbulent healthcare climate. Fundamental changes in organisational delivery systems, culture, values, quality and cost are only realistic ambitions if individual employees are enabled to discover fresh reserves of energy, creativity and confidence within themselves. The epiphanic language and management hyperbole used by some, to describe organisational transformation, deflects attention from the subtle yet profoundly important change required at the level of the individual. The process of 'personal transformation' describes a fundamental change in the way in which individuals comprehend themselves, their colleagues and organisation, the wider world and their capacity for taking each forward. Bohm (1980: 159–60) suggests that 'metamorphosis' more adequately captures its nature:

> The change is much more radical than the change of position of orientation of a rigid body, and that it is in certain ways more like changes from caterpillar to butterfly (in which everything alters in a thorough going manner while some subtle and highly implicit features remain invariant).

Like much in management, this is more easily said than done. The manager's objective therefore becomes helping to create an organisation served by individuals for whom work includes the possibility of accomplishing the seemingly extraordinary. Creation of such an environment is important, difficult and long term. It is not achieved by exclusive attention to an organisation's financial obligations.

Managers can contribute to the process of others' 'personal transformation' through applying organisational diagnostic skills. These skills help the manager make and implement more expert decisions while striving to create a more effective organisation. Experience of management research will sensitise the manager to the critical importance and complexity of effective implementation and how difficult it is to accomplish. The awareness may be expressed through carefully crafted organisational interventions to generate shared objectives by effective communication, education and training programmes, recruitment, selection and reward strategies aligned to the organisation's long-term purpose.

As individuals, we all need to be encouraged to discover and realise our potential rather than to have our contributions fossilised in outdated job descriptions. Often we assume too many constraints, when in truth, we are more constrained by ourselves than others. Outdated management practices need to be replaced with new methods determined by imagination, not conditioning. An approach used by one manager is to write job descriptions in a way that focuses on the contribution that the particular post makes to giving the patient the best possible experience and outcome. A cleaner's job description, for example, would include the important contribution that a clean environment makes to the patient's feeling of well-being. At the Leicester Royal Infirmary, job descriptions increasingly reflect the contribution made to the patient's process of care.

The manager is ultimately responsible for creating the environment in which individual growth may flourish focused upon fulfilment of the organisation's mission. Managers must also face this responsibility inwardly. Managers are responsible for managing themselves. Self-management includes extending personal effectiveness and the resolution of the uneasy tension between home and work, so frequently the least exercised accomplishment. Managers should prepare and implement personal development plans to close the gap between the competencies required of them today and those of the future. The Institute of Health Service Management's continuing professional development initiative provides an excellent framework for managers. Personal development can be discontinuous and sometimes uncomfortable, fashioned by the hammer of experience striking the anvils of knowledge and ignorance alternately. This provides the source of personal and organisational fulfilment, optimism and perhaps survival.

References

Ham, C., Hunter, D. and Robinson, R. (1995) 'Evidence based policy making', *British Medical Journal*, 14 January, vol. 310, pp. 71–72.

Sackett, D., Rosenberg, W., Gray, M., Haynes, R. and Richardson, W. (1996) 'Evidence based medicine: what it is and what it isn't', *British Medical Journal*, vol. 312, 13 January, pp. 71–72.

Dawson, S. (1995) 'Never mind solutions: what about the issues? Lessons of industrial technology transfer for quality in healthcare', *Quality in Healthcare*, vol. 4, pp. 197–203.

Bohm, D. (1980) *Wholeness and the Implicate Order*, Routledge & Kegan Paul, London.

2.2

Ethical Management

Brian Aird, Chief Executive, South
Staffordshire Health Authority

Introduction

Management in health services is often portrayed in public as 'the men in grey suits', intent on closing hospital beds, cutting back services, saving money and caring little about the sick, the aged and the disadvantaged. The NHS internal market, in the context of demand outstripping resources, has certainly brought rationing decisions more sharply into focus and has posed considerable dilemmas for managers and clinicians alike. It has also generated a debate about the basis on which such decisions are made, in parallel with, rather perversely, a growing suggestion that a comprehensive welfare state induces dependency and erodes individual freedom of choice.

Quite apart from the fact that the 'men in grey suits' are very often women, the truth is that those concerned with the provision of healthcare or the improvement of health are governed by a set of values which are essentially altruistic in origin. To be capable of practical and useful application, the values must be shared by society at large as such consensus provides the framework within which consistent and sustainable decisions can be made; otherwise each decision becomes a unique event. It is also true that managers are the custodians of the processes of decision making and are most ideally placed to make choices about the use of resources, as they are largely (though not always) removed from individual patient contact.

It is entirely appropriate for managers in the public sector to implement the policies of the government of the day, but to do so indiscriminately is to deny the public the benefit of the knowledge and experience of that manager in the context of the particular situation. If, therefore, a manager knows that a particular government objective may have an adverse effect on patients or the community, those doubts should be expressed. Yet it may not be sustainable to argue that management is, like medicine, intrinsically ethical. Managers are paid to manage effectively and that is what they should do. There is a body of knowledge, legislation and regulations covering the husbandry of public resources, staff employment, policy implementation, etc., which governs the practice of management, sitting alongside personal and organisational values. It is unrealistic to suppose that managers can also know and understand all the ethical dilemmas of medicine; that is for doctors to resolve, though increasingly with managerial assistance.

The value base

There are several sets of ethical principles which underpin the value base of the NHS, according to Andrew Wall[1] in his work for the IHSM. These are: utilitarianism, seen as the greatest good for the greatest number; individual rights, where individuals are seen as having rights whatever the circumstances; the ethics of care, which suggest that caring itself is virtuous and those who engage in this activity will therefore do 'the right thing'; and duty-based ethics, which is based on what 'ought' to be done and in which ethical behaviour becomes synonymous with obeying the rules. Quite clearly, all of these principles hold true in particular circumstances but none of them is without its weaknesses; for example, the rights based view does not address the issue of competing demands within finite resources nor does utilitarianism answer questions for managers about what should and should not be done.

In an attempt to give managers some framework within which to capture and work with these differing and often competing ethical forces, the Institute of Health Services Management introduced its Code of Professional Practice in 1997. This short and straightforward handbook sets out the personal and organisational responsibilities and the responsibilities towards individuals of every IHSM member and student. The contents are based explicitly on the Institute's own Statement of Primary Values, introduced three years earlier and derived from extensive consultation and discussion with practising managers. It provides a simple and clear set of signposts for every manager in health services faced with a growing number of seemingly insoluble dilemmas, and reminds managers of their wider responsibilities. Yet it also recognises that the statements contained therein are necessarily of a generalised nature and cannot provide a ready-made decision-making template. The fact is, managers routinely take decisions based on the assessment of a number of different ethical and other considerations and take responsibility for these decisions. That is the burden of management but it is also its freedom.

From theory to practice

Managers have a particular role to play in the overall organisation of health services, in acting as custodians of the process of decision making and for relating these to the public. In choosing what to do in any given set of circumstances, there are a number of approaches which can be taken. Management theory would have it that rational decision making which attempts, in logical order, to collect data, sort them, suggest options, act, then evaluate the outcome is the most credible way to proceed. The trouble is that this is seldom what people do.

Much more commonly, people decide what to do, often on the basis of experience and instinct, then seek a rationale or set of facts to support their conclusion. Only when the facts are widely divergent from the decision will a more thorough examination be set in train. In these circumstances, the underlying values and the process of decision making both need to be sufficiently visible to enable the public to understand how a decision was reached, as much as to understand the decision itself.

This is becoming increasingly important, if only for the defensive reason that the public is now more likely to challenge managerial decisions openly. This quite often takes the form of a judicial review, an approach which by its very nature concentrates on the process of decision making and not the decision itself. It is clear that as resource availability and demand continue to part company on the NHS graph, it is routinely impossible for commissioners and providers to meet their obligations to fiscal rectitude at the same time as satisfying the (legitimate) demands of their public for equitable access to the full range of high-quality care that modern science can provide. In such circumstances, and with an increasingly well-informed and articulate public, it is inevitable that many decisions will satisfy some but not all constituencies. Many managers have an increasing sense that in some situations there is no 'right' decision, only a set of trade-offs, an advantage here, a disadvantage there, all of which must be carefully weighed. Thus the way in which decisions are taken, the factors which are brought to bear in the decision-making process, the range of opinion sought (both professional and lay) are of the essence when the decision itself is viewed with that most reliable of all tools, twenty-twenty hindsight.

The essential role of managers in this context thus becomes one of creating the best conditions possible for 'good' decisions to be made. This is amply illustrated by reference to the concept of corporate governance. Managers have a clear responsibility to ensure that proper systems are in place to demonstrate that the principles of probity and integrity underpin all decisions relating to the use of resources; that everything done in the name of the NHS can stand the test of Parliamentary scrutiny, public judgement and professional codes of conduct; and that there is sufficient openness about activities to promote confidence between the organisation, patients and the public.

Inevitably, of course, not all situations present a clear set of guiding principles and a body of accepted good practice. Take, for example, the case of a health authority which sees the need to ensure its population has broadly equal access to a consistent level of mental health provision, requiring a redistribution of resources between two relatively small NHS trust providers; and some re-ordering of the service model to meet accepted best practice standards. Let us look at just two of the means of achieving this objective. One would be to describe a broad service model and configuration, consult widely, publish; then seek to implement its framework through the merger of the two trusts into one coherent organisation. This would enable the new trust to concentrate on the practical implementation issues, manage the changes properly, ensure a consistent service pattern and as a helpful byproduct release management cost savings for reinvestment in services in due course.

Another means, if the two trusts could not agree to merger, would be to specify services at a far greater level of detail, consult widely, publish; then seek to implement through a competitive tendering process, focusing on both qualitative and financial parameters. This second model would result in a 'winner' and a 'loser', leaving residual assets and liabilities to deal with. It would most likely also lead to a greater number of redundancies. Both models would result in major organisational disruption at the delivery end but the first model would enable a more orderly approach. In such circumstances, are the trusts behaving ethically in refusing to merge? Is the health authority being ethical in moving resources if it could result in the destabilisation of one of its providers? Is it, in the end, a straight choice between staff redundancies and patient services? Of course, if the authority was able to demonstrate significant benefit for its population, the utilitarian argument might apply. On the other hand, if the trusts could demonstrate that the organisational disruption was very likely to undermine delivery of patient care and result in substantial loss of professional expertise, the 'ethics of care' argument might win. In reality there is probably an argument for a judgement to be made by an impartial but interested party, such as the regional office. The role of managers is thus to focus very clearly on the benefits to patients, their relatives and carers; and to be able to marshal as much real evidence (as opposed to emotion or tribalism) as possible.

Take another example: a new drug is introduced which for the first time provides some treatment for a degenerative condition in a growing section of the population. This might be a cause for celebration were it not for the fact that it is not only very expensive per treatment, but it has been brought to market with only very limited trial evidence in support. Such evidence as exists suggests only very limited benefit, at certain stages of the disease, for a limited period. In addition, there is no evidence about long-term benefits or about side effects. What should commissioners, providers and doctors do? Recent judicial reviews indicate that a blanket ban on providing any licensed treatment is unacceptable, yet it seems to represent poor value for money. Demand will be high and resisting it will be difficult, publicly and politically. Meeting all demand would bankrupt most trusts and seriously skew the priorities of even the largest health authorities. In the circumstances, some method of rationing seems inevitable. The role of the manager must therefore be to ensure that the different rationing options are properly explored, that relevant clinical and research opinion is sought, that the views of patients, their carers and/or representatives are engaged through informed debate and that a clear decision is made and communicated. In so doing, it may also be wise to work with colleagues in neighbouring authorities/trusts in order to seek to establish a more consistent approach for a wider population. Indeed, there is an argument for such decisions to be made at national level for this reason.

The new NHS: modern, dependable

Will the changes to the NHS outlined in the late 1997 NHS White Paper make any difference to the ethical dilemmas in management? Arguably, they may become easier to handle in some respects, for example through the creation of a National Institute for Clinical Effectiveness. This body, charged with gathering, analysing and disseminating evidence on best clinical practice, could in time evolve a national approach to the introduction of new technologies as well as assessment of those already in use. Equally, the development of national service frameworks in the Calman/Hine mould will assist managers and clinicians alike by describing in practical terms an evidence base for local decisions about patterns of service delivery. In addition, the 'duty of partnership' on NHS bodies and the requirement for health authorities and primary care groups to engage a wide range of stakeholders, including the public, in the preparation of health improvement programmes could lead to greater acceptance of both the opportunities and the limitations of health services locally.

The emphasis on quality, as exemplified in the proposals on clinical governance and the Commission for Health Improvement, will, however, bring the cost versus quality dilemmas into very sharp focus; and will do so in a context which places increased emphasis on openness in decision making.

Finally, the intention to put GPs at the heart of commissioning decision making will give this group of staff, for the first time, an opportunity to experience the unenviable trade-offs which are an everyday part of the commissioning process. The first GPs faced with the prospect of closing their local community hospital to protect the level of services across the district may not relish their new freedoms and responsibilities and will need to muster all their understanding of ethics to help them through.

References

1 Wall, A. (1993) Future Health Care Options: Values and the NHS. Briefing paper given at the Health Services Management Centre, University of Birmingham, IHSM, London.

2.3

Primary Care Partnerships: 'What Counts is What Works'

Robert Sloane, Chief Executive,
Andover District Community
Health Care NHS Trust

The 'product of partnership' – more and better services for patients – is at the heart of the new collaboration culture expected of public sector agencies.

But the creation of strategic alliance goes far beyond the statutory organisations to embrace a wider community of interests. In the Hampshire town of Andover the power of community collaboration has delivered striking results and the promise of more to follow.

Introduction

Almost immediately after the 'third wave' Andover District Community Health Care NHS Trust was established on 1 April 1993, planning began to effect its transition into a primary care agency. Thirty GPs, then clustered in five main practices, had played a decisive role in both embracing fundholding and sponsoring the trust application. For the Trust, one of only a handful in the country without a previous directly managed unit history, the challenge was:

- to put in place the infrastructure with which to run the fledgling organisation;
- to meet all the mandatory 'must dos';
- to promote a series of 'driver' programmes designed to secure closer integration between primary and community care.

At the heart of this initiative were specific projects concerned with;

- epidemiological mapping (the Andover Health Project);
- consumer surveys (Local Voices);
- information management;
- integrated clinical audit.

The benefits of collaboration seemed strikingly evident, even in a climate where competition was the order of the day and purchaser–provider separation was regarded in some quarters as a universal truth. Early informal meetings between Trust Board and senior partners of the GP practices led in 1995 to a more structured co-operation arrangement between the two parties. Subsequent partnerships with social services, the local authority and local community have led to integrated models of care and an embryonic form of 'community governance' in which the Community Health Council also plays an important part.

A public planning inquiry in 1996, believed to be unique in the recent history of the NHS, pointed up the potential for the delivery of a primary care 'agency' in Andover. The specification of the 'agency' based on a combined commissioning/providing function fore-shadowed the primary care trust model introduced in the new NHS White Paper of December 1997.

Once the import of the new NHS White Paper was clear an expression of interest in establishing a primary care trust in Andover with effect from 1 April 1999 was lodged by the Andover GPs and the Andover NHS Trust.

A natural community

Andover is a natural community, described both by the geographical configuration and socioeconomic characteristics of the resident population, but also by a strong sense of community purpose which binds the urban core and surrounding villages. There are 70,000 people living in this part of north-west Hampshire.

The population base of the locality, said to be the fastest growing in the south of England, corresponds with the fifteen wards of Test Valley Borough Council and is equidistant from Basingstoke, Salisbury and Winchester. It also enjoys co-terminosity with the area structure of Hampshire Social Services.

Prevailing health issues

The multi-agency Andover Health Project, which began in 1994, has been instrumental in mapping the health needs of the locality. The project, facilitated by a health visitor, working closely with the Public

Health Department of North and Mid Hampshire Health Authority, was initially based on practice profiles which illustrated the nature of underlying health issues:

- the surprising extent of urban deprivation (and resultant health and social problems) concentrated in a few urban electoral wards;
- the specific health and social care needs of the highly transient military population which has had a long established presence in the area;
- the particular difficulties faced by the many rural communities in coping with isolation, unemployment, lack of amenities and information and inadequate public transport.

The early practice profiling work has increasingly been augmented by information provided from the Test Valley Borough Council, Hampshire Social Services and local voluntary groups.

In support of the Andover GPs' move towards total purchasing by 1 April 1998, a more comprehensive evidence-based health profile was compiled. This drew not only on epidemiological mapping, but also on extensive surveying of the local community to assess priorities.

Health services in Andover

The (now six) practices in the Andover locality have a registered practice patient population in excess of 50,000 patients. Fundholding is well rooted, with only a recently established single-handed practitioner not in the scheme.

The history of collaborative working between GPs goes back a long way. The dynamic is due in part to the need in times past when the policy emphasis did not smile altogether favourably on primary care – to exert collective muscle in the battle for resources.

Unity in adversity was also tempered by a more natural instinct to work beyond the practice for the greater good of the community. In this respect, the 100-bed Andover War Memorial Community Hospital, cosseted and cherished by the local community is a natural extension of and support to primary care. Although increasingly regarded by the professionals as a base from which integrated care is provided in the community, the hospital remains a potent symbol of what the NHS stands for in the eyes of the local community.

The service portfolio offered by the Andover NHS Trust is unusually broad for such a small organisation, encompassing a 'little bit of everything' from family planning to palliative care. The archetypal corner shop provides acute, community and mental health services within the hospital and community settings.

When separated from its parent in a 'disaggregation' exercise, the new Trust was credited with a budget line to 'buy in' a whole raft of services from the maternal home. In this very act the Trust was constituted (and thought of itself) both as a purchaser and provider service. With the adoption of fundholding by the five main practices the health system in Andover became effectively a federation of six small healthcare businesses each with purchasing and providing responsibilities.

Achievement

Perhaps the only material test of the Fundholding / Trust partnership is how well it has served the local community. Five years on, the residents of Andover benefit from:

- an increased range of new locally accessible services – ultrasound, mammography, endoscopy, cataract surgery;
- increased choice of referral hospital for more complex diagnosis and treatment as new relationships have been forged with neighbouring district general hospitals;
- improved access to local services with some of the shortest waiting times in the area (increasingly being referred to by GP fundholding outside of the area);
- service standards and quality ranking among the very best in the country;
- new approaches to meeting defined health needs witnessed by a 'pacesetting' podiatry project and multidisciplinary back service;
- restoration of services, such as chiropody, which had previously been cut by a sister organisation.

More recently, the extraordinary degree of interagency collaboration which exists in Andover has led to:

- the establishment of a fully integrated adult community mental health team – a joint enterprise between health, social services and the voluntary sector. The team has been very successful in maintaining clients in the community and reducing the demand for inpatient services. Pooling of resources has led to savings which have been reinvested in service development;
- the commendation of the health/social services/education-funded Early Years Centre by OFSTED inspectors;
- the mobilisation of a joint GMS/HCHS linked nurse triage service/minor injuries which could form the basis of a full primary care emergency service for the locality, including helpline provision.

The most remarkable aspect of these gains is that they have been achieved with almost 15 per cent less money in the local health system than on 1 April 1993.

This proud record of attainment (with not a single service having been cut in the period) is the product of:

- collective agreement among GPs about local health needs and the will to bring about change;
- ingenuity on the part of a small provider organisation to facilitate the implementation of new service models (drawing on the skills and competence as well as the good ideas of its well motivated workforce);
- the capacity of other local agencies, including the local community, to lend their support to enable new patterns of service to emerge.

In bringing about these changes, the wider community of Andover have experienced or observed a greater degree of involvement in the way their health services are planned and managed. The work already referred to in identifying local health need has been supported by special interest fora, public meetings and open days. The local health economy has benefited in large measure from two exceptional chairmen who have led the Trust through establishment and into next-step development. Their contribution has been augmented by the capacity of talented and public-minded non-executive directors.

A measure of the sensitivity with which the local healthcare system is geared to the needs of the community was the Charter Mark earned by the Andover NHS Trust in 1997.

Relationships with the local media are strong and health is very much a subject of civic interest. Although the Andover War Memorial Community Hospital inevitably remains an object of much local affection and support, the Health Promoting Hospital accreditation awarded in 1996 is evidence of the increasing role it will play in wider community-based health promotion activity.

Less visible to the public eye is the extent to which health outcomes are attempting to be measured. Since the inception of the Andover NHS Trust an active integrated clinical audit programme has been initiated. Well supported by primary and community care teams the Andover approach has been applauded in view of its multidisciplinary focus. This provides an ideal starting point from which to assess clinical effectiveness and move towards the concept of 'clinical governance'.

Rationale

The establishment of a primary care trust in Andover will bring further benefit to patients in the local community and wider health care system as a result of:

- devolving a greater proportion of the healthcare budget to the locality where the track record of providing needs-led value for money services is already excellent;

- ensuring and formalising local influence within an open and accountable framework evolving from the well-established model of 'community governance' involving GPs, local authority, NHS trust, social services and community health council;
- enabling even closer working relationships with statutory and voluntary sector partners building on the confident linkages that exist and producing community responses to *Our Healthier Nation* and adding to the portfolio of integrated services;
- tailoring primary care based services to local need allowing unified budgets to devise new patterns of managed care, utilising skills and competence of different team members;
- releasing economies of scale from the local healthcare system by avoiding duplication, making better use of resources and especially lowering transaction costs;
- easing pressure on acute services within the wider healthcare network by allowing each element of the system to concentrate effort on what they are best at;
- diminishing reliance on the private sector as a consequence of new service patterns and repatriating work which flows into the private sector at greater expense to the public purse.

Beyond these immediate benefits there is a clear expectation that the national policy emphasis will increasingly promote the health maintenance approach which fits the environmental characteristics of Andover perfectly. In this context it should be emphasised that the strengths of Andover lie in very good primary and community care. While there is a keen appetite to continue the development of locally accessible services, these must remain subject to the strictest tests of clinical and cost effectiveness and strategic fit.

Conclusions

No one in the local setting underestimates the difficulties that lie ahead, nor the formidable programme of work that has to be managed.

There is no ambiguity either about the dismantling of fundholding nor the voluntary winding up of the Andover NHS Trust – once the new primary care trust is legally constituted.

The drive for further change and the accompanying uncertainty it brings to a number of key individuals in the existing system is primarily about a belief in the potential to improve the health status of the local and wider population.

It may also be due to an outlook which favours shaping the future rather than being shaped by it.

Why Aren't We Waiting?

Stephen Day and David Lye,

NHS Executive

West Midlands Regional Office

The West Midlands Treatment Initiative began in July 1994. National action had successfully reduced the maximum waiting time for an operation to two years, but attempts to improve on this standard had failed. The treatment initiative involved a greater focus and degree of co-ordination across the West Midlands than before.

Over the next two years, the number of residents on waiting lists fell from 113,000 to 82,000, a drop of 27 per cent. The maximum waiting time fell to nine months; at the start of the initiative, 16,000 people had been waiting more than nine months for treatment. The number waiting more than six months for treatment fell from 32,000 to 4,500, a drop of 86 per cent. And patients waiting more than 13 weeks for their first outpatient appointment fell from 35,000 to 17,000 between December 1995 and July 1996.

So how did we achieve this and what lessons are there for other parts of the country tackling the same problem?

Crucially, there was a very strong commitment from the top. The chairman and chief executive of the regional health authority and their fellow directors made cutting waiting lists their top priority. The RHA set up a high profile project team led by the chief executive of a West Midlands NHS trust to promote good practice and manage performance, often to the level of individual patients. Much of the success of the initiative was based on improving standard procedures, for example the handling of referral letters from GPs to hospital consultants, or the management of consultants' workload – activities carried out at relatively low levels in most hospitals.

The project team had a strong analytical focus, and good timely information – not always a feature of the NHS – was one of the keys to success. The team made extensive use of data on performance, including bulletins on day case rates by specialty, average lengths of hospital stay and theatre utilisation rates in hospitals, as well as 'did not attend' and 'return visit' rates in outpatient clinics.

We also developed 'real-time' information on waiting times, based on use of contract minimum data sets (CMDS) which allows fast-track monitoring of trends, analysis of 'stocks and flows' of people on waiting lists, and analysis by specialty and procedure. It also inspired the development of the 'Golden Bullets' toolkit which allows detailed analysis of potential efficiency gains, looking at day case rates and lengths of stay down to procedure level.

The first task was to check the accuracy of existing waiting lists. This actually led to a temporary increase in numbers as the project team discovered patients who had been suspended from waiting lists or 'lost' in administrative cul de sacs.

Having established the size of the problem, the priority was to treat the 'tail; of people who had been waiting the longest for treatment. In some cases this was possible through laying on extra theatre sessions, but in some cases there was not the capacity locally to clear the lists.

This led to the creation of a Patient Options Service (POS) to offer patients the choice of quicker treatment elsewhere. The conventional wisdom in the NHS was that patients would prefer to wait longer for treatment near to home. But the POS achieved success by making it easy for patients to travel for treatment. It offered patients a package including transport and overnight stays for a relative. For example, cardiac patients transferred to a London teaching hospital travelled in a group and were encouraged to have a relative accompany them, who was accommodated free of charge in the hospital nurses' home. Particular care was taken to ensure that after-care was ready to be provided to these patients when they returned home. One of these patients, who travelled from Coventry to London for a heart bypass operation, said: 'I never believed the NHS could be like this.'

We also appointed a number of specialist surgeons on a short-term basis to help clear backlogs of long waiters. For example, a consultant plastic surgeon was engaged at the Royal Shrewsbury Hospital for several months. In addition, the initiative used private facilities where this was both necessary and cost-effective.

As a matter of deliberate policy, the region gave much publicity to our promise to reduce the maximum wait to nine months. This put pressure on the service to achieve its aims. Publicity initiatives included publication of average waiting times, by consultant, in local papers, a patients' freephone 'hotline' and public advertising, including advertising on West Midlands buses advising people to contact the hotline if they believed they had been waiting longer than nine months for treatment. Officials made many appearances on TV and radio to promote the initiative.

None of this was cheap, of course. The initiative cost £30–£20 million in 1994–95 and £10 million in 1995–96. This is a considerable sum, but a modest percentage of the total spend on health services, which was over £2 billion in 1995–96.

So what has happened since the initiative? The latest national figures indicate that the West Midlands continues to have the shortest waiting list for its residents and the shortest waiting times. But it has to be said that the figures have deteriorated. At the end of November 1997 there were 98,000 West Midlands residents on the waiting list, including 19,000 waiting longer than six months, 6,000 waiting more than nine months and 1,748 12-month waiters.

This is still significantly better than the position in July 1994 and the number of long waiters is substantially lower than in other NHS regions. Of West Midlands residents 98 per cent are treated within 12 months as opposed to 95.2 per cent nationally, and seven out of the ten best-performing health authorities are from the West Midlands.

However, the deterioration is real. It would be easy to blame underfunding, but the problem in the West Midlands and elsewhere hides a varied pattern, which suggests that other forces are at work. Of 25 general and specialist acute hospital trusts in the region, seven have no 12-month waiters, another four have fewer than 10, while six trusts have more than 100 12-month waiters (and over 75 per cent of the total in the region). Indeed, 23 per cent of all over 12-month waiters are on the lists of one hospital.

This disparity suggests that managerial lessons and changes in clinical culture have taken root in some hospitals but not in others, and that demands for extra funding need to be set against an imperative to raise the performance of the worst towards the best. There is no apparent correlation between numbers of long waiters and the size and complexity of the hospital. University Hospitals Birmingham, which includes the main teaching hospital in the region, has just 42 nine-month waiters in total including nine 12-month waiters, illustrating what can be achieved by effective management and clinical consensus, while another hospital with tertiary as well as local services has one of the worst records with 723 nine-month waiters, including 197 12-month waiters.

That said, waiting times clearly suffer when hospitals or health authorities get into financial problems. Of the six trusts with more than 100 12-month waiters, five have been managing deficits in 1998.

As well as the difference in performance between hospitals, there are differences between specialties. Orthopaedics is a widespread problem, and there have been local problems in general surgery, urology and ophthalmology. In one trust, for instance, which has a very good overall track record, there are very long waiting times for one complex plastic surgery procedure.

Where do we go from here? Health ministers are committed to delivering the manifesto promise of shorter waiting lists and are keen to see fewer long waits for treatment as well. The variations in performance give us hope that we can improve the position in the West Midlands, but this depends on maintaining financial stability where it already exists, and achieving it elsewhere. However, if we want to make major gains, the experience of the treatment initiative is that it will cost money over and above the improvements in efficiency and management performance.

A new West Midlands regional task force has now been set up, which will once more promote the good cause of minimising waiting lists and times. It will use the comparative information held by the region to encourage all hospitals and health authorities to do better. Achieving success will again require the commitment of managers and clinicians, but the treatment initiative and the continuing achievements of a number of trusts and health authorities in the West Midlands have demonstrated that it is possible to achieve and sustain major reductions in waiting lists and times.

This article was first published in the February 1998 issue of Health Management, *the official magazine of the IHSM.*

2.5

Mergers, Closure and the Way You Tell 'Em

Roy Lilley

'It's all right dear, doctor says you can go home now; we need the bed.' I heard those words from a nurse, in a hospital just recently. I think what the nurse meant to say was: 'Mrs Smith, the doctor says you've done really well. I expect you would like to finish getting better in the comfort of your own home and we are arranging for you to go home tomorrow. That's good news, isn't it?' In the words of Frank Carson, the comedian: 'It's the way you tell 'em.'

Communication

Communication, 'how you tell 'em', it is at the heart of it all. Certainly it is at the heart of merger. It is clear that service reconfiguration is on the government's agenda and that can only mean more mergers. In the wonderful, weird and wacky world of healthcare there is no other word that can be relied upon to excite more people to the edge of florid indignation than that six-lettered one. One whiff of it and everyone is under the ether of outrage, protest and demonstration.

At the first whisper of: 'We need to reconfigure services, with a speciality review, leading to merger', light the blue touchpaper, stand back and wait for the bang! Can we say it differently? Well, we could say: 'We think we should try to reorganise ourselves so that we can treat more people.' Or: 'We think we should try to make sure we provide a safer and more efficient service.' What about: 'We think we should organise ourselves so that we can put more money into treatment.' You might like: 'Merger is not something we are anxious to do but pressures of finance and huge improvements in medical technology mean that we can't stand still. The NHS is like anything else, we have to move with the times.' You see, it is 'How you tell 'em'.

What is merger?

Consolidate, centralise, concentrate, focus, integrate, combine, amalgamate, blend, fuse, unify, combine. There are a lot of words we can use. I guess we are stuck with merger. Merger mania. The word merger was first coined by the Conservatives, who used it as a euphemism for closure. Back in the health reforms of the early 1990s non-executive newcomers from the worlds of business and commerce immediately recognised what some NHS managers had been saying quietly for some time. There were too many hospitals in the system, too much capacity and some of it should be cut. In other words, close some hospitals and redistribute the cash and make two hospitals do the work of three. The public, waiting in queues and sleeping on trolleys in hospital corridors, found it incomprehensible.

'Closure' is a word no politician is prepared to do battle for and the invisible army at the Department of Health had no stomach for a fight.

'Merger', a word borrowed from the lexicon of business, seemed to fit nicely into the dictionary of healthcare. The trouble is the public read between the lines and came to the wrong conclusions. The whole reconfiguration argument got off on the wrong foot and the NHS has been on the run ever since.

The Thatcher NHS reforms were in gestation when Nelson Mandela was still in prison and implemented when Greta Garbo was still alive. We will shortly be flipping over into a new century and nothing looks any easier. Many of the same problems remain. We have learned that the NHS is not a business. In fact, to many observers, it appears to be more like a cult or a religion. A business it may not be, but who said it cannot be run in a business-like way: borrowing from business to bring the NHS closer to what the best of our businesses deliver to their customers.

Opening hours

Grocery stores, petrol stations, mail order companies and insurance firms have all realised it costs money to close the door. More and more service organisations are throwing away the front door key and keeping their entrances open, permanently. The fixed assets exist around the clock and the costs do not stop when you close.

However, if you drive past an acute hospital on a Sunday you will probably find that the doctors' car park is empty. It is likely to be relatively empty on a Saturday too. This is not because doctors jog to work at the weekend. It is because they are not there. The NHS is a 24-hour hotel and emergency service, but, after about four o'clock in the afternoon nearly everything else closes up.

Operating theatres, diagnostic equipment and pathology departments see most of their staff clear off after about 5.00pm. Theatres, kit and things that, were they the property of the private sector, would work around the clock. In the private sector there is a phrase that might make a lot of NHS staff turn pale: The phrase is to 'sweat the assets'. It means to make capital items earn their keep. An operating theatre that costs anything up to £5 million to equip and that is scrubbed up and closed up by 4.30pm does not work up a sweat. Working it around the clock, 24 hours a day, seven days a week, is how to get a proper return.

I doubt that many people on the waiting list for a new hip would object to being operated on at 3.00am on an Easter Monday. Mention the idea in the NHS and some doctors come up with an argument that says operating at 3.00am would be undesirable because they and their staff would not be at their best. Unsafe, some have told me. Tell that to airline pilots, long-distance coach drivers, train drivers and intensive therapy unit staff.

Organising the NHS on a three-shift system, working around the clock, would put more money into the scheme of things and take more people off the waiting lists. Close one out of three hospitals, shuffle the money saved between the remaining two and 24-hour working does start to look like a viable idea. The money goes further when it is not consumed by infrastructure expenditure, administration charges and back-office costs.

Closures

Closure – now there is a word. A word marinated in unpalatable truth. A word that comes with a razor-sharp edge and all the tact and diplomacy of a ram raider. Close a hospital and these days the articulate middle classes will wage war from the comfort of their sitting rooms, with their long-range, armour-piercing guns, called computers. Stand by to weigh the letters – you will never have time to count them.

Consultation will turn into a cross between Bedlam and Babel. The press will weave an intricate web of emotion and pain and spin the facts and figures into an unplayable delivery for anyone not used to a sticky wicket. Unwinnable. Ask anyone who has been through the process and they will show you their scars. At the drop of the 'c' word they will start to reminisce, like war veterans; pilots who had bailed out; or special services operatives, caught behind enemy lines – they will tell you their story.

Mergers, closures? It is all the same to a public that has an attachment to its local hospital bordering on the romantic. A public that, understandably, feels safe if there is a hospital in striking distance. Or driving distance. 'What happens if there is an emergency?' is a familiar question, bellowed from the back of a public meeting. It is hard to explain that advances in paramedic training, telemedicine technology and competence means getting to the patient quickly and stabilising them has almost eclipsed the need to get to hospital quickly. Times are changing. The days of the ambulanceman with a bandage and the driving skills of Stirling Moss are over. In inner cities, a paramedic on a motorcycle, arriving at the scene in minutes, is often more important than a blue light dash across town to A&E.

The location of the hospital is often less important than what it does. It is a joke, but a joke with a ring of truth about it; it is cheaper to pay for a taxi to take patients and their relatives to hospital than it is to build a hospital on the doorstep.

Political parties, likely to form a government, are not in the mood to increase taxes, and the evidence of the ballot box is that the public is none too keen to pay them either. In a world where technology is turning the workforce statistics on its head, it is getting harder to harvest the taxes to meet the insatiable demands of public services. The NHS, 50 years old, needs a make-over and may have to go on a diet; service reconfiguration, merger and closure just will not go away.

Merger and the manager

The NHS manager is going to have to a complex and difficult year. If merger is on your agenda, beware! All the evidence from the world of business is that mergers screw up more organisations than they sort out. The McKinsey study of mergers between 1972 and 1984 says only 23 per cent of them worked. A *Business Week* survey in August 1992 discovered that 'The average Bank merger in the 1980s didn't cut costs, didn't raise productivity and actually made the combined Bank less profitable.' It gets worse.

The Michael Porter Study of Modern Mergers discovered that following merger: 18 per cent of senior managers jump ship, 43 per cent of staff demonstrate lower morale, sickness rates increase by 30 per cent of current levels and 'customer' complaints shot up. Porter also says: 'Mergers are a drug that makes managers feel good in the short term but sap the energy of the organisation in the long run.'

Recent mergers have fared no better. The Glaxo Wellcome/SKB merger broke up in fiasco, when the bosses agreed to let 10,000 staff go but fought like ferrets in a sack for their own jobs; BT limped away from the MCI merger; the London Business School reported 75 per cent of British mergers failed to reach their financial targets; and the 1993 Volvo and Renault merger plan collapsed in a heap.

Someone else who knows a thing or two about business, Bill Gates, boss of Microsoft, says: 'Size works against excellence.' I first became interested in NHS mergers in 1993. I wrote at the time and feel it is just as true today:

- The first lesson is mergers are not a policy for tomorrow based on today's circumstances. If poor management or inadequate funding is pushing you towards a merger, sort the problems out and then think about the future.
- Second, they are not a euphemism for service reconfiguration, cutting manning levels and upping productivity, neither are they the political fig leaf of respectability, to disguise the need for closures and rationalisation.
- Third, mergers are a dangerous pastime that have demolished more organisations than they have built.

Having merged a trust and seen the outcome and understood the experience, I have come to realise that there are seven golden rules to remember:

1. Gossip and speculation about the possibility of merger can set the tone for the whole process. So move like greased lightning. Tell everyone as quickly as you can what is happening and keep them up to date with the outcomes.
2. Be honest about why the merger is to take place. Do not pretend it is about better services if the real task is to save money. People are not daft.
3. Get a handle on the size of the task and be realistic about timescales. What are you asking managers to do? Is it realistic?
4. Be straight with staff about their futures. If some are to go, help them move on if you can. People have families, mortgages and bills to pay. You cannot begin to understand morale and motivation until you understand that.
5. The project team must be properly resourced and not weighed down with day-to-day responsibilities as well as merger duties. Help them become a team.
6. Do not use the word communicate. Talk to people, go and see them and do as much as you can face to face. Explain what is going on and why, and share your vision of what the new organisation will look like. A clear leader, the sense of a 'third organisation' is vital.
7. Respect the past and take the best of it into the future.

Finally, crashing two lousy services together will not make either of them better – two turkeys do not make an eagle! You see, communication – at the heart of it all 'it's the way you tell 'em!'

2.6

Risk Assessment – What's It All About?

Gareth Watkins, Partner, Nabarro

Nathanson

Of all the legal changes which have overtaken the world of health and safety in recent years, none has created such a stir nor generated as much interest as the general obligation to carry out risk assessments – first introduced by the Management of Health and Safety at Work Regulations 1992. Some health and safety practitioners will tell you that there's nothing new about risk assessments. 'It's implicit in the general duties under the Health and Safety at Work Act,' they say. 'Assessing risk is a prerequisite for ensuring peoples' safety.' And so it is, in a rough-and-ready informal sort of way – but to nothing like the extent now required to be formalised and documented.

Risk assessments are also 'not new' in another, slightly different sense. Obligations to carry out specific risk assessments, intended to control the risk of particular substances or agents, have been in existence for many years. Exposure to asbestos, lead, noise and hazardous substances have all been subject to the requirement to perform suitable and sufficient or adequate risk assessments.

Yet the general duty ushered in by the 1992 Regulations on 1 January 1993 has been greeted with uncertainty and hesitation by many employers. Some have not yet completed their initial assessments, let alone kept them under review. Others have completed assessments, but in a way which seeks minimal compliance with legal requirements: the assessments may often be viewed as a bureaucratic chore and once completed they are filed away not to be looked at again until a formal review process begins.

The general obligation to assess risk is at the heart of an approach to workplace safety which is fundamentally different from what has gone before. More than any other single piece of legislation, risk assessments suggest a proactive approach to health and safety, which contrasts with a traditionally reactive philosophy to safety which has held sway since the beginnings of the Industrial Revolution. During that time, there have in particular industries been any number of success stories of declining accident rates and diseases being overcome. Many of these advances followed on directly from prescriptive legislation which was itself a reaction to major disasters or unacceptably high accident rates. The occurrence of serious harm was seen as a major agent of change – and in the absence of evidence of harm there was little motivation to change. In expecting employers to assess risks and to act on the basis of those assessments we are asking them to effect changes in the absence of any evidence of harm. We are challenging one of the basic tenets of management – 'if it ain't broke don't fix it'. It is not surprising that many employers have been slow to embrace this new philosophy.

The nature of the duty

Under Regulation 3 of the Management of Health and Safety at Work Regulations (MHSWR) 1992 every employer is obliged to make a suitable and sufficient assessment of the risks to the health and safety to which employees are exposed whilst they are at work as well as the risks to people not in employment arising out of or in connection with the conduct of the undertaking. The purpose of the assessment is to identify the measures which the employer needs to take in order to comply with statutory duties. Those who are self-employed are placed under a like duty.

Before the risk can be assessed, the hazards have to be identified. This distinction, between hazard and risk, is fundamental to successful risk assessment.

- A hazard is something which has the potential to cause harm. It may arise from plant and equipment, systems of work or the work environment.
- A risk is the likelihood of a particular hazard actually causing harm together with the consequences for those affected by the hazard – ie the chances of serious injury or death.

Assessing risk therefore calls for a quantitative exercise of judgment. It is more than an exercise in identification. One of the common reasons for inadequate or incomplete risk assessments is a failure to keep in mind the difference between a hazard and a risk, leading to an unhelpful list of risks without any real effort to evaluate them.

As with some other aspects of occupational health and safety management, there is a perception that assessments are more difficult and demanding to carry out successfully than is in fact the case. However, many of the problems recede if employers concentrate on the key distinction between hazard and risk and avoid overcomplicating the process.

The format of the assessment is one issue which occasionally gives rise to unnecessary levels of concern. What does a risk assessment look like and how do you set about filling it in? The great majority of assessments can be completed in a simple format. When completed the assessment is best regarded as a set of action points – a blue print for change. What it should not develop into is a set of documents to be deposited in a filing cabinet and forgotten.

Stages in risk assessment

Risk assessments are best approached in a sequential set of logical stages, as discussed below.

1.   Classifying activities

Question: How do you eat an elephant? Answer: In small chunks. Risk assessments are a bit like that.

There will be a surprisingly high number of separate activities, or types of activities, carried on. They have to be broken down into manageable chunks and tackled separately. Remember, what are being assessed are risks, not individual employees. Similar physical activities or processes may be the subject of generic assessments.

It is at this stage that an employer can legitimately address the issues of trivial risks – those risks which involve very minor hazards, whose consequences are mild or which are unlikely to materialise anyway. The Approved Code of Practice supporting the MHSWR 1992 (paragraph 9) makes it clear that trivial risks can usually be ignored. It is a matter of judgment as to which risks fall within this category. If in doubt, do not treat a risk as trivial.

The purpose of this preliminary 'risk assessment' is to ensure that the assessment proper concentrates on real, significant risks and does not become bogged down in a morass of very minor risks which would serve only to obscure the genuine dangers rather than highlight them.

It is vital that risk assessments do not become side-tracked into dealing with matters of no real importance, and the stage of classifying activities is a sensible time to carry out this exercise.

2.   Identifying hazards

The next stage is to identify and list the hazards which you can reasonably expect to cause harm in the conditions prevailing in your workplace. In particular:

- Look at hazards which arise from the *work activity* itself. Do not rely on manuals, internal codes of practice or permit to work systems; actual practices differ.
- Look at hazards which arise from the way the work is carried out – not just at the equipment or hardware.

List common hazards which may act as a guideline for hazard identification. Checklist the classes of people who may be affected by hazards. It is important to differentiate between these classes, as a hazard which will not be relevant to, say, members of the public may affect maintenance or repair staff.

3. Determining the risk

When activities have been classified and hazards identified, the next, and crucial, stage of the exercise is the determination of risk. This is the core activity of the risk assessment and calls for a high degree of judgement.

There exists a variety of methods for assisting employers in estimating the level of risk. As risk is the product of the likelihood of a hazard causing harm and the severity of the consequences, many of those methods involve a mathematical approach to the estimate. Numerical values may be ascribed to both likelihood and severity, and by multiplying one value by the other a 'risk factor' is arrived at. For example, if there is a high probability that a hazard will materialise it might attract a value of 4, on a scale of 1 to 5. If, however, the severity of its effects would be mild, then a value of 2 might be appropriate again on a scale of 1 to 5. Thus, the risk factor would be 8 (4 x 2) out of a maximum of 25 – i.e. a fairly moderate risk probably requiring some limited remedial action.

Although this method seems to be in regular use by employers, the use of numerical values seems to introduce a spurious element of scientific precision to what is, in the end, a question of individual opinion, albeit (hopefully) informed opinion.

For most organisations a less sophisticated method of estimating risk would be just as effective whilst being less time consuming. A simpler three-category matrix without numerical values has strong appeal as is shown in Table 2.6.1. This is the model which is suggested in the British Standards of Health and Safety Management – BS 8800. The advantage of this 'risk level estimator' is that it divides up levels of risk into no more than five separate risk banks, narrowing the scope for debate over categorisation of likelihood and severity and producing results in a simple and digestible format.

Table 2.6.1

	Slightly harmful	Harmful	Extremely harmful
Highly unlikely	Trivial risk	Tolerable risk	Moderate risk
Unlikely	Tolerable risk	Moderate risk	Substantial risk
Likely	Moderate risk	Substantial risk	Intolerable risk

4. Specifying action

Having estimated the level of risk, the action points necessary to eliminate and control the risk now need to be specified. In order to do this properly be clear on what each of the five risk bands means and what degree of action (if any) is likely to be necessitated by them. The parameters in Table 2.6.2 offer a useful guide, and again feature in BS 8800. On the basis of the actions and timescales set out overleaf, a risk assessment form can be completed with the appropriate remedial steps required to be taken, and the period during which they need to be completed. Those steps may then be monitored to completion.

5. Reviewing the assessment

The legal requirement is for risk assessments to be reviewed and where necessary modified when they are no longer valid or where there has been significant change in the matters to which they relate (MHSWR 1992 Regulation 3(3)). Although no set intervals are laid down for review it is sensible to build formal periodic reviews into the system, if only to guard against a failure to review in the circumstances envisaged by the legislation.

The fact that a regular review is due to take place at some stage should not be used as a positive reason for putting off reviews following changes in the workplace. The types of changes likely to generate a review of risk assessments are similar to those which will prompt a re-evaluation of the safety policy itself and include the introduction of different systems of work and new plant and equipment.

Table 2.6.2

Risk level	Action and timescale
Trivial	No action is required and no documentary records need to be kept. In retrospect, the type of risk which might have been identified during the classification process.
Tolerable	No additional controls are required. Consideration may be given to a more cost-effective solution or improvement that imposes no additional cost burden. Monitoring is required to ensure that the controls are maintained.
Moderate	Efforts should be made to reduce the risk, but the costs of prevention should be carefully measured and limited. Risk reduction should be implemented within a defined time period. Where the moderate risk is associated with extremely harmful consequences, further assessment may be necessary to establish more precisely the likelihood of harm as a basis for determining the need for improved control measures.
Substantial	Work should not be started until the risk has been reduced. Considerable resources may have to be allocated to reduce the risk. Where the risk involves work in progress, urgent action should be taken.
Intolerable	Work should not be started or continued until the risk has been reduced. If it is not possible to reduce risk even with unlimited resources work has to remain prohibited.

The assessors

There are a number of different views on the question of who should carry out the risk assessments. Provided that the assessor is both competent and trained to carry out the assessment there are no right or wrong choices: it is a question of who is best for the particular assessments in your hospital. The task will often be split up amongst a number of people, perhaps with the overall exercise co-ordinated by the functional safety department under the auspices of the Chief Executive.

There is much to be said for risk assessments being carried out by those employees whose jobs are the subject of the assessments. After all, they know the job better than anyone and should therefore be in a good position to make sound judgments about risks associated with the job and the necessary preventive action. Such assessments do, however, need to be viewed with special care, as there may be a tendency for some employees who are very familiar with a particular machine or process to become rather complacent and to fail to properly recognise hazards which an assessor bringing more perspective to the exercise would identify immediately as requiring attention.

Summary and checklist

Plan a risk assessment programme which is suitable and sufficient for your hospital or organisation. Build into the plan an assessment format, record keeping and regular reviews. Identify and train the assessors. In particular:

1. Classify work activities.
2. Don't overcomplicate the process; discount truly trivial risks at an early stage.
3. Identify the hazard.
4. Evaluate the risks.
5. Plan and carry out necessary remedial action.

Legal sources

General risk assessment

- Management of Health and Safety at Work Regulations 1992 — Regulation 3

Specific risk assessment

- The Control of Lead at Work Regulations 1980
- Control of Asbestos at Work Regulations 1987
- Noise at Work Regulations 1989
- Display Screen Equipment Regulations 1992
- Manual Handling Operations Regulations 1992
- Control of Substances Hazardous to Health Regulations 1994

Please note that an earlier version of this article was published in *The Health & Safety Handbook 1997*, Sweet & Maxwell.

Our Healthier Nation and the New Public Health

Gill Morgan, North and East
Devon Health

The UK has a proud tradition of public health. From the 1840s a focus on the determinants of health led to levels of health improvement, which dwarf anything since achieved by health services. The greatest gains long predate the availability of successful interventions. Health improved because of a broad vision and a systematic approach to improving housing, the cleanliness of water and increasing the availability of wholesome food. This required recognition of the link between public health, social justice and social reform and an acknowledgement that a wide range of factors determines health. Success was achieved by a broad coalition of interests. There was a recognition that public health transcended organisational and professional boundaries, required a wide range of skills and experiences and was not the prerogative of any one group. Sadly this focus on health was lost when effective treatments for sickness were developed. Social and economic trends over the past decades compounded the problem. The publication of the Green Paper signals the rediscovery of a broader and more traditional approach to health improvement and is greatly welcomed.

Our Healthier Nation – A Contract for Health was published in February 1998 as a consultation (Green) paper. It is a major initiative, building on the government's manifesto pledge to improve health. It replaces *Health of the Nation* published by the previous government and marks a change in emphasis with the acceptance that social and economic factors are major determinants of health in addition to individual and behavioural factors. It offers a more integrated approach to tackling ill health and inequalities in health status between different groups, reduces the number of priority areas and sets a limited number of national targets for health improvement. This holistic approach which brings together social, economic and individual strategies has come to be described as the 'new public health'. It is however very similar to traditional public health.

Policy context

The Green Paper is one of three major policy papers that will impact on the development of health and social care over the next ten years. It is unusual for a policy framework to set such a long time scale and reflects governmental confidence. This gives opportunities for a more radical approach to health and social care. *Our Healthier Nation* sets a framework for health improvement that must be addressed by the changes to health services signalled in *The New NHS: Modern, Dependable* and by any changes to social care and services identified in the anticipated social services White Paper. Whilst the NHS White Paper emphasised evolution rather than revolution, the changes implied are increasingly being recognised as fundamental and radical. The social services White Paper can be expected to set a similarly challenging agenda for change. Together the three papers give an enormous opportunity for politicians, clinicians, managers and the public to shape a more effective and better integrated health and social care system that has the goal of improved health at its heart.

Regrettably the Green Paper was not launched as the first of the three documents. The complexity of the issues and difficulties in agreeing robust targets, particularly for reducing inequalities, are rumoured to have delayed publication. The Green Paper does not fully resolve these issues and significant changes can be expected following consultation. Its publication was overshadowed by that of *The New NHS: Modern, Dependable* as many managers and clinicians were already enjoying the favourite NHS game of structural reorganisation and gave less attention to a document that focuses on health. Many of the changes required to improve health lie outside the NHS, are hard to influence and, for many managers who have spent all their time working in health services, can seem irrelevant.

Both papers must be seen in the context of the government's clearly articulated objectives for health and social care to:

- improve health and reduce inequality
- provide integrated services
- improve quality and responsiveness, and raise standards
- improve performance and efficiency

- enable staff to maximise their contribution
- improve public confidence in the NHS and social services.

Fundamental to this approach is a strong commitment to partnership both within and outside health services. Health and social care are very complex and have many key stakeholders. Better integration is needed in service planning and delivery, if access is to be simplified for users and carers.

Contribution of health services

Health services have a small but important role to play in improving health and reducing inequalities. Managers have a responsibility to ensure that services are targeted appropriately; that resources are used where they can produce the greatest benefits; that the quality of the services is improved and that vested interests are challenged for the benefit of patients. Managers must focus on health as well as health services. Whilst other organisations may have a greater influence on health, health organisations have a responsibility to convene, energise, harness and focus the necessary activity. This is a challenging management agenda and one that is very different to recent years. Cultural change will require more than the replacement of the rhetoric of the market to the words of partnership, collaboration and co-operation. In some areas there is no tradition of partnership working and new relationships will have to be developed and trust earned before the benefits of this new approach are seen.

The problem: ill health and inequality

Good health is a great asset and improves the quality of life for individuals. Ill health disproportionately impacts on the poorest in society and the level of inequity currently seen in the UK should be unacceptable in a civilised society. Ill health has a major economic impact leading to lost working days, increased costs and reduced ability to compete. It leads to unemployment, decreased income and to further disadvantage which is shared by all family members. Although overall life span is increasing in the UK, this is not the case for the poorest and most disadvantaged in society. For some groups there is a real decline in health status and the difference in health status between the richest and poorest is widening. An individual's chance of dying depends on his or her social class and reflects income, behaviour, education and other factors. In addition, whilst people are living longer this is associated with increased levels of disability, particularly in the least well off. The aim of a strategy for health must be to add 'years to life and life to years'. This requires good preventive programmes and equity of access to appropriate, responsive and effective health services. The more affluent often have access to better health services than the poor.

In addition to inequities between social groups there are marked geographical differences with people living in the north having significantly worse health status than those living in the south. People from some minority ethnic groups have particularly poor health experiences and positive action is need to deal with this. For example, whilst Asian people have high levels of coronary heart disease, they may face delays in treatment, meet cultural barriers and racism and have lower surgical intervention rates. Language, cultural and organisational barriers lead to worse health outcomes. Women too have lower intervention rates for coronary heart disease. Managers have a responsibility to ensure that systematic action is taken to break down these barriers and ensure that everyone, irrespective of race or gender, has access to responsive services.

Women can expect to live for 79.5 years and men for only 74.3 years. Compared with the rest of the EU however women rank only thirteenth of sixteenth countries, well below the average, whilst men are ranked sixth, above the average. This indicates that there are opportunities to do better. Whilst inequalities in health have been documented for many years, there have been few sustained and effective interventions identified. Finding sensitive measures to chart progress is difficult and complex. *Our Healthier Nation* focuses on a small number of key areas (heart disease and stroke, accidents, cancer and mental health) for which there is at least some evidence of effective interventions. Tackling these is important but to achieve real improvements in health and reductions in inequalities an attack on the underlying determinants of ill health including poverty will be required.

The causes of ill health

In line with the approach of the new public health, the Green Paper takes a broad view of the determinants of ill health; recognition of social factors is once again acceptable after the individual focus of the last decades. The paper identifies a range of influences, each of which needs different strategies:

- Fixed factors
  For example genetic makeup, age and sex over which there is little influence
- Social and economic factors
  Including poverty, employment status and social exclusion. Social exclusion involves social isolation, created by social problems such

as poor housing, unemployment, low pay, fear of crime and isolation, and also economic and psychological isolation. It is assumed that giving people support to help them participate more effectively will reduce the consequent problems. Tackling social exclusion is a key policy strand and the government has established a number of social exclusion units, which aim to develop comprehensive multi-agency approaches to the problem.

- Environment
  The importance of a safe sustainable environment, including air and water quality and the provision of good quality housing is stressed. The approach links in with 'Agenda 21' and the drive for more environmentally friendly policies. The green paper extends the definition to cover the social environment and the recognition of the importance of the quality of life in a neighbourhood is to be welcomed.

- Lifestyle
  The paper combines a broad social approach with a continued emphasis on behavioural issues including diet, physical activity, smoking, alcohol, sexual behaviour and drug misuse.

- Access to high quality services
  Five key areas for activity are highlighted including decent education, top quality health services, high quality social services and good local transport and affordable leisure services.

A contract for health

Our Healthier Nation integrates strategies focused on individual behaviour with more corporate strategies needing intervention by national government or local organisations. Some of these impinge directly on health services whilst others are targeted at other sectors. A new, National Contract for Health sets out the shared responsibilities for improving health. The national contract identifies four priority areas for action, heart disease and stroke, accidents, cancer and mental health, sets a national target for each area and identifies the key component of a national contract for each priority.

National responsibilities

Particularly welcome is the acceptance of the need for an interdepartmental approach to policy making. The appointment of a minister for public health has been widely applauded, as is the commitment to tackle the root causes of ill health. There is some regret however that a more aggressive stance to regulation and legislation has not been endorsed particularly with regard to smoking and fluoridation. Tackling the root causes of ill health will need effective partnerships between government, statutory agencies and non-governmental organisations to address a wide range of issues including:

- unemployment, low pay and social exclusion;
- the provision of decent housing and fuel costs;
- integrated transport policies;
- environmental issues;
- fluoridation;
- reducing smoking;
- the prevention of crime;
- better education;
- 'sport for all'.

Local action

Locally the emphasis is on partnership and joint working involving statutory bodies, business, voluntary and community bodies. The health authority is expected to provide leadership and to co-ordinate the production of a Health Improvement Programme, which identifies how the national contract for health will be delivered. All local agencies are expected to participate and a statutory duty of partnership is being placed on local government as well as health organisations. Effective partnerships depend on good personal relationships and trust, which take time to nurture. It remains unclear how a statutory duty will enable true partnership if there are significant political and organisational barriers. The Government does however expect local governments to take a key role in promoting the economic, social and environmental well-being of their area. The public health role of the NHS will be strengthened to support this activity. The key vehicle for local action is the Health Improvement Programme. The first programmes will be in place by April 1999 and will:

- describe how the national contract will be achieved locally;
- identify local priorities and targets including a focus on inequality;
- agree actions based on evidence of effectiveness;
- identify how progress will be monitored on local and national priorities;
- indicate which organisations are involved and what their role and accountability will be;
- ensure the plan is easy to understand and accessible to the public;
- set the strategy to shape local health services.

Performance will be measured locally and centrally through the new performance indicators and locally agreed measures.

Individual responsibility

The Green Paper also identifies that individuals are responsible for looking after their own health, by avoiding potentially harmful behaviour, and also for ensuring that they do not harm others.

Healthy settings

Three key 'settings' have been identified for special action, schools, the workplace and neighbourhoods. Healthy schools are expected to raise the health awareness of parents and children, provide healthy nutritional choices, encourage exercise and create an environment to support the emotional well being of children. Effective anti-bullying strategies are not specifically mentioned. The recognition of the importance of academic success as a future determinant of health is particularly welcomed. Employers are expected to ensure a safe working place, a smoke-free environment, flexible, family-friendly working arrangements, to reduce stress at work and facilitate healthy choices by workers. Finally a focus on the neighbourhood will give attention to people who are not in the job market including older people, carers and the jobless.

Targets for health

The Green Paper sets challenging but realistic health targets for four areas. Targets have been selected to be challenging but realistic. The national targets for 2010 are to be supplemented by a larger number of locally agreed priorities and intermediate targets are to be identified for 2005. Four areas have been selected for action:

1. Heart disease and stroke
2. Accidents
3. Cancer deaths
4. Mental health

Summary

Our Healthier Nation marks a change in direction for policy towards the broad view of health espoused by the 'new public health' movement. It takes a broad view of the determinants of health, acknowledging the major impact that social, economic and environmental factors have on health. It introduces the concept of a 'Contract for Health' which details national, local and personal responsibilities that encompass social and economic, environmental lifestyle and service approaches to improving health. This is underpinned by the identification of national targets for four key areas. The holistic approach is to be greatly commended.

PART THREE

MANAGING COMMUNICATION

Preparing to Collaborate – Public Participation in Healthcare

Suzanne Tyler, Deputy Director,

Institute of Health Services

Management

The NHS White Paper *The New NHS: Modern, Dependable* sets as one of its key objectives 'rebuilding public confidence in the NHS as a public service, accountable to patients, open to the public and shaped by their views'. Translating this into action will be a major challenge for a service that historically has not been good at working with its users. This chapter reviews some recent thinking in relation to engaging the public effectively and offers some practical examples for translating ideas into action, in the context of new policy initiatives.

History

Historically, the NHS has been a paternalistic doctor-knows-best service, run largely for the benefit of those working in it rather than using it. From the 1970s onwards a backlash started, fuelled by increasing scepticism of the ability of medicine to cure all, some disturbing insights into institutions and the intense concerns of small groups of users. By the 1980s 'patients' had been transformed into 'consumers', reflecting the principles of the market economy and consumer sovereignty with a focus on tailoring services to demands and promoting choice. Public accountability was seen as a managerial rather than a democratic responsibility, with non-executive directors chosen for their skills not their representativeness. At the same time national patient and user organisations played an important role in putting consumer concerns and perspectives on the national agenda. The end of the passive patient was evident in a population with increased knowledge about medicine, declining deference to experts in society and changing attitudes towards doctors.

With the symbolic ending of the market, marked by the White Paper, the notion of patients as rational economic decision makers who have complete sovereignty and are seeking to achieve maximum utility has been comprehensively rejected. But what will replace it?

The new NHS and collaboration

The 'new' NHS rests on a belief in users of healthcare as 'citizens', in which people are empowered to control and influence the provision of services themselves. Thus the NHS has a part to play in wider political agenda of improving democratic practice and improving social cohesion. The success of the White Paper will be judged in part by the openness and accountability of its new structures and processes and its ability to respect the autonomy of individual patients.

There are some very good reasons for putting greater effort into collaboration between the service and its users. We know that outcomes are improved when patients are active participants in decision making about their own care and treatment. We also know this results in greater satisfaction and fewer complaints. For the community itself, involvement in planning and delivery decisions leads to a greater sense of ownership. This is particularly important if we look at one major objective – the reduction of health inequalities. Here the focus given to interagency and intersectoral collaboration needs to be extended to the community itself, both in terms of defining problems, but also in working in partnership towards their solution. Finally, involving people and enabling them access to better information can be a way of improving the use made of health services, ensuring they are neither over- nor underused. Decreasing 'inappropriate' demand at an individual level and designing services on the basis of real rather than perceived need may also help to control the cost of services and improve cost effectiveness.

As a model of public involvement in the NHS, the direct participation of 'the public' either individually or collectively brings the unique perspective of the patient/user or carer to the policy and decision-making process at both macro and micro-level. The challenge lies in acknowledging that the user/carer/patient perspectiveness has a credibility and authority at least equal to the perspective of those who manage, run or provide healthcare. This can be threatening to the existing culture of staff groups within the NHS and will entail renegotiating and redefining the traditional power and status of particularly, but not exclusively, medical professionals.

In looking at public participation, managers should be focusing on both the direct involvement of individual patients/users/carers in planning, organising and delivering their own care and the collective involvement of groups of users organised into patient groups, voluntary organisations and self-help groups influencing the policy and provision of services.

Direct involvement of individuals

The key feature here is that the patient perspective should be integral to the care process at every stage of a patient's journey through the health system. This, of course, presupposes that health services are already moving in the direction of viewing patients in terms of their total experience rather than in relation to discrete episodes of care. Thus at the point of individual contact between an NHS user and provider, the patient perspective is given credibility and treated as of equal value, even when it is a perspective that appears to differ from or question the service's orthodoxy. Putting this approach into practice effectively means involving service users and carers at all stages – planning, delivery, review, reorganisation. Many techniques for successfully involving users have already been documented and the service should find ways to learn from existing best practice.

For individual users, direct involvement in their own care requires access to full and unbiased information and the time to digest such information before being committed to making decisions.

For the service, the direct involvement of users brings tangible gains. People who have a direct involvement in, or genuine opportunity to influence services are less likely to use it 'inappropriately', e.g. missing appointments, non-compliance, etc. There is also a greater likelihood of people understanding and exercising their rights and responsibilities as users and citizens. All of this adds up to a more mature relationship between the service and users/citizens.

Moving towards this approach does, however, require a significant culture shift throughout the NHS. Direct involvement of patients challenges some traditional service values, but is also more likely to help deliver the modern NHS than market-style consumerism. Achieving this culture change is the main barrier to its adoption. The key to shifting current NHS culture must lie in education and in-service training throughout the service. The patient perspective and the importance of patient involvement should be integral to the curriculum of medical, nursing and allied clinical staff, as well as managerial, administrative and support staff. It also requires an ongoing commitment to supporting mechanisms for direct patient involvement. One very obvious example is the tendency to consider patients' expertise, knowledge and contribution as a 'free good'. If patients are to be used in training staff, designing services and monitoring performance etc., their contribution needs to be adequately resourced.

Direct involvement by voluntary organisations and user groups

The UK has a well-developed, active and pluralistic community and voluntary sector. It is made up of a wide range of organisations, self-help and user groups with a spectrum of political ideals and organisational sophistication. At one end are large groups that have incorporated research, policy–making and campaigning into their agenda. They often have skills resources and access to decision making both at national and local level. At the other end are small specialist groups of individuals united around a common issue, with limited capacity to undertake anything beyond peer support and counselling.

Together, these groups offer the NHS enormous experience and expertise, for example, in relation to how diseases and conditions are actually experienced, how treatments and services are actually received, and what the real priorities and issues of concern are for health service users and their families. Incorporating these groups into decision making, therefore, clearly has major benefits for the service in terms of meeting real instead of perceived need, targeting and focusing on areas of neglected need, monitoring quality and performance etc.

The weakness of this approach lies, first, in the inability of the smaller groups to get their voices heard and, second, the tendency of most groups to reflect a limited, largely professional/non-manual and largely white section of society. The danger is that by involving only the larger well-established groups and the individuals within those groups, the service reinforces the inverse care law, whereby those with the most pressing health problems continue to receive an inferior service. The challenge for the service is to capture the knowledge and experience of existing groups and to find ways of reaching those individuals or groups of people who are not members of groups or are not represented by groups, or whose voices have not been heard. This could involve providing practical support to smaller groups, and disseminating information about their activities, while also ensuring that all groups retain their independence and do not become 'incorporated' within the established health system.

There are many effective ways to involve user representatives in policy and planning forums. For example, focus groups, partnering/pairing/buddying, users' forums, standing committees such as maternity services liaison committees. The service needs access to good information on the best of these methods and some guidance on which work best in which situations. Nevertheless, all of these methods do require resourcing and support. Not only should user expertise be recognised in financial terms, but many users will require support, training and guidance before they are 'empowered' to contribute on equal terms with health services professionals. One very simple technique of involving the public directly in policy making would be to encourage health services staff – both clinical and managerial – to negotiate visits to some user/public groups in their venues, and on their terms as a preliminary step to a more effective partnership. this kind of approach would lead to, or connect with community development approaches to service planning.

Moving forward on collaboration and public participation relies on a culture change, which respects and values the contribution of users. This needs a clear commitment from the most senior levels of the organisation in setting a direction of travel, including the NHS Executive, professional organisations and individual leaders and managers.

Conclusions

Rebuilding public confidence in the NHS means treating people as citizens, able to participate in the allocation and management of public resources. Managers facilitating this approach will need to demonstrate the following commitment to the following values:

- acceptance – of the validity of others' experiences;
- confidence – in the capacity of users and carers to make judgements;
- respect – for patients and carers as contributors both at an individual or collective level;
- honesty – a commitment to sharing all relevant information;
- reciprocity of duty – an understanding of mutual responsibility;
- reciprocity of interest – a commitment to pursuing the same goals.

In the context of the 'new' NHS there is plenty of scope for incorporating public participation into the heart of new structures and processes. For example, health improvement plans (HIPs) ought to be shaped by the experiences and priorities of those who use these services. Citizens' juries and citizens' panels are among the ways of encouraging local people to articulate values for guiding HIP development. Similarly community development allows local populations to articulate their own needs and shape the delivery of services within the HIP.

In terms of the primary care groups, community involvement ought to be one of the guiding principles with new arrangements embedded in local accountability agreements. Partnerships and collaboration across health and local authorities are strong themes in both the White and Green Papers and again public participation needs to be built into these new initiatives. Many local authorities already have well-developed methods for involving local people and it makes sense for the NHS to link with and build on these experiences. Finally, the whole public health agenda needs to include a public engagement perspective. The issue for public health is not whether, but how the public can be most effectively engaged in setting local targets for health improvement.

As the input of the public increases, the power of other NHS stakeholders decreases. To date most forms of involvement have focused on service improvements, with health services staff selecting the messages that are easiest to respond to. The challenge in the new NHS is to define those who were previously the object of policy as active subjects, involved as co-producers both at strategic and operational level.

[This chapter is based on work currently being undertaken under the auspices of the NHS Executive's Patient Partnership Initiative.]

3.2

Handling Complaints

Derek Day

New procedures throughout the UK for handling complaints about the NHS and its services were introduced on 1 April 1996. There are some variations to reflect the different management arrangements in the four territories – England, Scotland, Wales and Northern Ireland – but the procedures from the patients' point of view are very similar to those for England which are described in this article.

The new arrangements came into being because of growing concern about the handling of complaints in the NHS in the early 1990s. The Wilson Committee, which was set up by Virginia Bottomley in 1993 to carry out an independent review of the procedures, quickly concluded that the then existing complaints systems were extremely complex, difficult to use and often unhelpful in dealing with patients' concerns. The Committee said that the key to new complaints procedures must be to focus on satisfying complainants' concerns while also being fair to practitioners and staff.

It recommended that for future complaints the arrangements should be built on eight principles:

- responsiveness
- quality enhancement
- cost-effectiveness
- accessibility
- impartiality
- simplicity
- confidentiality
- accountability.

Thoroughness has since been added to the list.

The Committee recommended that the same basic procedures should apply to all parts of the NHS and to all types of complaint, although there would need to be some different features:

- to reflect the fact that the family practitioner services are provided by independent contractors while the rest of the Health Service is provided by health authorities, trusts and their staff;
- to cover complaints where the hospital care and treatment is provided by the private or independent sector rather than an NHS trust.

An important aspect of the recommendations of the Wilson Committee report, *Being Heard*,[1] and the government's response, *Acting on Complaints*,[2] was that they simply set out the basic architecture – the foundations – of the new complaints system, leaving the 'bricks and mortar' to be put in place following consultations with interested parties.

Outline of new complaints arrangement

The new complaints procedures are based on a three-tiered approach:

- local resolution as close as possible to where the complaint arose;
- an independent review, but within the Health Service;
- complaint to the Ombudsman.

The new procedures apply to all complaints – other than those relating to the Code of Openness – made from 1 April 1996. There are various transitional arrangements for dealing with complaints made before 1 April.

A series of directions[3] and regulations provides the legal framework for the new complaints procedures. These are complemented by a series of guidance booklets for trusts, health authorities and each of the four groups of family health service practitioners.[4] These set out how the new procedures are intended to operate. However, they are not designed to be all-embracing or to cover every contingency, so they may be supplemented at a local level. *The Patient's Charter*[5] was first published in 1991, and includes the right to have any complaint about NHS services investigated and to receive a quick, full written report from the appropriate chief executive.

Trusts and health authorities are required to have a designated complaints manager – although the title may be different – who is readily accessible to the public and is either accountable to the chief executive or, in the case of a large trust, at least has direct access. Family practitioners – GPs, dentists, opticians and pharmacists – must also identify a named person who is responsible for handling complaints. This is usually a senior partner or perhaps the practice manager.

Trusts, health authorities and family practitioners are all required to publicise their complaints procedures and to advise complainants and would-be complainants where to contact the local Community Health Council (CHC) for assistance in making and pursuing a complaint.

Local resolution

All trusts, health authorities and family practitioners have to establish a 'local resolution process', the aim of which is to try and resolve the complaint as quickly and as informally as possible. This might be:

- an immediate informal response by frontline staff or practitioner;
- an investigation;
- conciliation, perhaps meeting with the doctor or practitioner in a clinical complaint.

The Wilson Committee believed that 98 per cent of all NHS complaints could be satisfactorily resolved by an immediate informal response and that most of the remainder could be resolved by investigation or conciliation at the local resolution stage.

The key to making this stage work is the frontline staff – the nurses, receptionists, health visitors, practice managers. They should be trained and empowered to deal with complaints as soon as they arise, approaching them in an open, listening, helpful and non-defensive way. Where the staff member who receives a complaint is unable adequately to investigate it or give the complainant the assurance that he/she is looking for, the matter should be referred to the complaints manager for advice or handling. Of course the first responsibility of staff is to ensure that the patients' immediate healthcare needs are met. This may mean that urgent action needs to be taken before the complaint can be dealt with.

Not surprisingly, some complainants feel uncomfortable about making a complaint to the immediate staff involved – whether in a ward, clinic or practice – and, instead, prefer to contact the complaints officer or chief executive of the trust or health authority concerned. Where this happens, investigation or conciliation is used to try and resolve the complaint. In the case of family practitioners, the health authority itself has no power to investigate. It will either use conciliation or, acting as an intermediary, ask the practice to carry out an investigation and respond to the complainant.

Figure 3.2.1 shows the steps for local resolution of a complaint against a trust or health authority. The procedures are broadly similar for a complaint dealt with by a family practitioner.

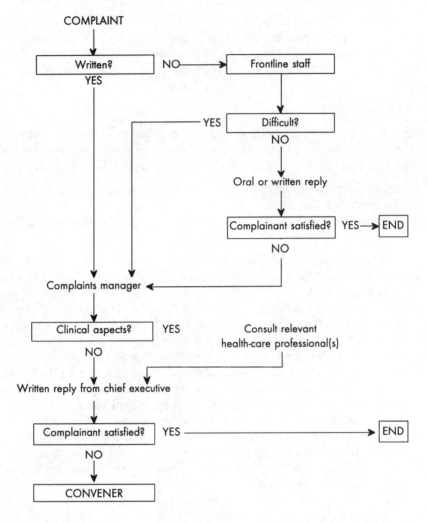

Source: Complaints: guidance on implementation of the NHS complaints procedures, NHS Executive, March 1996.

Figure 3.2.1 Flow chart showing the steps for local resolution of a complaint against a trust or health authority

Time limit

Complaints usually have to be made within six months from the event which gave rise to the complaint. However, if the complainant was not aware of the cause of complaint at that stage – for example, it was not known that inappropriate treatment had been given – then a complaint can be made within six months of becoming aware of it or within twelve months from the date of the event giving rise to the complaint, whichever is the earlier.

There is also a discretion to extend these time limits where it would have been unreasonable for the complainant to make the complaint earlier, for example, due to stress or trauma. Any extension will also depend on it still being possible to investigate the facts of the case.

Independent review

If a complaint cannot be resolved locally, the complainant can ask for a review by an independent panel, but there is no automatic right to this. The request is considered by the trust or health authority convenor, who usually is one of the non-executive board members.

The complainant is asked to set out in writing their remaining complaints. Based on this, the convenor, in consultation with an independent panel chairman, drawn from a list held regionally, will decide whether or not to set up a panel. If clinical issues are involved, advice will also be obtained from a clinical adviser, usually the medical director of the trust or medical adviser of the health authority. The convenor then has three choices:

1. If he concludes that further action could be taken short of establishing a panel in order to satisfy the complainant, he/she will refer the complaint back for that action to be taken. For example, the initial response might only have dealt with some of the issues raised by the complainant.
2. If the convenor decides that all practical action has already been taken and that establishing a panel would add no further value to the process, he/she will refuse the request.

   In either of these two cases, the complainant will be given the reasons for the decision and in the latter case informed of their right, if unhappy, to refer the convenor's decision to the Ombudsman.
3. If the convenor concludes that a panel would be useful, he/she will recommend to the trust or health authority that one should be set up and will also decide on its terms of reference.

The flow chart in Figure 3.2.2 shows the procedure for dealing with a request for an independent review panel.

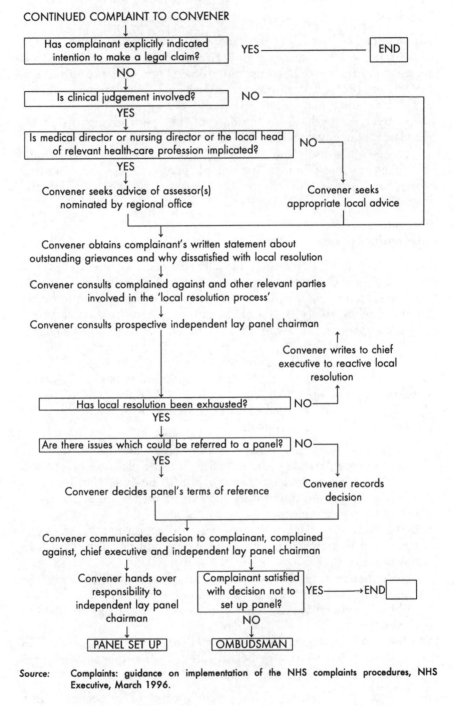

CONTINUED COMPLAINT TO CONVENER

Has complainant explicitly indicated intention to make a legal claim? — YES — END

NO

Is clinical judgement involved? — NO

YES

Is medical director or nursing director or the local head of relevant health-care profession implicated? — NO

YES

Convener seeks advice of assessor(s) nominated by regional office

Convener seeks appropriate local advice

Convener obtains complainant's written statement about outstanding grievances and why dissatisfied with local resolution

Convener consults complained against and other relevant parties involved in the 'local resolution process'

Convener consults prospective independent lay panel chairman

Convener writes to chief executive to reactive local resolution

Has local resolution been exhausted? — NO

YES

Are there issues which could be referred to a panel? — NO

YES

Convener decides panel's terms of reference

Convener records decision

Convener communicates decision to complainant, complained against, chief executive and independent lay panel chairman

Convener hands over responsibility to independent lay panel chairman

Complainant satisfied with decision not to set up panel? — YES — END

NO

PANEL SET UP

OMBUDSMAN

Source: Complaints: guidance on implementation of the NHS complaints procedures, NHS Executive, March 1996.

Figure 3.2.2 Flow chart of the convening role

Review panels are set up as a committee of the trust or authority and comprise: an independent lay chairman, plus two others, one will be the convenor from the trust or health authority involved in the complaint. The other will depend on to which body the complaint has been made. If it is a trust complaint, the third person will be a non-executive from the purchasing health authority, or a partner from the GP fundholding practice which purchased the care. If the complaint is about the health authority or a family practitioner, then the third person will be an independent lay person drawn from the regional list.

The review panel's function is to consider the complaint according to the terms of reference decided by the convenor, and in the light of the written statement provided by the complainant. Where clinical issues are involved, clinical advice will be provided by two independent clinical assessors. Extra assessors will have to be appointed if more than one profession is involved, for example, a complaint about poor medical and nursing care. The clinical assessors are also selected from regionally held lists – thus guaranteeing the independence of the panel and the advice it receives.

Panel proceedings are private and confidential. Each panel decides for itself how best to investigate the complaint, but the process is certainly not adversarial like a court case or the former service committee hearings for family practitioners. The parties may be seen together or may be seen separately. An opportunity will always be given to the complainant to express views to the panel. Complainants and those complained about may be accompanied by a friend, but legal representation is excluded so as to avoid panels becoming over formalised. Complainants may in addition be accompanied by a second person, such as a relative, to give them emotional support.

If clinical assessors are involved, they will advise the panel on appropriate issues and at least one will be present whenever the panel is dealing with clinical issues. The panel can disagree with the assessors' report, but if they do so they must set out their reasons in the final report.

The panel may send its draft conclusions to the complainant and those complained about for checking factual accuracy so that there is no dispute when the final report is issued. The panel's recommendations may be excluded at this stage.

The final report of the panel will set out the complaint; the results of its investigations; its conclusions, with any appropriate comments or suggestions. However, the panel may not recommend disciplinary action – that decision is entirely for the health authority or trust. The assessors' report will be attached to the findings of the panel at least for the complainant and relevant parties complained about. However, because of confidentiality issues it would not be normal for the assessors' reports to be sent to any parties complained about who were not involved in those clinical aspects – for example, a porter or receptionist who had been accused of being rude. The panel chairman has the right to withhold any part of the report and all or any part of the assessors' reports in order to ensure confidentiality of clinical information.

The panel's conclusions and any assessors' reports will be sent to the trust or health authority which will then decide in the light of the findings and recommendations what action to take and will write to the complainant informing them about this and of their right to take the complaint to the Ombudsman if they still remain dissatisfied. Where the complaint relates to a family practitioner or their staff the panel's report and any assessors' reports are sent to the health authority. The chief executive will then send the panel's report to the complainant and the practitioner. If the panel has suggested changes to the practitioner's services or organisation the practitioner will be invited to respond personally to the complainant on those matters as well as to the health authority. Again, the complainant will be advised that if not satisfied they have a right to refer their complaint to the Ombudsman.

The trust or health authority setting up the panel will be responsible for providing it with all necessary administrative support and meeting the costs of the panel and its assessors.

Figure 3.2.3 shows the procedure for an independent review of a complaint against a trust or health authority. Figure 3.2.4 shows the procedures where the complaint is against a family practitioner. The differences in the procedure for a complaint against a family practitioner are explained above.

Ombudsman

The Health Service Commissioner's remit has been extended by the Health Service Commissioners (Amendment) Act 1966 to cover all types of complaints within the NHS and complaints about NHS care provided by the independent or commercial sector. It also gives staff involved in complaints the right to complain to the Ombudsman if they consider they have suffered hardship or injustice through the complaints procedure.

The Ombudsman will not normally investigate a complaint until the procedures within the health service have been exhausted. Thus, for example, if he receives a complaint about a refusal to grant an independent review panel and concludes that further action can be taken within the health service either at local resolution level or by setting up an independent review panel he will recommend accordingly and take no further action on the investigation unless and until those stages have been completed and the complainant still remains dissatisfied.

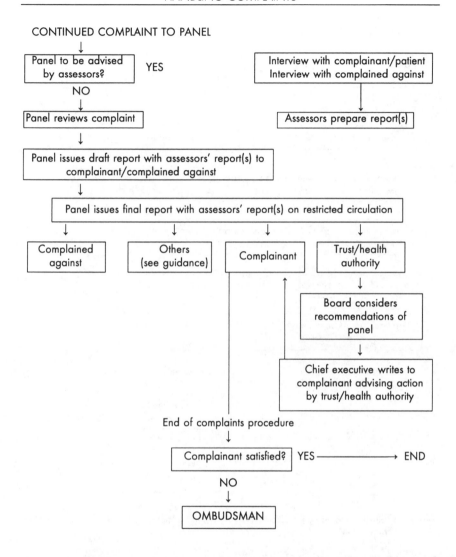

Source: Complaints: guidance on implementation of the NHS complaints procedures, NHS Executive, March 1996.

Figure 3.2.3 Flow chart for the independent review of a complaint against a trust or health authority

The Ombudsman's investigations are very thorough and take many weeks. He has the power of the High Court judge to compel the production of documents and the attendance and examination of witnesses. The final report will set out details of the investigations and the Ombudsman's conclusions, together with recommendations to the health authority, trust, practitioner or private hospital to put right

CONTINUED COMPLAINT TO PANEL

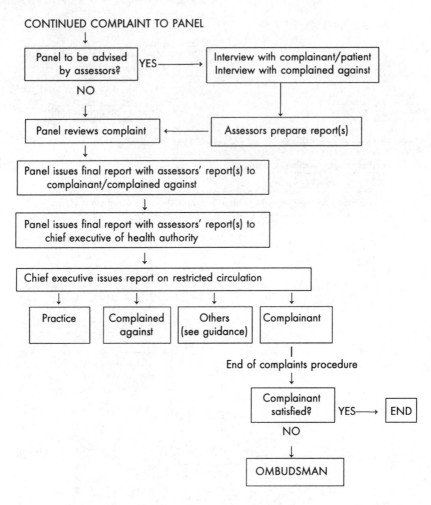

Source: Complaints: guidance on implementation of the NHS complaints procedures, NHS Executive, March 1996.

Figure 3.2.4 Flow chart for the independent review of a complaint against a family practitioner

whatever he has found to be wrong – for example, some organisational improvement. He may call for an apology and in some cases may recommend the granting of an *ex gratia* payment.

While the Ombudsman cannot require the authority or trust, etc. to act on his recommendations, most do so. In cases where this does not happen initially, he usually includes them in his annual report. These are then picked up by the House of Commons Select Committee on the Parliamentary Commissioner for Administration. In turn, they may call the body or person concerned to explain how the complaint arose and why they have not acted on the recommendations.

The Ombudsman publishes twice yearly a selection of the cases he has investigated. The aim is to enable those working within the NHS to learn the lessons from them. Unfortunately, this does not always happen. Instead, successive reports usually contain examples of similar types of complaints.

Performance targets

Tough performance targets for handling complaints have been set down in the guidance:

- Oral complaints are dealt with on the spot or referred on (in which case an acknowledgement should be given within two working days).
- A full response at local resolution stage should be given by a family practitioner within 10 working days, or by a trust or health authority within 20 working days.
- A convenor has ten days to decide whether to set up an independent review panel where that complaint involves a family practitioner, and 20 days in any other type of complaint.
- If a review panel is set up, it is expected to complete its work within three months of the request for a panel where the complaint relates to a family practitioner, or six months in other cases.

The reasons for the differences in timescales between family practitioner and other complaints are difficult to understand, since with the possible exception of the local resolution stage, dealing with complaints may be equally complex whether in relation to a family practitioner or other health service matter.

If it is necessary for any reason to go over the target timescale, the complainant has to be advised and given a revised timetable.

Separation of complaints from disciplinary action

The purpose of the complaints procedures is to look into complaints and try and resolve them. It is not intended to apportion blame among staff. Investigation of complaints is therefore kept completely separate from any disciplinary action. However, if at any stage a trust decides that disciplinary action is necessary, investigation of the complaint will be halted except to the extent that it also deals with other matters. On the other hand, in the case of family practitioners, unless patients are gravely at risk, any disciplinary action can only take place once a complaint has been dealt with.

Other investigations

If there is a need for any police or health and safety investigation or referral to the General Medical Council or other professional regulatory body this will take precedence over investigation of the complaint. Similarly, if the complaint relates to a serious incident this will be dealt with by an independent inquiry set up under section 84 of the NHS Act 1977.

If legal proceedings have already commenced, or there is a clear indication of doing so, based on essentially the same circumstances as the complaint, then no complaint investigation will be made. On the other hand, there is nothing to prevent complainants raising their complaints through a solicitor.

Purchaser complaints

Individual patients affected by a purchasing decision made by a health authority or GP fundholder can complain to them. This will be dealt with by the local resolution process and if necessary by an independent review panel. However, where the purchasing decisions have been taken properly and reasonably the panel will not be able to suggest an alternative decision.

Complaints about NHS care in the independent sector

Where the private sector is used to provide care for NHS patients, the contract will require that there should be similar internal procedures for dealing with complaints as the local resolution process already described. If the complainant remains dissatisfied after this, any request for an independent review panel needs to be made to the health authority, if it or a GP fundholder purchased the private care, or to the trust, if it purchased the care.

Monitoring

Trust and health authority boards are not only required to approve their local arrangements for handling complaints, but also to monitor at least quarterly how the procedures are operating; to look at trends and to ensure that the lessons learnt are being put into practice.

Some boards involve their local CHCs and least one GP in these monitoring arrangements, both as a means of getting an external quality input and also as a means of reassuring them and the wider public about how the procedures are working.

Trusts and health authorities are required to report annually on the handling of complaints against themselves but, interestingly, health authority reports do not cover complaints against family practitioners,

GP fundholders and independent providers. As with trusts, health authorities' reports go to the regional office and local CHC. Trusts also send their reports to their local health authorities, which then enables future contracts to reflect the lessons which have been learnt from the complaints.

Most trusts and health authorities also collect data locally on:

- oral complaints and on patients' comments and suggestions;
- the resulting changes in practices and procedures.

These data can be very important in identifying patterns of complaints and tackling them without delay so that more serious problems do not arise.

Patient representatives

In addition to the complaints arrangements, some hospital trusts employ patients' advocates or representatives to help patients and relatives with concerns. The aim is to tackle them before they develop into a complaint.

Professional standards

Each of the professions has a professional regulatory body, such as the General Medical Council, which deals with cases of serious professional misconduct and those professionals who may be unfit to practice because of illness. New powers have recently been given to the General Medical Council to deal with cases of doctors whose performance is seriously deficient. These latter arrangements will come into being in 1997. The proceedings of professional regulatory bodies are often lengthy – partly because they are usually dealing with the most serious cases. Poor performance, however, is best dealt with by preventative measures or early action as soon as it occurs. There are various procedures in place within the Health Service, including clinical audit and peer review to help tackle such problems.

Access to Health Records Act 1990 and Code of Openness in the NHS

A person who has a complaint arising from a request for access to health records can make the complaint under the NHS complaints procedures as an alternative to making an application to the courts. Complaints records should be kept separate from health records, subject only to the need to record any information which is strictly relevant to the patient's health.

Complaints about non-disclosure of other NHS information are dealt with under the Code of Openness in the NHS.[6]

References

1 DoH (1994) *Being Heard: report of the Review Committee on NHS Complaints Procedures*, chaired by Professor Alan Wilson.
2 DoH (1995) *Acting on Complaints: The government's revised policy and proposals for a new NHS complaints procedure in England.*
3 DoH (1996) *Directions to Health Authorities on Procedures for Dealing with Complaints about Family Health Services Practitioners.*
   Directions to NHS Trusts, Health Authorities and Special Health Authorities for Special Hospitals on Hospital Complaints.
   Directions to Health Authorities on Miscellaneous Matters Concerning Complaints.
4 NHS Executive (1996) *Complaints: guidance on implementation of the NHS complaints procedures*, EL(96)19. Also guidance pack for general practitioners; general dental practitioners; optometrists and pharmacists.
5 NHS Executive (updated 1995) *The Patient's Charter.*
6 NHS Executive (1995) *Guidance on Implementation of Openness in the NHS*, EL(95)60.

3.3

Press Relations

Hazel Brand, Communications
Manager, Doncaster Royal Infirmary &
Montagu Hospital NHS Trust

The press and media can be the health service manager's ally or enemy. This chapter will consider how to use the press to advantage – effecting a change from adversary to ally, and creating good relations in the community through the media – and how to deal with the press in a crisis. Central to this discussion is the role of local newspapers. Local TV and radio stations have a wider catchment area and are, on a day-to-day basis, generally less intrusive on the health service manager's time than local print journalists. Specific reference will be made to the broadcast media when appropriate.

Disaster, drama, misappropriation of resources, the procedure that went wrong (or result that did not come up to the patient's expectations), bureaucrats *vs* 'angels', faulty equipment, human error – all are the lifeblood of the press. The journalist's adage is good news is no news. Bad news makes headlines, which sell papers. If there is nothing else to write about, the papers will only carry negative stories. And the role of the papers as opinion formers should not be underestimated: patients read them, as do their relatives; so do GPs, CHC members, and key staff in health commissions. Newspapers also reflect public opinion through letters columns, feature articles and so on.

Greater scope for mistakes is undoubtedly found in acute trusts, though the principles below apply to all health agencies. Without condoning complacency, there are bound to be things that go wrong, however small, in an environment where there are thousands upon thousands of interactions each year between staff and patients. Controlling the flow of information, both within and across organisational boundaries, is the first step to using the press to advantage. It is wise to invest responsibility for all press relations in a single individual of sufficient seniority to have a 'place at the top table' and early access to information, both operational and strategic. This staff member should also have responsibility for internal communications to ensure that information is co-ordinated and messages consistent and that staff 'don't read about it first in the newspaper'. However harmless an event might be – inviting the press to a cheque presentation, for example – were a story to break suddenly, reporters are there, inside the organisation, just when they are least wanted. The press officer should, ideally, be the single point of contact with the press; at the very least, s/he should know about any and every occasion that the press are on the premises. An organisational climate that does not encourage leaks to the press is an advantage – and systems need to be in place to be able to react quickly and professionally to a call out of the blue.

- If the press contact is not available, who takes the call?
- Can the PR manager be reached to deal with the enquiry?
- Are junior or secretarial staff taught and trained not to be drawn into conversation with journalists?
- Are more senior staff aware of the procedures for handling press calls? Do they respect and honour the need for these procedures?

The press officer may need to issue a 'holding' statement – or defer comment at all, with a commitment to return the call – until such time as the full facts are at his/her disposal and a more informed press release or statement can be written. The confidence and competence to deal with such press enquiries, at times under great pressure from the journalist, are prerequisites for the postholder.

Bad news is the lifeblood of the press – and journalists are out to make their name with exclusive, front page lead stories: bylines are one way to impress the editor of a bigger, better, larger circulation, regional or national paper when seeking promotion. But most local papers do not have a specialist health correspondent: the reporter can be dealing with relocating the bus station one minute, with a health story as their second job that day, and the theft of a prize parrot to round off the afternoon. Local reporters tend to work from 8.30am to 4.30pm, filing stories as they are written, and, as the publication date approaches, deadlines become tighter. Health service activity does not often match reporters' work patterns and it is all too easy to dismiss a request for information by x o'clock as 'their problem – the reporter's deadline, not mine'. But in effecting a change from the press as enemy to ally, the constraints under which reporters work must be respected and every attempt made to respond on time. Because reporters tend to finish work earlier in the afternoon than most health service staff – but the late afternoon and early evening are often the best time to hold events, such as opening of a new unit, etc. – it may be difficult to attract reporters and photographers to cover these activities. If so, use a medical or freelance photographer and supply the papers with a photo and copy afterwards.

Be helpful to a reporter consistently over time and s/he will have much more difficulty in 'stabbing you in the back' when bad news arises. Non-specialist reporters need all the help they can get to find their way around the structure of the health service in general, and local organisations in particular. The role of hospitals is fairly easy to comprehend – but less so health commissions. Medical and management jargon should be avoided at all costs – or at the very least explained in layperson's language.

Get to know local reporters in whatever way is appropriate to the organisation and individuals concerned. Sitting down to brief journalists over a working lunch is some chief executives' (and PR managers') worst nightmare – the PR officer should find a way to get messages across that is not excruciating to all concerned and in keeping with organisational culture.

Local reporters tend to be of two types – those who have been with the paper for years and are at the pinnacle of their careers as, for example, a news or features editor, and those who are at an earlier stage, and are ambitious. The latter group move on more frequently with changes among junior reporters. There is probably little that the PR manager, possibly new to the area, can tell the established contingent, which may have all sorts of preconceived ideas about the organisation and its management, and have a depth of historical knowledge that is churned out every time there is a bad news story: 'This medical blunder is the latest in a catalogue of disasters at X Hospital: in 1985, there was a fatal accident in the hospital laundry, where staff were found to be negligent in health and safety standards. Two years later, the chief executive was convicted of... And now, questions are being asked about the death rate.'

Understanding the press is the first step towards an alliance – giving them what they want is another. Journalists have pages to fill – help them to do it. Press releases are the easiest way, and keep control of information in the sender's hands. They should tell an interesting story and be well constructed, to avoid being consigned to the bin. In the last six months of 1995–6, every press release issued by Doncaster Royal Infirmary & Montagu Hospital NHS Trust was used by local press and media; the success rate in the preceding six months was 95 per cent. Below are some guidelines to writing effective press releases:

- Identify the organisation sending the press release: headed paper is quite adequate;

- Print 'PRESS RELEASE' in large bold letters across the paper;
- Date the press release (right hand side);
- Also on the right, indicate if it is 'For immediate release' or embargoed, or not for publication but for information only. Include the date and time of the embargo (e.g. Embargo: 12 noon, Wednesday 24 July 1996),
- The heading should be factual (in bold print and including an active verb) and not 'clever' – writing catchy headlines is the sub-editor's job.

The less the journalist has to do to modify the press release, the better s/he will like it so write for the paper's readership: probably an average reading age of twelve years. The average length should be four to six paragraphs: the first paragraph should tell the story in summary. The second and subsequent paragraphs will expand on the points made in the first, developing the story in descending order of these points' importance. A quotation is helpful, if appropriate and from someone with standing or about whom the press release is written, in the second or third paragraph. The final paragraph should give the press officer's name and phone number for further details. After every press release, include a standard paragraph (Note to Editors) that describes, in summary, the organisation: name, when established, main aims and services provided, population served, number of staff, and mission statement.

Whenever possible, include a photograph with the press release. But be imaginative about photographs of cheque presentations that are the bane of newspapers. Instead of a picture of one party handing over a cheque for £x raised through a sponsored walk to another, get the walkers to sit in a row, feet towards the camera with boots on, etc.

Never offer one paper an exclusive: all media must be treated equally. Of course, judicious timing of mailings may be to the advantage of one paper over another, but there should never be overt favouritism. You will earn no credit from the paper which has had the advantage (that reporter will know that you are just as likely to favour another next time) and those who are disadvantaged will not trust your impartiality.

What should be the subjects of press releases? Press releases put the power of information in the hands of the health organisation and provide an ideal opportunity to disseminate positive news. So, anything and everything that is even slightly better than the norm can go out in a press release. Whenever possible, major on the 'human interest' angle. Likely topics include:

- new consultant and senior staff appointments;
- retirements (say, three senior staff with 100 years' service between them);

- 'medical miracles';
- commencement of a new service, or development of an existing one: a new aquanatal class, refurbishment of a clinic area, new outpatient 'outreach' service. What does it mean for patients?
- launch of the organisation's own Patient's Charter;
- extra-curricular achievements of staff (prize-winning orchids, winning a poetry competition);
- community groups' fund-raising;
- Christmas Day/New Year's Day births.

If a known 'problem event' is forthcoming, press releases can be timed so that there are plenty of positive stories in the papers in the run-up to press coverage.

Dealing with the press in a crisis situation calls for all the examples of good practice outlined above – and more. Most health organisations will have a well-rehearsed plan for major incidents. Generally, the health services are seen in a good light at such times when 'heroic' deeds are recorded and equally 'heroic' medicine may be practised. More difficult to deal with is the unexpected event that is likely to catch the organisation unawares and have the potential to put it in a very poor light.

Recent health service history is littered with such events, not all of which resulted in adversely affecting the organisation's reputation: the abduction of Abbie Humphries, the Beverley Allitt affair, swabs left inside a patient, accusations that a consultant gynaecologist illegally procured an abortion by carrying out a hysterectomy on a pregnant woman, allegations of misuse of public funds in the former Yorkshire Regional Health Authority. Good relations with the media can be critical to weathering such media storms – but building good relations is a lengthy process and will not stop even the friendliest journalist from going for the jugular when there is a good story to be had. But a good impression of the organisation, built up in the minds of journalists and the public beforehand, can be influential in conveying the idea that the 'problem event' is a one-off mishap rather than a symptom of organisational malaise. Organisations without in-house PR staff may find it a struggle to improve a damaged media profile – and, at the end of the day, it is rarely the bought-in PR company that ends up with a poor reputation but the organisation that has hired it to reverse media opinion. In fairness to PR agencies, it is an almost impossible task – and their very involvement can be a public relations disaster in itself.

It is advisable to have a 'crisis management' plan for just such incidents, which may differ little from the PR manager's role in the major incident plan:

- Identify the PR contact or substitute if s/he is not available;

- The press operate twenty-four hours a day; similar press support will be necessary;
- Inform staff, first those most closely involved with the incident then all staff through internal briefing mechanisms;
- Alert staff to be vigilant to the presence of the press;
- In particular, inform reception desks, switchboard operators and security staff;
- Arrange counselling or support systems for staff, if appropriate.
- Inform the regional office and NHSE (Corporate Affairs);
- Organise 'receiving arrangements' for journalists who arrive on the doorstep: large room, power supplies, refreshments, parking spaces and room for outside broadcast vehicles;
- Keep the press regularly informed;
- Decide if a spokesperson will be provided or written statements only;
- Identify the spokesperson.

A press conference is the common way to brief journalists. However, these events usually suffer from journalists vying with each other to ask the most outrageous, difficult, or even impossible questions. Disaffected relatives, patients, etc. may turn up at a press conference, making it difficult for the spokesperson to maintain credibility when media have the opportunity to film, photograph or interview disabled, disadvantaged, or damaged 'victims'. Though more time-consuming, consider individual press interviews, one for each paper/TV company/ radio station. This is much easier to control and less intimidating for the spokesperson.

When the pressure is on, film crews wandering around the organisation is the last thing the PR manager wants. Despite entreaties from TV crews, refuse permission for filming – they have had plenty of time to come along and shoot 'library footage' and the sight of TV cameras can increase anxiety among staff.

Unless the chief executive is uncomfortable in front of reporters s/ he, or the medical director or DNS if more appropriate, should face the press. The spokesperson should have had prior media training. Have a 'trial run' with the spokesperson: his/her own staff can ask much more piercing questions than the press. The spokesperson should have three key points to make – and, whatever questions are asked, these three points must be made. Media training will teach the techniques to achieve this. Of a half-hour interview, two minutes may be broadcast – continuously making the key points is, therefore, essential so that they feature in the selected 'soundbite'.

Give thought to the transmission times of the broadcast media and, if possible, enable broadcast journalists to do their interviews first, in time for their programmes; print journalists can usually wait a little longer. TV crews will want a spokesperson or, at the very least, someone from the organisation to read a statement. The latter is inadvisable, as this individual may unexpectedly, and without prior discussion or agreement, be asked questions to which s/he does not have the answers. Filming a health service employee in obvious discomfort will not help the cause. If the decision has been taken only to issue a written statement, adhere to that decision – the TV reporter will find a way round this inconvenience: 'In a statement issued by the hospital'.

Provide a written statement (not a press release) for anyone not able to attend the press conference; the spokesperson's 'script' and the statement should carry the same messages. Never say 'No comment', which gives the impression that there is something to hide. It will be turned into 'Refused to comment' by the reporter. Patient confidentiality must be respected but do not use this or the threat of legal proceedings as an excuse not to comment: legal restrictions are an added challenge to journalists.

If a patient/relative has 'gone to the press', anything that he or she has said is in the public domain and that information can be used by the health organisation. Difficult though it may seem, there is often the possibility of agreeing a statement with the patients/relatives involved in the incident and deciding how to handle the press. The public are unaware of how to deal with journalists – or how the journalists will deal with them – and the expertise of the PR manager may be appreciated.

Use 'off the record' briefing with caution – you need confidence in the journalist first. Then be exaggeratedly clear about what is on and what is off the record. If printed or broadcast, correct factual errors immediately and demand a public apology or correction. Daily access to up-to-date press cuttings, and links with a TV/radio monitoring service, will ensure timely information on whether such action is necessary. A published correction is not worth the paper it is printed on unless it appears at the first possible opportunity, for example, in the next edition of the paper.

Just as health service managers have a duty of confidentiality towards patients and staff, so journalists have codes of conduct overseen by the Press Complaints Commission for print journalists, and the Independent Television Commission for TV and radio journalists. Both codes of conduct have aspects of particular relevance to the health service, which are usefully summarised in *Health Service Public Relations: A Guide to Good Practice.*

In summary, the press can be an important ally in informing the public about developments within the organisation. A newspaper can actively support fund-raising – in Doncaster, the Free Press has been a major player in the Diagnostic Mammography Campaign – and will provide an extremely cost-effective means of publicity. The 'down' side is that print journalists will seek out the negative stories but will be happy to use the positive ones if supplied. It is the PR manager's role to make sure that the balance tips in favour of the health agency and to use his/her skills as a 'newshound' to identify and develop stories from all corners of the organisation. Reading favourable articles about themselves and their employer can only have beneficial effects on staff morale. An organisation that has, and develops, good ideas is a healthy one and recognition of staff achievements further generates interesting and imaginative ways of delivering healthcare.

References

Jefkins, Frank (1977) *Planned Press and Public Relations*, International Textbook Company,

Silver, Roger (ed.) *Health Service Public Relations: A Guide to Good Practice*, Radcliffe Medical Press, Abingdon, Oxon.

PART FOUR

MANAGING FINANCE AND PLANNING

4.1

PFI Watch

Richard Meara,

Meara Management Consultancy,

Co-ordinator, IHSM PFI Watch

Following its 1997 annual conference the IHSM established the Private Finance Initiative (PFI) Watch. This arose both from the growing importance of the private finance initiative as the major route for capital investment in healthcare, and from the publication earlier in 1997 of a report entitled 'Building Services and Servicing Buildings'. (Meara Management Consultancy, 1997).[1] The purpose of the report was as a policy paper for consultation throughout the IHSM membership and as a touchstone for the wider debate on PFI which occurred as part of the run-up to the May 1997 General Election.

Contrary to the expectations of some and the hopes of others the Labour government embraced PFI and indicated that it would continue to form the means by which the majority of capital investment would take place in the NHS. Figures produced by the NHS Executive's Capital Review Group in 1996 showed a steady decline in publicly funded capital investment over the coming years, and the arrival of a new government has not changed the picture. However, the shortfall was more than made up for by massive forecast increases in private finance totals. So the NHS faces a future in which its traditional sources of capital investment are sharply declining. This has been made worse by the recent reductions in block or minor capital allocations to trusts. These are discretionary allocations which trusts have traditionally spent on minor refurbishment schemes and on major maintenance projects often in relation to meeting fire precautions and other statutory standards. The reduction in minor capital allocations has also led to a squeeze on expenditure on medical equipment, needed to replace outdated plant or to keep pace with technological change.

Issues arising from the application of PFI

It is possible, therefore, to paint a depressing picture of a health service which faces a starvation of capital at the same time as it struggles with a backlog maintenance bill of £10 billion. Is the real picture as bad as this implies? No wonder that managers in the NHS tried for some time to pretend that PFI did not apply to them and could be side-stepped. In spite of being introduced in 1992 it was not until 1994 that Kenneth Clarke, then Chancellor of the Exchequer, required that all schemes be tested through the PFI process, and as late as the winter of 1996 some NHS trust boards believed that they could bypass it and gain access to Treasury capital.

The arrival of the Labour government heralded a reappraisal of the selection process for schemes and the launch of a major review of the policy. There are already a number of important issues to emerge from the new government's attempts to sharpen up the policy and to speed up the process.

First, it had to be admitted that too many major schemes were competing for PFI approval. Anecdotal evidence from senior staff in regional offices showed that both they and the relevant health authorities were aware of significant numbers of weak business cases which were being driven through the system by political pressure. With the PFI's greater emphasis on affordability this was unsustainable. One of the first steps in summer 1997 was to halt all 43 major schemes and to assess their viability under PFI. By August fourteen schemes had been chosen to proceed, to which was later added a fifteenth (Greenwich). This was both an indication that greater rigour needed to be applied to the issue of affordability, and that there was a real issue about how many schemes the PFI market could bear at any one time. Behind the need for robust business cases lies the fact that much greater service rationalisation and change is needed in order to deliver the cost reductions and the income streams on which capital investment in the NHS increasingly depends. This has lessons for both managers and politicians over the next few years.

Second, while the approach to more rigorous prioritisation of major acute schemes began to bear fruit in late 1997 and into 1998, the PFI process failed to deliver any community and priority service schemes. Although announcements for some pathfinder schemes may be made in late spring 1998, there remains a real concern that such schemes cannot be put together under the standard PFI model. Such schemes often involve a mix of refurbishment and small-scale development. Because of past decisions land sales may not always be available to improve the affordability of the package. Although with some schemes there may be good residual value in the smaller domestic-style assets, problems arise because inadequate income streams are available from outsourced services. In some cases it is clear that it would be helpful to the PFI deal, and possibly also to the quality of service delivered, if clinical services could be included in the services to be outsourced. Although the government has yet to pronounce on this aspect of policy, it seems unlikely that it will agree to allow services that involve direct patient care to be managed in this way. What is clear is that there is no single bullet solution to dealing with this kind of scheme, and the PFI Unit continues to explore a number of routes from conventional PFI, public/private partnerships, as well as Treasury funding. The advantages of bundling a number of smaller schemes into one large package are also being explored in order to create the requisite critical mass.

Somewhat surprisingly, there are no plans to create a priority list of schemes from the large numbers in various stages of preparation, on the same lines as the major acute schemes. It is possible to make a similar assumption, namely that some of these projects are based on weak business cases and should be weeded out. Because of the disparate nature of the schemes, however, it is more likely that regional offices will be expected to wield the red pencil.

The issue is a troubling one because the reshaping of mental health and learning disability provision and investment in new forms of service provision are far from complete. A publication in late 1997 from Pathways Research for the NHS Estates R&D programme described the difficulties in applying the PFI process to community care schemes. Palmer and Watson[2] in a report titled 'Hospital Reprovision, Learning Disabilities and the Private Finance Initiative' argued that community care planning processes were seriously flawed, that NHS community trusts were not best placed to lead that process, and that conventional PFI was too much of an 'all or nothing' route which prevented best value for money solutions in hospital reprovision schemes. They concluded that:

> The PFI process as it presently applies to the procurement of housing and residential care within the health service is complex and cumbersome. However, application of the PFI approach within the NHS for the procurement of housing is in some ways a red herring, because it seems probable that this is not an appropriate task for health bodies to be undertaking in the first place.

It is therefore essential that a number of models for financing such schemes, which will include variants of the standard PFI model, are developed and tested in 1998, before a serious log jam is created in the priority services.

A third issue concerns the approach by the NHS Executive since mid-1997 to impose strong central control over large schemes, and in general to lower expectations within the NHS. Central planning of capital investment to a degree not seen since the 1970s has been introduced through the establishment of the Capital Prioritisation Advisory Group (CPAG).

The CPAG

The remit of the group is to advise ministers on national priorities for major (over £25 million) capital investment on the basis of shortlisted schemes put forward by regional offices. It is not yet clear whether this will be an annual process, but for the first round regions were restricted to putting forward two schemes each to CPAG.

The arrival of CPAG introduced a new hurdle into the approval process – the strategic outline context (SOC) which must be completed in relation to each bid and be supported by the health authority and regional office. This precedes the outline business case and outlines the health need for the investment, and the service model on which the investment is based.

It is difficult to overestimate the importance of the new centralist approach to capital investment. It raises a number of issues, including:

- the need to reinvent good strategic planning at regional offices and health authorities;
- the definition of 'health service need'. This is attempted in the annexe to the FD letter but in such an all inclusive way that most schemes could be justified. It is certain that further work needs to be done to refine and narrow the criteria;
- the extent to which strategic decisions can be taken which just focus on large schemes, without defining what smaller investment decisions should be made within a comprehensive regional or subregional strategy;
- the implications of a culture change within the NHS towards capital investment, which involves spreading the jam more thickly but to fewer recipients. NHS capital investment reality over the past 30 years has been to give as many localities as possible some investment – in other words to spread the jam thinly. One implication of this change is that many trusts stand no chance of a major new development and must explore radically different options: from small-scale upgrading and refurbishment, rationalisation of services without capital investment, or rethinking long-held assumptions of what assets are needed to deliver the services required locally.

In addition to the problems posed by schemes in the priority field, many NHS trusts are looking for capital investment which falls between the very minor and schemes over £25 million. These small to medium-sized projects which involve acute and elderly care services also have their difficulties. As a typical example, it is possible to consider a medium-sized general acute trust in southern England. Redeveloped in phases, the newest block (Phase II) opened in 1997 providing 72 beds and associated operating theatres. This was a conventionally funded scheme, and incidentally at planning stage 120 beds were demanded by the clinicians. Seventy-two beds were provided and the hospital is currently running on 60, at double the previous throughput. This gives the lie to the criticisms of PFI, by the British Medial Association among others, that it alone has been responsible for major acute bed reductions.

Completion of Phase II has left the trust with a requirement for Phase III – the final and unfashionable bits. These include kitchen and boiler house replacement, a new CSSD and mortuary and some office accommodation. As a PFI scheme it would have been unworkable. It offered too much refurbishment and too little opportunity for outsourcing services. As a result, a radical rethink of the package to be privately financed was put together. An improved development control plan was constructed for the whole site; this involved substantial demolition of recently constructed buildings and the construction of a single new block, which allowed a sizeable land sale along one edge of the site. Capital charges on the remaining site were reduced and the resulting package just covered the unitary payment needed.

This may be typical of the aspirations of many trusts for smaller scale tidying up schemes which struggle to meet the technical criteria of the PFI process. In this case it may have proved possible to create a viable scheme by radically rethinking the scheme internally. In other cases, however, even more dramatic re-examination will be necessary, drawing in other trusts and reconfiguring across sites.

Conclusions

The PFI process has developed rapidly over its short life, and further changes are inevitable. Spring 1998 will see publication of new guidance on the process in four volumes. The aim has been to simplify and speed up the process, to strengthen competition between competing private sector consortia, and to begin a process of standardisation which will avoid individual trusts inventing their own wheels. Whether it succeeds in these aims is as yet unclear. What is certain is that PFI is encouraging the development of new skills and the reinvention of old ones among NHS managers. These include the ability and willingness to think and plan in strategic ways; project management of large complex change over extended periods; skills in presentation and negotiation; and skills in partnership working between public and private sector players once the first schemes are operational. As is often the case what seems to be a largely technical issue peripheral to the concerns of many general managers is beginning to usher in profound change in the management of health services.

References

1 Meara Management Consultancy (1997) 'Building Services and Servicing Buildings, IHSM, London.
2 Palmer and Watson (1997) 'Hospital Provision, Learning Disabilities and the Private Finance Initiative.' NHS Estate R&D programme report.

4.2

PFI Procurement – Managing the Legal Process

David Anderson, Partner, Nabarro

Nathanson

Introduction

It is a fact of life that no Private Finance Initiative (PFI) project can successfully be concluded without a significant amount of legal documentation. While the legal documentation is fundamental to any such project it should, however, be regarded as a means to an end rather than the end itself.

In managing the PFI process, the overall strategic planning to be carried out by the Trust team at a very early stage will itself have direct impact on controlling the process of drafting, negotiating and finalising the legal documentation.

Strategy and prioritisation

The changes in NHS PFI procurement which the Labour government has brought in have specifically emphasised the need for early planning in respect of PFI procurement. In particular for major schemes (over £25 million) a Strategic Outline Case (SOC) is required to provide the necessary information to enable the NHS Capital Prioritisation Advisory Group (CPAG) to assess those schemes which are to be recommended to ministers for development. This additional step in the process of developing major schemes is required even before preparation of the Outline Business Case (OBC) which is itself required prior to proceeding to advertise the scheme to the private sector.

The NHS circular announcing the establishment of CPAG acknowledged that the only information required in the SOC is that which will enable CPAG to assess the national priority of schemes; but the requirements for inclusion in the SOC include assessments specifically to cover project management arrangements, timetable/deliverability and 'PFI-ability'. It is impossible to consider these aspects of a proposed PFI scheme without taking into consideration a number of key issues and the way in which these issues should be managed through the overall procurement process. Particularly in the context of demonstrating 'PFI-ability', the Regional Office is required to make an assessment of the Trust's own supporting information in respect of the risks that will be expected to be borne by the private sector and the scope of services to be provided by the private sector within the scheme. The key risks expected to be borne by the private sector are required specifically to be listed as part of the Regional Office's assessment.

As the negotiation of PFI contracts is all about confirming in writing the responsibilities for allocation and management of the consequences of risks inherent in a long term contract, it is advisable, therefore for the Trust to consider at an early stage (at least in a broad sense) the way in which a contract structure for the delivery of the scheme should be put together.

This approach applies equally to smaller schemes below £25m which will be outside the CPAG requirements but which, as a matter of good procurement and to enable regional offices to support such schemes, should also identify strategic, project management, timetable/deliverability and PFI-ability at a very early stage.

The benefit of experience

This early strategic planning represents good practice in the development of the project and should enable the Trust to remain firmly in control of the process with the Trust having a very clear idea of overall structure, negotiating strategy and required outputs which will enable the relationship with private sector bidders to be developed efficiently.

On the major front running schemes, much time has been spent in the detailed negotiation of the contract documentation and this has led to many schemes taking far longer to reach financial close than was originally anticipated. Guidance from the NHS Executive based on lessons learned and strategy developed from the early schemes will provide invaluable assistance. On the assumption that, with the benefit of this experience and guidance a Trust will be developing its PFI project within a well planned strategic context, there are a number of aspects which a Trust should take into account in respect of specifically managing the legal process itself.

Identifying the contractual issues

As part of the overall project management process, the Trust should put itself in a position where it enters into the stage of legal negotiations with preferred bidders fully prepared for the issues to be resolved through to contract signature and financial close.

In preparing for the development of the legal documentation and contract negotiations, the Trust should identify at an early stage the key contractual issues which will need to be addressed as part of the process. Broadly speaking these can be separated into core issues and project-specific issues.

Core issues

The core issues include those aspects of the scheme which may be beyond the control of the Trust or the consequences of which the Trust may not be in a position to manage without support from the centre or which are regarded as key to the overall structure which will enable a scheme to be approved. The resolution of these issues will require specific reference to guidance issued by the NHS Executive.

The core issues are essentially those issues whose significance and importance goes beyond the day to day aspects of managing the relationship between the Trust and the private sector consortium.

Examples of core issues include the following:

- **Legislative change** – over the lifetime of a long term contract, legislative changes can have an impact on the performance of the parties' obligations under the contract and significant cost implications for the parties in complying with changes in the law. The starting point in a PFI contract is that the private sector should bear the risk of the cost implications of providing services over a long period of time; but there will be exceptions, for example where a change in law is discriminatory against PFI schemes or relates specifically to NHS hospitals.
- **Force majeure** – force majeure relates to the occurrence of circumstances beyond the control of either party which will have an impact on the performance of contractual obligations. Guidance dictates a narrow definition of events of force majeure to include a very limited range of circumstances where, even though the consortium is unable to perform its contractual obligations, the Trust may still be required to incur expenditure either by way of ongoing payments to the consortium or as lump sum compensation if the circumstances have, in effect, brought the contract to an end.
- **Relief events** – in a long-term contract where significant per-formance risks are allocated to the private sector, there will be circumstances falling short of a force majeure event where it is

reasonable for the consortium to be relieved from its obligations to the Trust and will not be held to be in breach. An acceptable list of these events has been developed through negotiation on early schemes.

- **Termination and financial consequences** – the circumstances in which either party can terminate the contract will need to be carefully considered and documented. The nature of a long term service contract where the consortium and its financiers are dependent on the ongoing stream of payments from the Trust requires that the contract should not easily be capable of being terminated. These provisions need particularly careful attention as, whether the agreement is terminated as a result of default by the Trust or by the consortium, the Trust is likely to be required to pay some form of compensation to the consortium.
- **Application of insurance proceeds** – in the event of substantial damage to the hospital facility, the method of application of insurance proceeds will need to be clearly specified to take account of the respective interests of the Trust, the consortium and the consortium's financiers.

These are (non-exhaustive) examples of issues where the Trust should seek and follow central NHS guidance as to how they should be handled. Based on precedent, experience and guidance, the Trust should be in a position to negotiate a position which has proved to be acceptable in the wider context of NHS PFI deals in the knowledge that the approach is supported by the NHS Executive.

Project-specific issues

Project-specific issues relate more closely to the day to day running and management of the contract and the ongoing rights and obligations of the Trust and the consortium respectively.

Examples of project-specific issues include the following:

- **Output specifications** – these need to be considered in the context of the overall service to be provided by the consortium to the Trust to meet the Trust's requirements. These requirements will have been identified earlier at the strategic planning stage. In developing the output specifications the Trust will need to consider not only its requirements in respect of the consortium's design and build responsibilities but also the ongoing provision of services by the consortium over the life of the contract.
- **Design and construction obligations** – these will need to be determined by the Trust's particular requirements and will need detailed specification and negotiation.

- **Payment mechanisms** – at the centre of the contract, for the purpose of risk allocation to the consortium will be the payment mechanism. While precedents are developing for the structure of payment mechanisms, this is an area where PFI contracts may continue to evolve and, depending on the specific nature of the project, different payment mechanisms may apply from project to project. These will be based on the principle that the Trust should not pay for services which it does not receive and that poor service should result in a reduction in payments by the Trust.
- **Performance requirements** – these will be closely linked to the payment mechanism. Failure to perform to agreed standards will result in reduced payments being made by the Trust for the services being provided by the private sector. The performance requirements are, of course, closely linked to the output specifications and will again need to be specifically tailored and negotiated on a project by project basis.

Distinguishing the issues

Whether issues are core contractual issues or project-specific issues, guidance will be available from the NHS Executive as to how these matters should be approached. The key difference is that, in respect of core issues, the NHS Executive is likely to have certain minimum requirements which should be adhered to in the structuring and negotiation of the transaction. The project-specific issues on the other hand, will be capable of being separately and specifically negotiated by the Trust and the consortium on the basis that they are resolved in a way which demonstrates sufficient risk transfer to the private sector whilst delivering value for money in meeting the Trust's specific operational needs.

Managing negotiations

Early identification of the contractual issues will significantly benefit the legal negotiation process. While the specific contractual issues will set the framework for negotiations, there are other important aspects of the process over which the Trust can and should be prepared to exercise significant control through being prepared for key aspects within the negotiation process.

Consortium composition

The composition of the consortium will have a significant impact on the way in which negotiations are conducted and progressed. A PFI contract will typically involve five key aspects of input from the private sector:

- design;
- build;
- finance;
- building maintenance;
- provision of other services (eg portering, catering, cleaning, linen and laundry).

These disciplines and inputs from the private sector will necessarily be provided by a variety of consortium members or sub-contractors; how the relationship between these parties is managed will have a direct effect on negotiations. In particular, while it may be agreed in principle between the Trust and the consortium as to how certain risks should be allocated as between the Trust and the consortium, the consortium then has to determine how those risks should be allocated between the respective consortium members and sub-contractors.

It is therefore important as part of the negotiating process for the Trust to understand and test the relationships within the consortium itself. In particular, the Trust should make it its business to understand how risks are being allocated amongst the consortium members and sub-contractors. If these aspects are not addressed and understood at an early stage, issues which appear to have been resolved between the Trust and the consortium may get reopened if the consortium deals with internal risk allocation at too late a stage.

Financiers

All PFI schemes depend on finance. On smaller schemes this will not necessarily involve the obtaining of external finance by the consortium if the consortium members are able to finance the basic design and build obligations from their own resources. In most cases, however, an external financier will be involved. The Trust, in negotiating the contractual documentation will need to be aware of the need to strike the right balance in risk allocation to the private sector to ensure that the scheme is sufficiently attractive to external financiers.

The responsibility for obtaining finance is, of course, principally with the private sector partner, but in negotiating the contractual documentation, both the Trust and the consortium need to work together to ensure that the transaction is 'bankable'. External financiers are essentially looking for a secure income stream such that the risks of this income stream being diminished are significantly minimised. Here lies the delicate balance in the negotiation of the PFI contract where the Trust needs to ensure sufficient risk transfer in the contract to meet PFI requirements whereas the financiers will require the risks being borne by the consortium to be minimised to ensure the security of their income stream.

This gives rise to detailed and specific negotiations particularly in respect of the payment mechanism and the circumstances under which the Trust is entitled to make deductions or withhold payments and, equally importantly, the basis on which the Trust may be able to terminate the agreement for poor performance and thus terminate the financier's source of income to service its investment.

Much time and detailed negotiation was involved on the front running major schemes to establish the correct balance. While the management and negotiation of these aspects may vary specifically from scheme to scheme precedent and guidance should now assist schemes in striking the right balance.

The mechanics of negotiation

A PFI contract will have numerous different and interrelated strands and it is important as part of the negotiation process to ensure that these are effectively and efficiently managed.

Early strategic planning carried out by the Trust should enable the Trust to have a clear understanding of how the contractual documentation should be structured and negotiated to deliver the Trust's requirements. In conducting this exercise, the Trust should have regard to the need to identify the major substantive issues which are central to the overall structure of the scheme. These will include both the core issues and the project-specific issues.

This approach should enable the Trust to ensure that key related issues are negotiated together. For example, the output specifications and performance requirements will need to be considered specifically together with the payment mechanism. If the Trust agrees to less stringent performance requirements, this could be balanced by greater deductions to be made to payments to the consortium if these requirements are not met. By identifying the issues in this way, the Trust is in a position to link compromises and concessions which may be made by either party as part of the negotiation process and ensure that the overall balance of the contract is maintained.

In managing this process it is important to separate these major substantive issues which are central to the scheme as a whole from issues of detail. This is not to underestimate the importance of getting the detail right, but detailed operational issues, for example, should be dealt with separately within the overall structure of the contract which should itself be determined by the resolution of the major substantive issues.

Adequate preparation should ensure that committing the detail of the contract negotiations to writing is a means to an end rather than the end itself. It is important to ensure that the principles are negotiated and agreed with the detailed drafting following the agreed solutions. This avoids the detailed paperwork getting in the way of the resolution of the major substantive issues. The role of the project documentation should be to record the parties' intention rather than developing the documentation as a method for resolving issues through the detailed wording. The detailed wording is, of course, important and does take time to get right but can only be dealt with once the major points of principle are clearly considered and agreed in the context of the transaction as a whole.

The management of meetings is also particularly important in controlling the process. Wherever possible, negotiation meetings should have a clear and concise agenda to enable the Trust's negotiating team to be adequately prepared and to ensure that the meeting is properly focussed. This preparation should involve the Trust's team working with the Trust's professional advisers to construct recommended solutions to issues in advance of negotiation meetings.

Conclusion

The management of a PFI procurement is a lengthy and complex process. The success of an efficient procurement is dependent on adequate planning on the part of the Trust at an early stage. The clear emphasis from the NHS Executive on early strategic planning sets a sound base from which to progress the detailed legal process. Identifying and understanding key legal issues at the earliest opportunity will enable the process to run both efficiently and cost effectively.

What is Business Planning?

Maureen Devlin and Anne-Toni

Rodgers, Glaxo Wellcome

What is business planning?

The word 'business' seems a curious fit in today's NHS. The language of business that hallmarked the reforms of the late 1980s introduced the concept of boards, directors, chief executives and, of course, business plans.

The reforms may be melting away to make room for an emerging NHS based upon a different set of values, a set of values more in tune with the late 1990s, but of all the facets that were learned at the time business planning remains as one of the most useful management tools we have.

Business planning highlights the old motto: none of us plans to fail, we simply fail to plan. Business planning is a tool, fixed in the cycle of the NHS year as well as making a business case it is, essential for helping us to think clearly about what is ahead of us and the milestones we must pass to reach our goal.

In the movies when someone announces 'I have a plan', it usually means they have found a cunning way out of a sticky situation. In the language of business, a plan should help to prevent you getting into sticky situations in the first place; the art of planning means constant assessment of the situation and an understanding of the environment in which the activity will take place.

It was the author Rudyard Kipling who first spoke of his 'friends, trusted and true; who, what, where, when and who'. Kipling's friends are the friends of the business planner. They give us a hint of the key questions to ask and focus our thinking on what is important. Who is involved, what do we want to do, where are we trying to get to and who will do it?

If planning is like going on a journey, there are various things you need to decide.

Where are we now and where do we want to get to?

Coupled together the answers to these questions help us to shape the vision for the future. 'How and what needs to be done to achieve the end?' and 'What might the finished product look like?' Product might seem like a misplaced word; in truth 'product' can be a finished scheme, bricks and mortar or an opening day; or it might mean the product of our imagination in changing a service, or just doing things differently. Whatever the purpose of the plan, a clear vision of where you are now and where you want to end up is vital.

How you are going to get there?

The how is as important as the where. We have the vision and now we need to ask ourselves the question 'How do we get there?' How do we achieve our vision, or our goal? In the language of the business planner, this is the 'strategic cycle'. We need to marshal our strategy and think about the tactics and techniques we will need to employ as we move through our journey.

It may be that when you check where you are, you need to revise your direction in order to achieve your objectives. But that's OK – in life we do this all the time.

Business planning is a stepwise process that enables you to have a successful journey, using the resources you have set aside. But it is not a one-off.

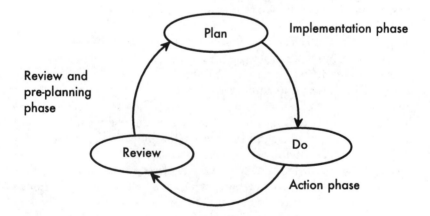

Figure 4.3.1 The planning cycle

Planning is cyclical. What does that mean? Figure 4.3.1 shows you how the planning cycle works. First, the plan is put together, it is implemented and the outcome evaluated. The process is reviewed, and fed into the pre-planning phase before the next plan. Planning the plan is as important as the plan itself. What you can learn from what has gone before is a useful ingredient of the next one. There is no substitute for experience.

Why business planning in the NHS?

The NHS is a complex organisation, comprising many separate and diverse local organisations. Each part, be it general practice, trust or health authority has, to a greater or lesser extent, an idea of what they are trying to do, with what staff and with how much money.

NHS business planning is a tool to:

- justify changes in resource allocation;
- adapt skills, staff and resources to meet the organisations aims;
- clarify decision making;
- motivate staff;
- map progress/development year on year.

Why you are making the journey?

Why make the journey in the first place? Good question – do you have a good answer? Put another way: what are our objectives? To build a building, to change a service, to justify funding and finance or just to 'do things better'? The reasons make no difference to the process. A stonemason was once asked 'what was he doing'. He might have said laying stone, or making a wall. He actually said, 'I'm helping to build a cathedral.' That was vision and objective all rolled into one!

Can you clarify your objectives?

What is vital for a successful trip?

Sometimes called 'critical success factors', they are a way of determining benchmarks along the way. To achieve the goal certain things must be done, without them there is no chance of success. What are your benchmarks? Think of them as foundation stones: without them in place, the roof falls in.

Who is going to do what?

A great plan is a great plan, but it is still a plan until someone does something. Sounds obvious, maybe, but the real message here is an 'action plan'. Who is going to do what, and when? You may discover you do not have all the skills needed to finish the project (or even start it). Identifying the tasks to be completed and the skills required produces a kind of audit. Thinking through the jobs to be done creates its own list of the skills required and the talents needed. But, it does not stop there. It is not just about skills and talents; it is also about key players having the time to deliver. If they are currently holding down a big, routine workload, how are they going to find the time to work on this project? The answer might be, they cannot. What are the answers? De-couple them from the routine, or bring more people in. Expertise and time are two of the vital ingredients in forming the plan.

Checkpoints and signposts of where you are against where you want to be

There is an old story of a lost tourist who stops a local and asks for directions. 'Well,' says the local, 'I wouldn't start from here!' For the business planner, there is a lesson in the story. Knowing where you are, all the time, is vital. It means you can judge your progress and make sure you do not get to the end of the allotted time and find you have six weeks' work to do in ten days.

A good plan will have checkpoints, 'must be complete by' dates to help everyone involved know where they are up to and how much time they have left. If it looks like there is slippage in the timescale you need to know early. Complicated plans will have to build in a contingency for slippage and overruns. Remember, everything takes longer than you think and everyone lets you down in the end. That is not corrosive cynicism, it is just commonsense based on hard-bitten experience.

Although the 'internal market' is no longer, and competition between trusts for 'business' will soon give way to 'co-operation', each NHS body still has a duty to strive for efficiency and have rigour in its decision-making processes through contestability. The thought processes that an organisation has to go through when business planning are still as valuable. Competition or co-operation, a good plan is the badge of efficient management and a cohesive organisation (see Figure 4.3.2).

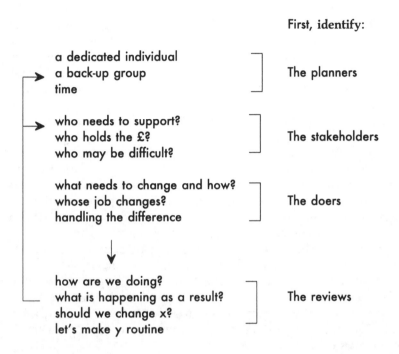

First, identify:

a dedicated individual
a back-up group   The planners
time

who needs to support?
who holds the £?   The stakeholders
who may be difficult?

what needs to change and how?
whose job changes?   The doers
handling the difference

how are we doing?
what is happening as a result?   The reviews
should we change x?
let's make y routine

Figure 4.3.2 The planning network

Checklist 1

1. Is the plan concise enough yet long enough to give a clear understanding of what is intended? A good question to ask is: Who is the plan for and is it written in a language they can understand? There is a vast difference between the business plan for a capital development and plan put forward to improve chaplaincy services. Try to read your plan through the eyes of the decision maker.
2. Does it have a purpose? A good plan outlines the purpose and sticks to it. The temptation is to wander off the main issue. A good plan is the result of good *discipline*.
3. Is there more than one course of action considered? The so-called SWOT analysis, strengths, weaknesses, opportunities and threats, has been a management tool since business began. What are we good at, what are we not good at, where is the real opportunity and where are the threats coming from? In a public sector environment this may seem out of place, particularly in an NHS that has turned its back on competition. Nothing could be further from the truth. Understanding your organisation, your department, your job, and being honest about what is good and what is not so

good takes courage and insight. Opportunities and threats in the NHS come, mostly from politicians and technology. They are not opportunities and threats in the conventional sense of the word, but a shift in policy at the top, the invention of a new wonder drug, or an extension of what can be achieved as a day case may throw, as the saying goes, the 'best laid plans of mice and men' (and women) off course.

4. Is the chosen course of action properly defined and reason for choice understood? Comprehensive planning, involving a good evaluation and a SWOT analysis may point the planner in an unexpected direction. Check the definition of the plan, are you asking yourself the right questions? Picking answers to options is seldom something to be done alone. The other stakeholders must 'sign up' to what is expected and they can only do that if the reasons for the choices you have made are clear to them.

5. Does the plan show that the purpose can be attained? There are some who argue that the best plans are the ones that point to failure. It seems a negative approach but there is a grain of truth in it. Better to paper test the aeroplane on the desk, rather than see it fall out of the sky. Better to see that there is not enough time, skills, talent, money or capacity for the plan to work – up front. Better than egg on the face later!

6. Are results expected from the chosen course of action specified? What timescales?

7. If the plan is to result in individual tasks, are responsibilities allocated?

Everyone wants everything yesterday. Timescales are important. End results are often tied to finance cycles, the beginning or end of a financial year or the chance to bid for new resources. Does the course of action in the plan really deliver what is wanted? It may sound silly, but planning to get it right first time is not easy.

We end where we started, with Mr Kipling. Yes, he probably does make exceedingly good cakes and his namesake, Rudyard, helps us to make exceedingly good plans. But no plan is worth the paper it is printed on without the 'Who', the right people to make it work. That means assembling the right talents and skills, making sure everyone knows what is expected of them. Enabling them to work in an environment where mistakes are not bawled out, people are encouraged to be frank about where they are up to and what their problems are. Planning is about teamwork and so is delivering. Good luck.

Figure 4.3.3 shows how to instigate step-by-step planning.

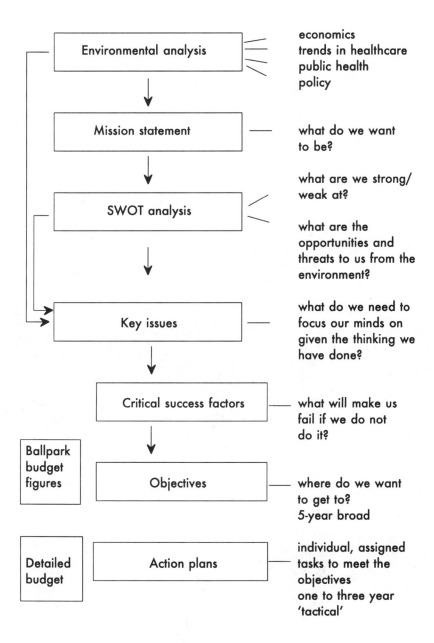

Figure 4.3.3 Step-by-step planning

Further reading

Semple-Piggot, C. (1996) *Business Planning for NHS Management*, Kogan Page, London.

Lilley, R. *Trust, Management and Strategy – 101 questions for the board*, Radcliffe Medical Press.

PART FIVE

MANAGING INFORMATION

5.1

Can You Afford to Ignore the Internet?

Keith Pollard, Acumen Solutions

If you read the newspapers this morning, the likelihood is that somewhere, someone was writing about the Internet. Like it or not, in your daily life or in your role as a healthcare manager you cannot afford to ignore the impact of the Internet.

What is the Internet?

The Internet is a network of computer networks. Government, academic, commercial, and research networks around the world are connected together so that users of any one of the networks can use the Internet to access information or reach users on any other network. The beauty of the Internet and one of the main reasons for its success is that users with different types of computer can communicate effectively. It does not matter whether you are a fan of the PC or Macintosh, or that you are connected to a mainframe computer, you can communicate with any computer user anywhere in the world at a remarkably low cost.

What is the World Wide Web?

The Web provides a user-friendly interface to access the wealth of information that exists on the Internet. Using a web browser such as Netscape Navigator or Microsoft's Internet Explorer, you can access resources from around the world incorporating text pages, pictures, audio files, and even digitised video clips. The Web is simple to navigate (or 'surf') and enables you to jump from one 'hypertext' document to another using 'hyperlinks'.

How can I access the World Wide Web from my office or home computer?

What does this involve? Let us assume you have a PC or Macintosh of a reasonable specification. (A 486 PC with 8Mb of RAM is a minimum sensible configuration.) You will need a modem (cost, around £100), an Internet connection package from a company such as Demon, Virgin Net or Pipex. Typical costs are around £10 to £15 per month for your connection – the software is free. Of course, while on-line, you will pay local telephone call charges.

If you are based within an NHS facility then you may have the advantage of being connected to NHSNet. NHSNet is the NHS Intranet – a closed Internet environment that is only accessible by people within the NHS. The Department of Health intends that every NHS facility – general practices, hospitals and clinics – will be connected to NHSNet by 2002. If you are based within an NHS facility, then you can ask your network administrator to provide you with access to NHSNet and through this connection, access to the Internet at large.

So, now you are on-line. The next step is to go on a training course. Even if you are an experienced computer user, a one-day course is a really worthwhile investment.

What is happening with healthcare on the web?

Once you are on-line, you will realise why the Internet, and the Web in particular, is receiving so much attention. Here are a few examples of healthcare applications on the Web together with the web addresses. (This chapter is available on-line at: http://www.ihsm.co.uk/article.htm if you would like to hyperlink to the example sites.)

I want to save my hospital from closure

If you go to the Kent and Canterbury Trust site, you will see how this Trust is using the Web as a focal point for its campaign against service closures. (http://www.kch-tr.demon.co.uk)

I want to know how my hospital is performing

The Department of Health provides an on-line version of the NHS. (performance tables http://www.open.gov.uk/doh/tables97/index.htm)

I need details of an EL or DOH circular

The DOH COIN database (http://www.open.gov.uk/doh/coinh.htm)

provides the text of all Department circulars including Executive Letters.

I want to give up smoking

Quitnet (http://www.quitnet.org) will help you to give up smoking. You can work out a programme for giving up and even acquire an on-line buddy to help you through.

I want to track down a patient support group

Many of the UK's patient associations and self-help groups provide information on the web. On the Patient Information site you can find links to most of those in the UK (http://www.patient.org.uk).

I want to provide an on-line educational programme

The Web can be used to provide interactive medical education. On the Epulse site (http://www.epulse.co.uk), general practitioners can undertake PGEA approved courses.

It is estimated that around 15 per cent of the information on the Web is health related. Patients, doctors, nurses and health managers are making increasing use of the resource. Patients are arming themselves with information about their condition before seeing their consultant. Medical students are using the Web to aid their research by accessing Medline and similar services on the Web. Nurses can view an electronic version of Nursing Standard (http://www.nursing-standard.co.uk/). And on the IHSM site (http://www.ihsm.co.uk), health managers can search a database of healthcare consultants, find the latest news on NHS issues and buy healthcare publications through an Internet bookstore.

Finding the needle in the Internet haystack

So, there is a wealth of healthcare information on the Web. But with over 60 million Web pages now in existence, how do you find the information you are looking for? You are faced with something akin to seeking a very small needle in a very large haystack.

For general searches, most people start with one of the Internet 'search engines', such as AltaVista (http://www.altavista.telia.com), Hotbot (http://www.hotbot.com) or Yahoo (http://www.yahoo.co.uk). These sites operate like computerised library catalogues and enable you to submit a search term and come up with a list of likely pages from their databases. Usually the site asks you to enter one or more keywords, subject headings or names that you are looking for. When the input you have made has been processed you will be sent back a page containing a list of sites which contain material matching your request. These are usually listed in order of relevance. Those that most closely match your request will be listed first. There are normally links to each of the sites directly from this list.

Making the most of a search engine

It is not that easy as the results from a search engine can be both overwhelming and confusing. For example, a search for the phrase 'health management' will produce a listing of the top ten or twenty out of over 7,000 Web pages containing the phrase. Search engines compile their results on a variety of criteria with the result that a lot of what you find may be irrelevant to your search. A search for the phrase 'health management' on AltaVista lists a Web page on critical reviews of potato health management at number three and one about NASA's Space Vehicle Health Management Program at number nine in the search results. Will these help you to become a better health manager?

So what is the solution? First, get to know your search engine. It pays dividends if you spend some time reading the help pages for one search engine and 'making friends' with it. Once you know what you are doing, your Web searching will be much more productive.

My favourite search engine is AltaVista. Let us suppose you are looking for information on the Web about the e coli bacterium responsible for a number of recent food poisoning scares. These are the results you will obtain from AltaVista, based on different ways of entering the search phrase.

Search term "e coli"
Result 18,674 pages
Comments Putting the phrase within "..." finds pages where e and coli appear together on the page, but there is a lot to choose from.

Let us make the search term more specific, and focus on the bacterium involved in recent outbreaks.
Search term "e coli 0157"
Result 590 pages
Comments Making the phrase more specific is obviously worthwhile, but there are still over 500 related Web pages.

And if we make our search even more specific.
Search term + "e coli 0157" + "food poisoning"
Result 87 pages
Comments Using + to combine two phrases in your search is highly effective. The results include instances of both terms on a page. Now we have a manageable result.

Search engines such as AltaVista are incredibly sophisticated. But as with any tool, the more time spent reading the instructions, the better the results.

One final recommendation: If you are looking for UK information, use the UK or European versions of the major search engines. Although the Internet grew up on the other side of the Atlantic, many of the Internet search sites now provide a version especially for us, and the Web address is different. Try these:

Altavista Europe
http://altavista.telia.com
Yahoo! UK and Ireland
http://www.yahoo.co.uk
Lycos UK
http://www.lycos.co.uk

Useful resources for healthcare managers

Rather than use a general search engine, you may save time by going to one of the dedicated medical and healthcare sites on the Web. Of course, many of these have an American bias but the UK is beginning to make its mark.

Many sites provide links pages which categorise worthwhile health-care resources. The IHSM Health Centre (www.ihsm.co.uk/health.htm) will guide you to some of the essential health management resources on the Web. There is also UKMedW3 (www.ncl.ac.uk/~nphcare/ GPUK/a_herd/topmenu.htm), Healthindex UK (http:// www.healthindex.co.uk), the Swiss-based Health on the Net Foundation (www.hon.ch) and in the US, Medical Matrix (www.medmatrix.org/index.asp) which provides a searchable database and categorised links for over 4,000 clinical resources on the Web. Probably the ultimate US resource is the National Library of Medicine (www.nlm.nih.gov) where they are not only creating a complete, anatomically detailed, three-dimensional representation of the human body but also offer a free Medline service. Medline provides access to all the key professional medical databases such as Cancerlit, Healthstar, Aidsline etc.

Government resources

For UK government resources, the starting points are the DOH pages at http://www.open.gov.uk/doh/dhhome.htm and the NHS Executive at http://www.open.gov.uk/doh/nhs.htm although you are going to have to do some digging to find what you want.

Publications and libraries

An excellent source of health-related publications is the British Official Publications Current Awareness Service (http:// www.soton.ac.uk/~bopcas/). The NHS Centre for Reviews and Dissemination at York (http://www.york.ac.uk/inst/crd/) now provides open access to their searchable database of healthcare effectiveness (DARE) and the NHS Economic Evaluation Database. A good starting point for good-quality UK biomedical resources is OMNI (Organising Medical Networked Information) at http:// www.omni.ac.uk. This site is run by a consortium of dedicated librarians and researchers centred at the Queens Medical Centre in Nottingham.

Current health management issues

What about health management issues? With the exception of the IHSM site, the UK still has some way to go. An excellent US focus for IT issues in health management is Health Management Technology (http://www.healthmgttech.com). In the UK, worthwhile starting points are the academic centres at Birmingham's Health Services Management Centre (http://www.bham.ac.uk/HSMC/), the Nuffield Institute for Health (http://www.leeds.ac.uk/nuffield/home.html) and Kent's Centre for Health Services Studies (http://snipe.ukc.ac.uk/ CHSS/).

Keeping up to date

Do you want to keep up on the latest healthcare developments? Then bookmark Reuters Health (http://www.reutershealth.com), CNN (http://www.cnn.com/health) and Achoo (http://www.achoo.com). And if you are short of dinner party conversation the Cool Medical Site of the Week (http://www.maxface.com/~wcd/cmsotw.html) should give you something to talk about.

Information for Patients and Health Service Users

Bob Gann, Director, The Help for

Health Trust

Access to information

Over the past decade patients and carers have had an increasing expectation of access to information about their own healthcare, and this has been encouraged by NHS policy. There are at least four good reasons why this should be the case.

It is ethical to do so

Honesty is an ethical imperative which is fundamental to any social contract. Truth telling is not only a moral absolute but also produces the best kind of social relationship, one based on mutual trust.

People want it

There is abundant evidence that people want more information about their own healthcare and treatment. Poor communication is the most common cause of dissatisfaction in many patient surveys and opinion polls. Not all patients want to be given information and to share in decision making but many do, particularly younger people, better educated people and those living with long-term illnesses and disabilities who have become experts in the management of their own condition.

Research shows it works

In clinical trials it has been demonstrated that better functional and physiological health status is closely connected to good physician–patient information sharing. (Coulter, 1997) There is some evidence that information sharing can lead to better health outcomes. Rather than increasing the expectation of treatment, research indicates that informed patients may be less likely to seek interventions. Patients seem to be more averse to risk than doctors when in full possession of the facts on risk and benefit.

Legislation requires it

Rights to information in the UK have, since 1991, been set out in the *Patient's Charter*, due to be replaced in 1998 by the new *NHS Charter*. Rights to clear information on treatment and research are already based on the fundamental common law principle of informed consent. The right of access to health records was established by two Acts of Parliament, the Data Protection Act 1984 and the Access to Health Records Act 1990.

Partnership, openess, effectiveness and quality

More recently new agendas have emphasised the need for improved patent access to information. These include:

- *NHS Code of Openness;*
- *Patient Partnership Strategy;*
- *Promoting Clinical Effectiveness;*
- *NHS Research and Development;*
- *The New NHS* White Paper;
- *Our Healthier Nation* Green Paper.

Health service managers are increasingly aware that sharing information with consumers (patients, carers and the wider public) can be a significant factor in:

- encouraging informed and discerning use of health services;
- creating public awareness of the concepts of effectiveness and uncertainty when considering treatment options;
- helping set priorities in purchasing and clinical care which reflect consumer values;
- encouraging professionals to develop skills in communicating with patients.

Openness

Published in 1995, the NHS Code of Openness encourages both purchasers and providers to enable public access to information about NHS services, costs, quality and performance; proposed service changes and how to influence decisions; decisions and actions affecting their own treatment; and what information is available and how to get it.

More specifically, purchasers should ensure mechanisms for public access to information on:

- healthcare services purchased;
- clinical performance of providers;
- lists of GPs, dentists, pharmacists, optometrists;
- late opening – family health services;
- complaints, numbers and response times;
- *Patient's Charter* information;
- people's rights as patients.

NHS trusts should be providing information on:

- performance against *Patient's Charter*;
- waiting times by specialty;
- information about clinicians (including special interests);
- clinical performance by specialty;
- patient information literature.

Patient partnership

NHS Executive medium-term priorities as set out in *Priorities and Planning Guidance 1998–99 Medium Term Priority D3* include 'Ensuring good quality information is made available to patients to enable them to look after themselves better, know when and how to seek help, and play an active part in decisions about their own care.'

Achieving this in practice is not easy. Patient surveys and health service ombudsman reports repeatedly highlight concern about lack of information, poor communication and absence of real partnership in decision making. As a first step towards remedying this at all levels within the NHS, the NHS Executive in 1996 published the first comprehensive *Patient Partnership Strategy*. The strategy, with points for action at local and national level, focuses on the work that needs to be done in four main areas:

- production and dissemination of information for health service users and representatives;
- structural, organisational and resourcing requirements for patient partnership and involvement including skills development and support for users

- supporting staff in achieving active partnership and user involvement in service development;
- research and evaluation into effective mechanisms for patient partnership and involvement.

Effectiveness and research based evidence

Sound information is an essential prerequisite for promoting clinical effectiveness and supporting decision making by patients as well as professionals. There are now a number of information-gathering and dissemination initiatives funded as part of the NHS R&D programme, including the NHS Centre for Reviews and Dissemination, the UK Cochrane Centre and the Health Technology Assessment programme. The *Promoting Clinical Effectiveness* framework for action recognises the importance of patients and carers having access to this information alongside clinicians and managers. A number of projects (e.g. at the King's Fund and NHS CRD) are developing evidence-based patient information materials to support informed treatment choices. Furthermore, a Standing Advisory Group on Consumer Involvement in NHS Research and Development has now been established, beginning its work advising the Central Research and Development Committee (CRDC) in 1996.

Health information services

In response to these changes in public expectation and driven by explicit NHS policy, there has been a major growth in information services for patients and the public over the past ten to fifteen years. (Gann, 1991)

There are now specialist health information services for the public in many settings including health shops, hospital enquiry points, health information mobiles, patient libraries etc. A single national freephone number for health information was established in 1992. Callers dial 0800 665544 and are automatically routed to their nearest health information centre. The local centres operate under an umbrella service name: the NHS Health Information Service (HIS). Health Service Guidelines HSG(95)44 require health authorities to provide access to information for their residents covering:

- common illnesses and treatments;
- self-help groups;
- healthcare services;
- waiting times;
- keeping healthy;
- patients' rights and how to complain;
- charter standards.

The Health Information Service now deals with almost one million calls a year across its network, and has provided the public information contact point for a number of health alerts, including public concern on hip replacement operations.

Centre for Health Information Quality

The new NHS White Paper promises a health service 'with quality its heart'. This approach extends to information for patients. In December 1996 an earlier White Paper *Primary Care: Delivering the Future* set out the NHS commitment to a national resource centre which would 'act as a source of expertise and knowledge for the NHS and patient representative groups on all aspects of patient information with the aim of improving the NHS's capability, competence and capacity to provide good, evidence based patient information' (Para 4.19).

This new resource centre, the Centre for Health Information Quality was launched by Baroness Jay in November 1997, with three years' funding through the NHS Executive Patient Partnership strategy. The work of the Centre for Health Information Quality is being developed in a number of ways:

- a database of people in the NHS working on patient information initiatives, to support networking of good practice and avoid re-inventing the wheel;
- a database of references to articles, reports and evaluations of patient information work;
- a training programme on identifying and producing good quality information for patients;
- promoting awareness of a range of tools and checklists for testing the quality of information;
- a programme of quality testing of patient information materials;
- production of a range of information resources including a newsletter, topic bulletins and Centre website. (http://www.centreforhiq.demon.co.uk)

Towards 2000

Managers (and clinicians) are coming to accept that the patient of the new millennium is likely to be more assertive, more questioning and in some cases more sophisticated in understanding of risks and benefits, clinical uncertainty and effectiveness. This consumer demand builds on existing policy and provision, including the freephone Health Information Service and the Centre for Health Information Quality, but will be strengthened over the coming years by commitments in the *New NHS* White Paper.

Policy relevant to information for patients will include:

- publication of a new Information Management and Technology Strategy for the NHS including 'providing knowledge about health, illness and best treatment practice to the public through the Internet and emerging public access media (e.g. digital TV)';
- a new 24-hour, nurse-staffed national helpline called NHS Direct;
- a National Institute of Clinical Excellence responsible for production of clinical guidelines for a range of audiences;
- establishment of a national network of healthy living centres.

The *New NHS* White Paper has now been complemented by publication of the Green Paper on public health, *Our Healthier Nation*. This looks forward to the day when all schools and colleges are linked electronically to the Internet. A new website Wired for Health will link students and others to 'accurate, clear and credible websites on a variety of health issues'. Through the National Grid for Learning it is the intention that every young person in the country will have access to the information they need to make responsible decisions about health. In the 21st century we can expect a new generation of health service users with much greater access to information sources – and the skills to use information for their own health and for involvement in service planning and policy.

References and further reading

Blaxter, M. (1995) *Consumers and Research in the NHS*, Department of Health, London.

Coulter, A. (1997) 'Partnerships with patients', *Journal of Health Service Research and Policy* **2**(2), 112–21.

Deber, R. (1994) 'The patient physician relationship: changing roles and the desire for information', *Canadian Medical Association Journal* 151, 171–6.

Gann, R. (1991) 'Consumer health information: the growth of an information specialism', *Journal of Documentation* **47**(3), 284–308.

Kaplan, S.H. *et al.* (1989) 'Assessing the effects of physician–patient interactions on the outcomes of chronic disease', *Medical Care* **27**(3 Supplement), 110–27.

NHS (1996) *Primary Care: Delivering the Future* Cm 3512 HMSO, London.

NHS (1997) *The New NHS: Modern, Dependable*, Cm 3807 HMSO, London.

NHS (1998) *Our Healthier Nation*, Cm 3852 HMSO, London.

NHS Executive (1995) *Code of practice on openness in the NHS*, HMSO, London.

NHS Executive (1996a) *Patient Partnership: Building a Collaborative Strategy*, HMSO, London.

NHS Executive (1996b) *Promoting Clinical Effectiveness: A Framework for Action in and Through the NHS*, HMSO, London.

NHS Executive (1998) 'Research: What's in it for Consumers?' First Report of the Standing Advisory Group on Consumer Involvement in the NHS R&D Programme, HMSO, London.

5.3

Healthcare On-line

Peter Cochrane, BT Laboratories

Introduction

Early in the new century the number of people needing healthcare and
support will more than double, while the number of potential carers
and those gainfully employed will fall. Worse still, we may see most
people failing to provide adequately for a longer period of old age,
and siblings refusing to pick up the tab. And all brought about by a
combination of demographic change, falling education standards, and
our expectation to live longer. We already suffer the California
Syndrome, expecting treatment no matter what the cost, and see death
as an unnatural act.

How is a diminishing band of healthcare professionals to cope in a
world of exponentially growing customer expectation and demand,
when resources and funding will at best remain static, and most likely
fall? No doubt clinicians and carers will continue to refine their
techniques and processes to become ever more efficient, whilst
administrators desperately cut corners, shave costs, reduce bed
occupancy, and push patients back into the community ever faster.
But none of this will stem the tide of demand and the growing
inability to respond. Something radical is required to change a
paradigm that has fundamentally been in stasis for over a century.
Compared to leading industries healthcare appears to be in desperate
need of change.

How IT can help healthcare

Industry is busy delayering and reducing the number of managers,
embracing IT and radical change, whilst healthcare goes in the
opposite direction. The height of this absurdity has been reached in

some US hospitals, where each patient now has a dedicated administrator.

As a prime target for change, consider patient records and the number of times information is entered into the system. GP, nurse, specialist, consultant, radiologist, anaesthetist all gather the same basic information during just one illness. This process is then repeated for successive illnesses and visits. The biggest single innovation in patient records during the last century has been to redesign the cart in which the papers are carried. We should be looking at IT and new ways of working.

Patients, doctors and specialists travel to meet at some hospital, surgery or home. This is wasteful. With head and hand-mounted cameras it is now possible to affect remote diagnosis and A&E support of paramedics at a remote site. The technology has moved beyond the experimental stage and affords great advantage and economy in dermatological examinations, foetal scanning, endoscopy, and operations of all kinds. Using standard dial-up ISDN lines the scanning of pregnant women in the Isle of Wight, with remote diagnosis in London, is routinely saving thousands of pounds per patient. It also affords the dual advantages of reducing diagnosis delays to hours instead of weeks, patient stress, and transport costs while increasing the effectiveness of the medical staff involved. IT classically delivers much more for much less — better patient care, better results with fewer people and less time and money.

The teaching of medical and surgical techniques is often limited by the number of students that can crowd around a subject. However, with miniature head-mounted cameras above each eye, and microphones, it is now possible for thousands of students (wearing VR headsets) to stand inside the surgeon's head looking out to experience the scene. Reversing the process means that a student, or surgeon, performing a procedure for the first time can have the support of an expert 'standing' inside them.

Similar successes with endoscopic examinations have also been recorded and the problem of bringing expertise and patient/customer together can be solved for almost every situation faced by the healthcare community. At a simpler, and more prolific level, consider the nurse with a laptop computer, digital camera and GSM mobile phone. At the push of a few keys the abilities of a GP can be extended with an image of a wound or infection captured on screen and transmitted back to the remote surgery.

Beyond direct medical care, we will see a rise in the number of single people and of loneliness. The technology for video conferencing is now fundamentally inexpensive and available. Support communities on the Internet already exist for most diseases or conditions. Thousands of people worldwide communicate and compare notes, offering advice and experience beyond that available via traditional routes. Extending this facility to everyone is potentially inexpensive, via a set-top box.

Beyond all of this, there is, however, a potential threat. Smart patients will use IT to get ahead of the medical profession. By accessing on-line databases, they can become better educated, ask more perceptive questions, demand the latest treatments and be more demanding customers. But perhaps worse still, countries will export their medical services to compete in other marketplaces. Interestingly, whilst the UK has been ahead of the game in demonstrating the benefits of telecare and telemedicine, it is US hospitals that are already delivering on-line services into the Middle East.

Using the net it is already possible to bypass UK restrictions on the drugs and medicines available over the counter. Soon it may be diagnosis and treatment that is on immediate offer as the technology becomes more sophisticated, cheaper and available. After all, I already have one wrist watch that can record my ECG, another that deals with my heart rate and blood pressure. Soon it will be blood glucose, salinity, temperature and more – all in one low-cost unit plugged into my PC or phone line.

PART SIX

MANAGING PEOPLE AND PERSONAL DEVELOPMENT

6.1

New Skills for a New NHS

Keith Holdaway, Mayday

University Hospital and

Bournewood Trust

How to tell the future

There are two ways to approach foretelling the future. You can lie on
your back on a grassy hummock, looking up at a blue sky, letting your
imagination run riot. Alternatively, you can look at trends: what linked
sequences of events can you find which seem to be heading in a
particular direction, or what issues are becoming increasingly important?
Extrapolating this into the future can indicate what will happen next.

No, there are three ways. You can look at what is happening in the
USA now and expect it here soon. Lists like this are always likely to
end up expanding (there are four ways ...) as all fans of the Monty
Python film 'Life of Brian' know! The danger is believing that any
answers to complex problems might be limited in their scope, or that
they might even exist at all.

Some might argue that the surreal humour of Monty Python itself
provides clues about the skills needed by health service managers.
Dealing with people who say one thing but mean something quite
different or who sit in rooms ready to have an argument (or is it
merely contradiction?) with the next person who comes through the
door. As a professional adviser on management development I feel
that I ought to use phrases such as 'political awareness' or 'ability to
cope with ambiguity in the workplace' to describe such skills, using
the jargon to 'establish professional credibility' with others. The
trouble is that I have grown weary of jargon and wary of lists. Lists of
skills, knowledge, attitudes, competences or lists of anything which

are claimed to describe the 'correct' manager. Such lists seem to be another symptom of the problem of believing that there exists one best solution, and that management is the task of finding and implementing it.

Give up trying

The idea that there exists one, predictable future has its own history of going in and out of fashion. Chaos theory and our own personal experiences of trying to predict what will happen suggest that such a view of the future is currently very much out of fashion. Yet, as managers, we do have to prepare ourselves for the needs of the future health service and our future careers. The resolution to this dilemma is to give up trying. It is remarkable how liberating it can feel to give up on a task which you know in your heart is a lost cause, or one that you carry out merely because others expect you to do it. The liberation releases energy and gives an appetite to do other, more productive, things.

The alternative to trying to predict your future needs for specific skills is to be able to learn new things very quickly when you have to. This requires:

- a good set of baseline abilities to build upon;
- good learning skills;
- a knowledge of resources and methods available to you;
- rapid and accurate diagnosis of your shortfalls;
- personal flexibility;
- feeling 'OK' about not yet being able to do something;
- openness to the need to change and develop;
- changes in work experience to generate new needs;
- developing now for the known future;
- access to money and time.

The irony of presenting a list, given my introductory remarks, is not lost on me. My only defence is that I do not claim it to be complete or a total solution. It is at least all in the 'here and now', things to make sure are in place before meaningful development can take place in the future. I believe that to be able to do your job well in the future you need to be doing it well now, you need to be confident in your ability and to have made plans and allocated resources for your personal development. Re-reading that sentence as I write this it seems self-evident. Yet how many can claim that it is all true of us? Worrying about future needs may well be blocking our very ability to meet them, by diverting attention from building a really sound foundation at the moment.

The management skills of the future are those of the present.

The motivation to learn new things

My experience of working with adult learners of all kinds shows that motivation is more important than teaching. When adults are convinced that they *need* to learn something and, crucially, know how to go about it, then the training manager's best option is to get out of the way and let them get on with it. That person will do all they need to learn. The motivational aspect is extremely important when working with managers on their own development. The urge to learn comes from the belief that it will be useful. Such a belief must exist in the stomach as well as in the head; thinking something will be useful is not at all the same as feeling it, and nowhere near such a good motivator.

The motivation to learn a new skill grows as the meaningfulness or salience of the need increases. The salience is greatest at the moment you find you have to do something new. That is the time to develop the new skill, find out new knowledge, change your mind about the importance of something. That is the point at which you should embark on your new learning. The learning will also take less time and effort.

It will take less time because you will push yourself to learn what you need as quickly as possible. The issue of effort is less obvious. You will probably put in hours of study, working extremely hard. But because you want to do it and can see an immediate benefit, you will not need to make a huge 'effort'. Effort is the perception of how hard the work is. Getting up in the morning to do something boring can be a big effort. Getting up to go to the airport to fly off on holiday requires just as much work, but who would describe it as an 'effort'? The same applies to pre-programmed courses of study. They are often a huge effort to attend because the salience of the need is too small to maintain enthusiasm for the work.

What skills might be needed?

It is not useful to try to advise on what you need to learn. It is personal and different for every reader. What I can try to do in the next section is to point out some of the likely causes to make you want to learn, to increase the salience and decrease the associated effort of personal development.

The PEST framework of politics, economics, social and technological trends is as useful as any for my analysis.

Political developments

Primary care groups

The White Paper and its implications throughout the UK has been extensively covered by other authors in this book. The proposed development of primary care groups (PCG) as the mechanism for commissioning healthcare brings together a group of staff who have not been used to working in this way in the past. Managing change and building teams are well-established skills, what will change is the context of their use. Getting community nurses and GPs to agree on anything has always proved difficult. Moving the staff out of old mindsets about hierarchy and personal worth will require a profound understanding of their values and sensitivities on the part of anyone leading the changes. Understanding GPs is valuable, as is understanding district nurses; the real knack is to be able to predict how these two groups will interact in a PCG. Add to this situation social services, voluntary sector representatives and a general manager or two and it becomes highly complex. You cannot set out to learn this in advance; everyone involved will need to learn quickly as they go along, possibly using the services of a skilled facilitator who can help self-diagnosis of behaviours which cause blockages.

Evidence-based practice

The insistence upon evidence-based practice will be the source of much game playing by clinicians from all professions and specialisations. Each new piece of research evidence will be used to lay claim to further investment to bring a service up to scratch. Managers will need to be able to assess the quality of clinical research, assess the risks of not changing practice to match that suggested and persuade others to follow the decision.

Clinical governance

Placing greater responsibility for clinical governance and the quality of medical treatment onto the chief executive, will further test the balance of delegation and control between trust boards and doctors. Clinical audit will become less of an educational exercise and more a managerial quality assurance tool. The practical need to understand the process and its reliability and to manage the political ramifications will become important for clinical and chief executives.

The formulation of a set of national healthcare standards (a kind of 'national curriculum' for hospitals), and a demand for benchmarking and consistency across the country will benefit management styles which are open, communicative and keen to share. Competitive cultures will only survive where there has been a recent history of high achievement which trust managers seek to emphasise or gain recognition from. The habit of competitiveness among NHS staff was easier to develop than many seem keen to admit. Losing the habit may be a little more difficult than many imagine.

Human resources issues

Frank Dobson seems keen to 'tackle racism head on'. In my experience, few managers understand the complex mechanisms of institutional racial (and other forms of) discrimination, or what can be done to counteract it. Human resources specialists will need to learn how to get anti-discriminatory policies and actions to the top of board agendas dominated by financial problems.

The redesign of Whitley around core and non-core terms of employment but with a national pay scale seems highly likely. Local pay was seen off largely by an unwitting alliance between NHS managers unable or unwilling to take on the work and unions unwilling to lose national collective bargaining. It is unlikely to happen that way again. Trust managements will need to acquire the skills to build and maintain local negotiating arrangements which are central, rather than peripheral to staff reward systems. Understanding different types of pay systems (there are others apart from the long pay spines and rigid grades found in Whitley), negotiating with unions, implementing changed terms and conditions will all be needed.

Economic developments

Efficiency through mergers

Roy Lilley, earlier in this volume, is not alone in his determination to 'sweat the assets' of the NHS and to make them work around the clock. In London, bed closures have not been accompanied by hospital closures, putting up the cost per bed of the service. Rationalisation and mergers of trusts and of health authorities to reduce management costs are increasing. Senior managers must be able to manage these projects, confident in their own future, ensuring that the synergy in the new organisation overcomes the accompanying damage to staff morale. Career management and outplacement must replace the expensive and destructive round of early retirements and redundancies. The sight of displaced staff leaving with somewhere to go more than makes up for the financial cost in terms of improved corporate morale and reduced guilt, the so-called 'Survivor Syndrome'. Senior managers and human resources specialists will have to overcome their reluctance to use outplacement consultants or to pay the going price. Middle managers will need to look ahead at other jobs they would like to do and plan career moves rather than applying in secret and feeling disloyal. These attitude changes need to be accompanied by career and succession planning skills.

Social developments

Education contracting consortia

These are still unfashionable. Chief executives are not rushing to take up the chairmanship of such bodies, yet they control so much money. And of course they are so important to the future supply of staff, our most expensive cost. Thomason (1990)[1] has argued that true personnel work has never been undertaken by trust management. Job design and professional boundaries are decided by outside bodies, grading and pay are determined nationally. Even staffing levels are often decided by the needs of professional education. All trusts have had to do is assemble a workforce from pre-defined parts within pre-determined limits. If workforce planning does become more local, the skills to do all these things will be needed. The extent to which this will change depends on how tenaciously Ministers in the Department of Health insist on attending to the 'softer, HR issues' in the health service.

Customer care skills

Rising expectations of patients and relatives will demand greater concentration on non-clinical aspects of care. Managers and staff will need to improve their handling of complaints to ensure satisfactory outcomes as well as hitting the deadlines set out in procedures. Writing in clear, customer-friendly terms will no longer be an optional extra, it will be a must.

An ageing workforce

The demographic rise in the elderly population is always portrayed as a demand problem in the NHS. It will also mean an ageing workforce and reduced numbers of school leavers. Workforce planning and job re-design will be necessary skills to respond to these pressures.

Technological developments

This part of the analysis is the most difficult to predict. Who knows what technological improvements could be made to remote working or even remote treatment?

Communications technology

The drive to improve efficiency and improvements in communications technologies will press for truly radical changes to patient records and information systems in general. The history of unsuccessful IT projects in the NHS is an embarrassment. It adds weight to criticisms by zealous reformers of the NHS who point to it as a symbol of weak or amateurish management. It will soon reach a point when IT illiteracy will be a serious disadvantage at work.

Expert systems

The development of expert systems, capable of diagnosing conditions, prescribing treatments and monitoring progress against predicted outcomes of treatment seems only a short way off. The staff whose status is most at risk from such systems are those who depend most highly on expertise for their position such as doctors and pharmacists. Staff who are employed for their physical or interpersonal skills (e.g. surgeons, nurses, therapy helpers, receptionists) or their caring approach to others will be the most in demand. Managers will have access to better decision aiding tools and will need to learn to trust and use them.

Conclusion

The pursuit of excellence (à la Tom Peters) as a managerial strategy is only useful as a competitive advantage in established services. If something is new, doing it early and coping by the skin of your teeth is usually advantage enough. Do not let a desire for perfection (or fear of failure) prevent you from doing well or even adequately in a new field. Give up the belief that you can train in advance for things that only might happen, you will have no energy for them. Instead, ensure that you are good at your current job and confident in it, get as much good feedback on how you are performing as you can arrange. Vouchsafe a budget should you need it and find out what development activities (not just courses) are available to you. Be prepared to respond to changes.

References

1 Thomason, G.F. (1990) 'Human resource strategies in the health sector', *International Journal of Human Resource Management* **1**(2), 173–94.

Continuing Professional Development for Managers

Miranda Coates, The Amalfi
Partnership

Introduction

Throughout my career, both within the NHS, and as a manager in other sectors, continuing professional development (CPD) has been of central importance to me. Whenever I take time out to review my own development, I am delighted by the wide range of individuals and events which have contributed to my own CPD and how both planned and spontaneous opportunities have helped me towards my goals. CPD is not an optional extra, it is vital to our professional well-being as managers.

The world of work continues to evolve at a dramatic pace and it can feel like more than a full-time job simply to keep up with these changes. What is certain is that the changes will neither slow nor stop and we will not have time to 'catch up' later. Development opportunities missed now are lost forever. We are increasingly aware that no-one else can (or will) manage our careers. It seems clear that, in the future, the fit between personal development objectives and your organisation's plans for you (assuming that you are part of an organisation) will be further apart than ever. Continuing professional development emphasises individual responsibility for development and asks the fundamental question, 'If not you then who?'

How important to you is your career? Why?

This question is clearly the place to start in any approach to continuing professional development. I believe that personal development should not be ignored in the rush to maintain and improve your marketability. As the concept of 'lifelong learning' gains wider public recognition, CPD should become easier. Weekend conversations with friends might hinge around how the next week at work will contribute to your development plans and how you will be able to apply what you learned last week. Easier perhaps, but not easy, CPD will continue to require both effort and imagination.

Effective CPD should increase your employability and provide a framework for you to consider how you can develop into new areas or improve your most important skills. CPD enables individuals to develop their careers by focusing on current and future needs and aspirations in two main ways.

1. CPD can relate to securing a different post by helping answer the question, 'What skills/knowledge/experience will I need to have in order to take my next career step?'
2. CPD can be used to enable individuals to contribute more effectively within their current role by focusing on areas where performance could be improved or where the role could be extended.

CPD is relevant to you whatever your career stage; however much development you have 'done'. For managers, increasingly, there will be no employment without development.

Why is CPD important to you at the moment?

CPD, by its very nature, is individual. What is important for your development may be of little interest to a colleague even if they have a very similar role to you, since their background and their aspirations will be quite different. A new appointee to a trust board from outside the NHS is likely to have very different needs to an internally promoted manager going into the same position. Two internally promoted managers will also have different needs reflecting their past successes and what motivates them for the future.

IHSM defines the process of continuous professional development as:

The individual manager taking responsibility for the development of his/her own career by systematically analysing development needs, identifying and using appropriate methods to meet these needs and regularly reviewing achievement compared against personal and career objectives.

The impact that your CPD activities have will depend upon your particular objectives and might include, for example: building upon opportunities in your current role; dealing proactively with imminent redundancy; making an appropriate sideways move into another directorate; moving to a position within a health action zone; or setting up your own business. A common impetus for increased CPD activity is starting in a new role — as a result of organisational restructuring there are now larger gaps between organisational levels so that the step up is a bigger risk both for your employer and for you.

It can be especially difficult to bring together immediate development needs and long-term needs or those strategic issues with a bearing on your career. Longer term development needs tend to be harder both to identify, and, once identified, to generate achievable objectives from. As with any objective setting exercise, it is vital that your plans are manageable. For example, if you want to work on health education policy development across Europe and you are currently a ward manager in Dumfries then you need to plan specific steps that will take you towards your goal.

In planning for long-term development needs it is often useful to think about wider trends in the sector. For example, what impact will an increased emphasis on primary care within the NHS have on your CPD? How much emphasis will there be on project team working in your future? What impact will information technology have on your role as a practice manager? What impact will medical technology have on your desired work of designing hospitals of the future? Participants thinking as far ahead as they can visualise will be able to put their current CPD into perspective, and thus avoid objectives which take them in the wrong direction.

For CPD to be effective it is important to find a balance between identifying a wide number of possible options and making realistic choices between all those possible options. The IHSM has developed the concept of the career climbing frame. This image is used to show that the environment is more complex and that managers have many choices available to them. Clear development objectives can help you to find your way.

In this case there will need to be a partnership between the employer and the manager to meet the immediate needs but the individual will also need to keep one eye on their own future plans.

Your continuing professional development activities should help you to:

- reflect on your work and development experiences;
- identify your professional (and personal) goals;
- recognise your development needs;
- implement realistic plans to meet these needs and accomplish these goals;
- review your success in moving towards your goals;

- deal with personal and organisational change in positive ways.

In addition, for CPD to be successful, participants need to base their decisions about priorities and development choices on a clear understanding of how they learn and develop most effectively and they need to improve the ways in which they learn.

How can I integrate my short- and long-term development needs?

If your longer term plans are quite different from your current role there could be tension between your immediate development needs and where you can see yourself going in the future. You need to strike a balance between improving your performance in your current role and addressing the future possibilities that you have also identified.

Most people find that between three and five specific objectives gives them enough variety and coverage. However this depends upon the detail and the challenge in each of the objectives: a participant may have only one CPD objective which is very complex and very important or may choose to attempt eight or more at a simpler level.

Who else do you need to involve in your CPD plans?

You should think creatively about the different ways in which any particular objective might be achieved. There are many options available to meet any identified need; CPD is not simply about attending courses or about access to training budgets. A little imagination, some thoughtful advice and a good knowledge of what works for the individual will enable effective choices. Organisations such as IHSM can help with (among other things) networking, publications and events.

In order to choose an effective development method you may need to clarify further what it is that you really need. Often a chosen topic is too wide for you to be able to generate realistic development methods with which to address the need. You might use the following questions to refine your needs:

- What specific topics are important to you? (Try to express this in terms of training objectives if you are having difficulty);
- What attainment level? (Where are you now; where do you want to be?);
- Within what context will you apply what you learn? How?;
- What other objectives are important to you? (e.g. team building, networking).

If, for example you want to address your 'writing skills', precisely what topic(s) do you need to consider?:

- report writing skills;
- minute taking;
- summarising long reports;
- graphical presentation;
- grammar and use of English;
- writing business cases;
- issues of style and impact;
- creating articles for newsletters and journals;
- visual aids for oral presentations.

You are in the best position to decide which development methods are most effective for you and most appropriate for your situation. I have found mentoring to be particularly effective. It can be used in a very wide variety of situations and helps to develop your reflection on current skills and competences. In addition it can be used to help signpost issues and individuals outside your normal orbit; for example when you want to explore a new sector or area of work.

Another valuable source of development can be any voluntary roles or tasks that you have undertaken. Offering your services as a member of a management committee for example, can contribute to your understanding of, and skills in agreeing difficult organisational budgets. Alternatively, if you are in a senior management position you might find real development opportunities in a hands-on volunteering role providing care.

What happens once I have made my plans?

It is important to review CPD activity systematically and in a regular manner. CPD is not a once a year activity, but needs frequent work to be really effective. This evaluation activity contributes directly to the next year's CPD plan. It is important to evaluate success with CPD effectively, covering both positive and negative issues. As part of this review, participants should identify areas of future importance and also any areas of concern.

With CPD you choose both what you work on and how you accomplish it. CPD reinforces the message that professional development is necessary for every manager. Giving structure to your professional development helps makes it effective. It has never been more important to pay attention to your development needs and to be able to aim confidently for what you want from your career and in your life.

I will leave you with three important questions:

- When you have retired (however near or far that seems) what sort of career do you want to look back on and do you need to make changes to your plans to facilitate this?

- What do you need to achieve in your career in the next three to five years to feel satisfied with your own development?
- What three actions will you take *this week* to advance your continuing professional development now?

6.3

Family-friendly Organisations – Myth or Reality?

Karen Baker, Head of Personnel,
Imminus Ltd

On Karen Caines' accession to the directorship of the Institute of Health Services Management, she was reported as saying, 'We have to change the culture of the 80-hour week, 500 miles commuting and not seeing one's children. It's not a sensible or healthy way to work.'[1] Some months earlier her predecessor, Ray Rowden, expressed his views, 'It is a badge of pride to work seven till seven (but) in today's world, with the pressures on the service, a lot of it is regrettably necessary.'[2] When one also takes into account the issue of junior doctors' working hours, and the advent of the European Directive on Working Hours, it is perhaps not surprising that the concept of the 'family-friendly' employer has recently become an issue of debate in health service circles.

What is a family-friendly organisation?

There is no accepted definition of the 'family-friendly' organisation. The concept seems to have evolved in the late 1980s, when a number of large UK employers decided to introduce measures to make it easier for their staff to combine work with family responsibilities. This was for business, rather than philanthropic, reasons. With the pool of available labour expected to shrink over the next few decades, those organisations that were able to offer the most attractive packages to employees would be better placed to retain their competitive edge.

The family-friendly employer is likely to offer a range of additional benefits to help staff cope with their domestic responsibilities. Examples include:

- enhanced maternity leave and pay provisions;
- paternity leave;
- special leave for carers of sick dependants;
- job share schemes;
- career break schemes;
- assistance with childcare;
- annual hours contracts;
- term time working;
- teleworking.

The overwhelming emphasis has been on provisions that are attractive to working mothers. This group has been targeted because many of its members remain at home if they are unable to cope satisfactorily with the often conflicting demands of work and childrearing. They literally vote with their feet. To date, much less attention has been paid to the needs of working fathers and to staff who care for elderly relatives.

How does the National Health Service fare?

Public opinion seems to be that the NHS must be a family-friendly place to work (presumably unless one is a junior doctor). After all, its staff are predominantly women, many of whom work on a part-time basis, and local initiatives to introduce workplace nurseries, holiday play schemes and career breaks are regularly reported. However, many health service human resource practitioners are not so sure. There is considerable evidence that, while most health service organisations have introduced a range of family-friendly benefits, the NHS culture remains essentially family unfriendly.

'It was far more acceptable to say I had a problem with my car than a problem with my child.'

(Former NHS marketing director)

'You get to the stage where even if you are at home on Saturday you feel guilty. The pressure just builds up inside you until the only activity you consider legitimate is work.'

(Accountant working in a large acute trust)

There is a tendency for boards to introduce family-friendly policies on a piecemeal basis. The driving force might be union pressure (or the need for a trade-off in negotiations), the determination of an individual director, or the desire to be able to report some concrete progress in the annual return to the Women's Unit. Only very rarely, does it seem, do boards debate what being a truly family-friendly organisation might mean. The focus is almost exclusively on how to help people in times of particular crisis, rather than any recognition of the fact that family life goes on 365 days a year and that balancing it with work commitments is a constant (and extremely stressful) battle for many staff, and that the worst casualties are usually their dependants.

Ironically, it is likely that the rubber stamp is put on the new carer's leave policy at nine o'clock at night.

The same trust that opens a workplace nursery and upgrades its maternity leave provisions, probably also holds informal management meetings during 'happy hour' at the pub, expects its staff to attend training courses in far-flung places without demur, and praises those who forego their full annual leave entitlement. In short, staff receive extraordinarily mixed messages.

The culture of 'presenteeism'

'Presenteeism' is an expression coined to describe the belief that the longer one remains behind one's desk, consulting couch or reception kiosk, the better one's performance will be rated. Many NHS staff complain about a culture that forces them into staying at work longer and longer. There is a growing tendency for contracts of employment to contain the euphemism 'such as are necessary to carry out the job' under the heading 'hours'. And it is a brave soul who steadfastly leaves the office at 5.30 pm, knowing that her colleagues will have their heads down for at least another two hours and will then converge on the local pub to mull over the day's business, bounce ideas off one another, and reach group decisions. It is an even braver soul who regularly leaves on time if the financial situation is looking grim and another round of job cuts is in the offing.

The need to be able to spend time with one's family is paramount for many people, but we should perhaps question the type of existence where anyone (irrespective of whether or not they have family commitments) exists solely to work. Long working hours make it particularly difficult to feel a part of the community in which one lives – whether finding time to vote in the local elections, chat with the corner shopkeeper, or participate in fundraising. It can be argued that being in touch with local issues is particularly important for staff whose business is caring for local people.

There is little doubt that hours of work in the health service have been adversely affected by staffing cuts and 'delayering' exercises in the face of ever-growing patient expectations. Even in those organisations where work processes have been re-engineered, new technology introduced and the best time management training given, fewer pairs of hands do not make for lighter work. Among managers it is also possible that there is the desire to overcome a poor public image by working ever longer and harder to try to square the circle.

Another factor that seems to have gone largely unexplored is the impact of the personal beliefs and modus operandi of the top decision-makers in any given organisation. People who hear Ken Jarrold, Human Resources Director of the National Executive, firmly state that he will have no part in the long hours culture, might feel temporarily uplifted, but depression descends all too rapidly if they return to a workplace dominated by a workaholic chief executive.

The impact of individuals

The impact that senior individuals can have on 'the way we do things around here' is well illustrated by Jane McLoughlin in her book *Up and Running*.[3] In the following extract she quotes a female employee of an advertising agency:

Company policy is based on the personalities at the top. Three years ago two top men here were divorced and going through the 'bimbo' stage. They took clients on horrible male nights out which deliberately excluded female colleagues.

Both of them have just got married. It's had a very definite effect on the agency. It's a much more family atmosphere. The CEO showed interest when I took my baby to work one day, because his wife is pregnant. That's why I've been able to do my job on a part-time basis – it's acceptable now, but if I'd got pregnant in his Jack-the-Lad phase, it would have been different.

There are two other directors who are having affairs and they're the ones who had a problem with my part-time. The business is their cover for the single lifestyle and they don't want any overlap between family life and work. But suddenly they're out of tune with the company ethos and because they're not comfortable they're not particularly effective.

Focusing once more on NHS decision-makers, it is interesting to study the review of top female managers carried out by the Executive in 1992.[4] Clearly some of these women are trying hard to create a family-friendly culture in their organisations:

Some of the women were passionate in stating that their personal lives mattered more than work and that this should be true for everyone. These women are champions of working arrangements which enable parents to manage better their work and domestic responsibilities. They eschew evening meetings without reasonable prior notice. They have no desire to join their male colleagues at the pub after work. They dislike the workaholic culture which dictates that you should prove your worth by hanging around the office until nine-thirty each evening. As managers, they want to know and understand the people below them as whole people, with personal lives and domestic constraints.

Conversely,

> Others keep their personal lives invisible from their colleagues in the belief that their domestic concerns will detract from their professional standing. At best their commitment will be questioned and, at worst, any work difficulties they or the organisation are confronting will be attributed to their domestic problems. A few women described hiding tragedies or difficulties with their children's health or education for this reason.

If some women at this top level feel unable to reveal (let alone seek help with) their personal difficulties, how much harder it must be for their junior colleagues, and how much it emphasises the role that key managers' individual attitudes play in determining corporate culture.

Policies are only as good as the access to them

A common complaint among human resource professionals is that they put considerable effort into developing initiatives to help staff balance work and family life, only to find that, once implemented, take-up is minimal. One possible reason is that few staff have the financial resources to take advantage of extended maternity leave, job share and career break schemes. There is evidence that over the next decade unemployment will continue to escalate among young and middle-aged men and that in many more families the woman will be the major breadwinner. If one also considers the rise in single-parent families, it might well mean that fewer and fewer women are able to access family-friendly provisions that involve loss of income.

It seems likely that cultural pressures manifest themselves here as well. In a climate where good jobs are at a premium, staff might well succumb to (sometimes subtle) pressure by line managers not to exercise their rights to new leave provisions. If line managers make it clear to staff that they see maternity leave as a necessary evil, paternity leave as ridiculous and special time off for people caring for sick dependants as political correctness gone mad, employees might well think twice about using their entitlements. The culture of presenteeism is not confined only to long hours; it can also involve taking minimal annual leave, struggling into work when totally unfit, even deferring childbearing. In a survey carried out at the North Middlesex Hospital Trust in 1994, more than 50 per cent of those line managers who responded said that they felt existing leave provisions were difficult enough to accommodate and that more generous arrangements would be impossible to absorb without the injection of additional resources.

One can have some sympathy with these views. Looking again at an extract from *Up and Running*,[5] Rosemary, the managing director of a manufacturing company, explains some of the difficulties she faces as a manager:

> I have a couple of senior directors working for me who've taken maternity leave in the last three years and it was really dreadful. One was in a creative job, involving a future range, and we couldn't replace her. She had a lousy pregnancy so we had a year of her out or one under par. In the event I doubled up and did it badly. I admit my sympathy was tested. Her job involves travel, and after the baby was born it had to be left at home. I'm still making allowances for her, even without her knowing and it's not easy. It's seriously affecting the business.

Less easy to justify, however, is the petty personal prejudice that sometimes emerges. A good example of this can be the attitude towards breastfeeding. It would seem that many managers would rather their staff remain isolated and out of touch while on maternity leave, than be provided with the simple breastfeeding facilities (a quiet room and comfortable chair) that would enable them to call in and attend team meetings. Indeed, figures collected in 1990 showed that a fifth of all mothers were back at work by the time their baby was four months old, and of this group 18 per cent were still breastfeeding.[6] Some health service organisations have begun to recognise this as an issue, but the majority (along with other UK employers) have done nothing to address it. Given the economic factors outlined above, good breastfeeding facilities might be a greater necessity for some staff than extended maternity leave provisions. The National Childbirth Trust is able to cite some appalling examples of women whose employers throw every obstacle in their way to prevent them from continuing to breastfeed their babies.[7]

Another problem which some employees face is their line manager's unwillingness to allow them to take annual leave at short notice, for example, when a child is ill or if a domestic emergency such as a flood occurs. The survey carried out at the North Middlesex Hospital revealed that nurses were experiencing this as a particular problem, and that, at all grades, they were forced into dealing with it by reporting sick. Ironically, although this course of action pushed up their total annual absence from the workplace, it was seen by some managers as culturally more acceptable than 'bringing their domestic problems to work'.

An area where many NHS organisations have tried valiantly to provide support is childcare. However, the provisions are perhaps not always well thought through. The vast majority of NHS nurseries are based on hospital campuses. However, ten years ago the clearing banks were beginning to realise that on-site workplace nurseries necessitated many users transporting babies and toddlers long distances, sometimes by bus or tube. In response to this, Midland Bank bases its nurseries off-site in places where a high concentration of Midland staff live. For example, their St Albans nursery is in a college five minutes' walk from the station and the centre of town, so parents can drop off children, park the car and catch a train to central London with a minimum of inconvenience.[8]

NHS organisations are disadvantaged by being unable to offer the significant nursery place subsidies of many large private sector companies. As a result, quite a few trusts are embarrassed by the fact that their nurseries are oversubscribed by their highest earning staff and that places have to be offered up to non-health service employees. The Boots Group has overcome this problem by setting up its own network of childminders, who are offered additional training and facilities.[9] The large corporate organisations cited certainly benefit from a co-ordinated approach, whereas in the health service it is left to individual organisations to find their own solutions. At very least, a central source of advice and support could be set up for trusts and others who wish to re-evaluate how they could best help staff overcome childcare difficulties.

Men have families too

The focus in most organisations has been on helping working mothers. Many provisions are of equal benefit to working fathers (support with childcare, carer's leave, etc.), but there is little doubt that if the culture can dissuade women from taking these up, it can make access for men extremely difficult. Brian Booth, clinical nurse adviser with Kingston and District Community Trust explains, 'if you are a man, a manager will ask whether your child's mother is going with him to the appointment. If she is, the attitude is – well, why do you need to go then? They don't understand the father's contribution.'[10]

Some trusts, such as Worthing and Southlands Hospitals, are beginning to look at fathers' needs as part of the drive to improve recruitment and retention. However, the Institute for Public Policy Research in its report *Men and their Children*[11] concludes that little is being done to help fathers. The IPPR believes that father-friendly employment would result in reduced absenteeism, lateness and employee turnover and increased productivity. They come back to the vexed question of working hours, stating that fathers in the UK work on average 47 hours a week, with many seeing next to nothing of their children.

Conclusion

The bad news is that life for most NHS staff who have caring responsibilities continues to be a daily battle. The better news is that the family-friendly organisation is topical and that improvements can be expected. Unfortunately, some individual initiatives have fallen on stony ground, but useful lessons can be learned from these.

Common stumbling blocks

- Some organisations believe that by introducing a few embellishments to staff's terms and conditions they qualify for full family-friendly status, and sit back on their laurels. They fail to recognise that they are only tinkering at the edges of the problem.
- Provisions are usually introduced out of the best of motives, but little assessment is carried out of their appropriateness, accessibility and impact. Many of the most creative ideas (term-time working, career breaks, etc.) are more accessible to staff who live in two-parent families and have relatively high family incomes. Managers are often expected to accommodate new arrangements without any recognition of the operational and financial consequences.
- The focus is primarily on helping staff during times of crisis or life change. Little is done to improve the day-to-day quality of people's lives by looking at working hours and making them feel comfortable about admitting that work is not the be all and end all of their existence. Indeed, there seems to be no acceptance of the fact that all staff, irrespective of whether or not they have families, need time and space to do other things and that this will make them better and more productive employees.
- The attitude (and, indeed, whim) of senior individuals has a marked effect on the culture of the organisation. It is fairly pointless for boards to introduce family-friendly arrangements if, as role models, they continue to work 60 hour weeks, take minimal annual leave and erect firm barriers between their work and personal lives.
- Family-friendly is seen as synonymous with working mother-friendly. Little is done to explore the needs of working fathers or of people with elderly dependants.

Tackling the problems

Key factors in tackling the problems are:

- accepting that initiatives will fall on stony ground if the culture remains unchanged;
- establishing what staff would really find helpful;
- being realistic about resources and operational impact.

Rather than rushing in with ad hoc policies, a co-ordinated, strategic approach is called for. Ideas such as setting up a working parents support group (with a small budget to spend on speakers, etc.), supporting national Go Home on Time Day (co-ordinated by The Long Hours Institute), and featuring articles in staff newsletters about how individuals manage to balance their lives, cost next to nothing, but might help to convince staff that change is afoot.

> Repercussions of the general life overload the employees experienced and evidence of its severity can be seen in how they spend their time outside work, and the kind of social lives they developed. Most did very little during the week apart from work, unwind, microwave an evening meal, and go early to bed. Weekends were hardly more hectic – catching up on housework and preparing for the following week at work. Family and friends had to be 'coped with' and 'made time for' rather than enjoyed.[12]

How many of us and our staff will identify with this quote and how long will it take us to do something about it?

References

1 'Caines and able', *Health Service Journal*, 25 April 1996.
2 'Is the 56-hour week good for you, your family or the NHS?', *Health Service Journal*, 13 July 1995.
3 McLoughlin, Jane (1992) *Up and Running*, London: Virago Press.
4 NHS Management Executive (1993) *Women Managers in the NHS – A Celebration of Success*.
5 McLoughlin, Jane (1992) *Up and Running*, London: Virago Press.
6 White, Freeth and O'Brien (1992) *Infant Feeding 1990*, London: HMSO.
7 'Work and feeding', *New Generation*, March 1996.
8 'Family values', *Human Resources*, Autumn 1994.
9 'Family values', *Human Resources*, Autumn 1994.
10 'Wait until your father gets home', *Health Service Journal*, 16 May 1996.
11 Institute for Public Policy Research (1996) *Men and their Children: Proposals for Public Policy*, London: IPPR.
12 Marshall, Judi (1990) *Women Managers – Travellers in a Male World*, Chichester: John Wiley and Sons.

Women Managers: Career Obstacles in the NHS

Valerie J Hammond, Chief

Executive, Roffey Park Management

Institute

NHS today

The reformed health sector is a highly complex system. The purchaser–provider split and the creation of Trusts has fuelled the demand for more and different skills of increasing levels of sophistication. Responsibility for forecasting and planning is firmly based at the local level, as is growing and allocating the necessary staff and facilities to meet the need.

However, it is unlikely, that resources can ever match the potential demand for quality healthcare in its entirety because, in marketing terms, health is an extremely successful sector. Advances in medical science and practice creates huge levels of expectation and demand from the public. Yet, this success sows the seeds of disillusionment. The possibilities for treatment inevitably outstrip the supply of funding and other resources. In such a situation, it is vital that there is true alignment between the strategic goals and operational practices of the service. Those who take the strategic decisions must have a real understanding of the consequences. The top team in each organisation benefits from experience drawn widely, from across the whole service.

These pressures and changes are matched by the desire and ability of many more NHS women to enter into mainstream management and to achieve at the highest level. They want to apply their specialist knowledge and skills in a strategic context, reflecting the situation that exists in society more generally where women want and need to play a full role in line with their ability. One might think that this would be easier in the NHS than elsewhere because of the huge proportion of women employees in health. Based on numbers and occupational spread alone, one would expect a management cadre largely comprised of women. This is so far from the case that one needs to explore what other forces are at play in preventing what should be natural from being achieved.

Continuing functional segregation

There are some unique features of the situation in the NHS. Although women are the majority employees, there is functional segregation between the professions: for example and at its simplest more women are nurses, more men are clinicians. There are divisions on gender lines within the professions: women clinicians are less likely than men to be surgeons; women are more likely to be in senior positions in community and priority care than in acute providers. Probably the most significant factor is the predominance of women in nursing and the way this particular profession is perceived.

Nursing has been the foundation of modern concepts of healthcare since Florence Nightingale. The greatest proportion of employees in the service is nurses. They are an acknowledged key resource and are highly esteemed by the public. However, power has progressively slipped. Nursing is struggling to emerge from its status as a supporting profession. The slippage is reflected even in the way in which official statistics are gathered where nurses are referred to as associate professionals. Doctors are the professionals.

But what has this to do with the role and status of women managers in the NHS? Everything. If the major source of women managers is regarded primarily as a support role, then this compounds the difficulty women encounter in being regarded as credible candidates for management roles. It has nothing to do with individual competence or respect for nursing *per se* but is related to perceptions of an appropriate role for the group as a whole. Further, it is distinctly possible that this view of the predominant group leeches out and is unconsciously applied, so that women more generally are expected to be in support roles. A significant obstacle to women's progress is therefore bound up with the perceived standing of nurses within the service *vis-à-vis* other groups of staff.

Numerical measures as barometer

The Creative Career Paths project studied the careers and work experiences of more than 2600 senior managers in the NHS. Significantly, the findings show:

- disproportionately high number of men in senior management and among senior nurses;
- disproportionately high number of women in junior management and among leavers;
- disproportionately high number of single and childless women in all groups studied;
- relatively young age profiles, particularly of top managers;
- virtual absence of people from ethnic minority groups and disabled people.

The Agenda for Action developed as a result of this research makes it clear that 'vigorous action' is needed 'to ensure that the NHS selects and keeps good managers, regardless of age, gender, race, disability, family circumstances or professional background'. It includes many recommendations for specific actions some of which are included here.

By completing the following 'quick check', organisations can uncover the basic situation for their women and gain clues as to the possible areas to investigate to uncover obstacles to women's development.

Table 6.4.1 Quick check on women's development

Group	Total nos	% Women	% Men
All managers			
Top team			
Senior managers			
Middle managers			
Junior managers			
Managers from ethnic minorities			
Managers registered as disabled			

Briefly, if, for example, the quick check shows that women form 50 per cent of managers overall but that at senior or top levels this dwindles to something much less, then clearly there may be factors around development and/or selection processes that need to be investigated. Similarly, small numbers from the ethnic minorities or disabled groups when compared with the source population may stimulate enquiries into the cause.

It is also useful to compare the age profiles and salaries of women and men in comparable grades. At a minimum this should be gathered with regard to the top team together with the academic and professional profile of this group. Data of this kind can prompt enquiry into the subtle as well as the overt obstacles that women have to overcome in order to achieve parity with male colleagues.

Recruitment and selection

NHS organisations are sometimes rather underdeveloped in terms of recruitment and selection. There may be inadequate attention to job definition and to preselection processes, for example, screening applications against specified requirements. There may be a lack of clarity which is not helpful to recruiters or applicants. Often there is a reliance on panel and social interviews. Clearly, interviews do have a part to play and skills training can make these more effective. However, the addition of appropriate selection processes, varied according to the role and including activities and tests, can give a more complete picture of the individual. This can be helpful in challenging assumptions and in overcoming obstacles related to existing role labels.

As indicated NHS women are well or even over-represented at junior management levels. They then tend to move up within their specialisms and so may not gain broader experience. This can result in situations where, when women do achieve senior management, they are still typecast within the functional framework. They may be appointed director of nursing rather than clinical director, for example, or director of personnel/HR rather than finance or IT, and these roles may be perceived as 'softer' or more 'supportive'. However, directors must be able to transcend functional roles and take on the broad range of responsibilities for steering the organisation towards its goals. Women must be advised and encouraged to take lateral moves at early stages in their career to broaden their range of experience and avoid typecasting.

Entering a new role

Each individual brings her or his own mix of talents to a new role; this is a natural, desirable factor. The woman manager often will have to get used to having things ascribed to her because she is a women, rather than because she is a new person in the role. There is no easy way to avoid this form of labelling. It is best ignored but colleagues, male and female, can help in working through this stage.

This is a period when working practices and norms are quickly established so it is vital to challenge discriminatory practices or language. Usually such things are unintentional; an all-male group may have developed a particular way of working or speaking, for example, or of timing meetings so that they run into the evening. Any new member of a group should feel able to negotiate for changes in established practices. There may be good reasons why these cannot be changed, but there is no reason why they should not be challenged. The group can help by providing a forum for an open exchange with new members at the outset and again after some months in the role. Also, it is a good idea to have a formal or informal mentor for the new member who can check out some of these issues. Explicit processes ease potentially difficult situations because delicate issues can be explored with no loss of face. For people coming together as part of a team but with very different orientations, this can be immensely helpful.

Developing for and within management roles

It is essential for all managers, including women, to develop a broad range of experience and to be prepared continually to retrain to meet new demands as they arise. This does not always happen and a number of factors contribute to inadequate development processes, the most obvious of which is perceived lack of funds.

Although the total spend on training and development in the sector is huge, local provision is often at risk. This is especially so at Trust level where there is often a perception of having to make a choice between funding patient care or staff development. This, together with the social doctrine of the sector, makes individuals acutely aware of training costs. They may aim to fund their own development but at the more junior levels where, for example, a management qualification might support a career move, individuals may find the funds involved are beyond their personal resources.

The arrangements made by the Women's Unit to fund nurses and other groups to study for MBAs have made a significant impact here in opening development opportunities to numbers of women who would previously have been excluded. This process should be maintained and extended. It is important for all managers but especially for women who may be more reluctant to stake a claim for personal development funds.

Flexible working patterns

A major factor in the career progression of many women who are experienced and active in health services is the fact that they may need to balance work and family responsibilities. It is significant that many studies show that high achieving women are frequently single or, if married, without children. The opposite is true of men for whom a family is seen as a symbol of stability. A key obstacle is the implicit expectation that women will make a choice between career and family. Yet women are increasingly unwilling, and indeed unable, to make this choice. Many are sole or main earners in the household and equally committed to career progress.

The NHS must provide for more flexible work patterns at all levels. Against a persistent culture of long working hours which, in itself, needs to be challenged, women may need, for family reasons, to work part-time during all or part of their management career. In other cases service may be on short-term contracts. In both situations the effect is often to exclude women from management roles. This is not usually because the women do not want this kind of work. Rather, those making the appointments find it difficult to comprehend how a management role could be less than full-time. To some extent this is a generational issue since research shows that younger people, especially those who have experience of employing managers who work part-time, are willing to appoint others.

As a fluid and flexible workforce becomes the norm, there is less justification for saying that management roles cannot be performed in this way. It is vital to ensure that contract and part-time staff have access to training and development so that they can form part of the resource for future management roles, full- or part-time. Contract and part-time workers, who are mostly women, are too large a part of the whole to be neglected.

Career paths

The Creative Career Paths Project, and indeed the much earlier report, A Celebration of Success which charted the careers of 27 senior women in NHS, demonstrated that fast-track routes and golden pathways are largely the figment of dreams. Successful people, men, and especially women, arrive at their positions in a variety of ways, taking opportunities as they arise. This may include significant experience gained outside the service as well as within. The unpredictable nature of organisational life, the fragmentation of national approaches to staffing and the emphasis on personal responsibility for career development suggest this opportunistic approach will continue or escalate.

To assist, there should be an explicit understanding between the NHS and the individual about what each can reasonably expect of the other in relation to careers. If individuals must take more responsibility for shaping their own careers, the NHS must provide appropriate support and counselling. Successful managers of the future will need to be politically astute in managing their own careers

At a practical level, when competing for jobs women can overcome obvious obstacles by:

- presenting personal information, CVs, bio-notes, in ways which help the reader immediately to access relevant past experience. A professional qualification gained ten years ago is less relevant than management or project experience directly relevant to the job in hand;
- presenting an image that is in keeping with the role, one that inspires colleagues and staff to feel confident and comfortable;
- treating the job competition as a learning process; finding out

information in advance about the job, about the selection processes and the people involved; thinking from their shoes; afterwards, asking for feedback and working through this with a mentor or counsellor.

A range of initiatives has been introduced through the Executive to give effective support and feedback. These include:

- Career Development Registers – through which women, and now men, can obtain personal, objective advice on how best to develop and present themselves for career opportunities;
- Development Centres – to experience a series of tests and activities leading to personal development plans;
- Peer Centres – where individuals learn how to evaluate their own and others' performance and to give feedback as well as ongoing counselling and support to colleagues;
- Executive Coaching schemes – whereby experienced usually external mentors provide ongoing coaching to new appointees.

All these initiatives, in their different ways, support individuals in their quest for development and feedback. Demand for these services is likely to increase in the continuing uncertainty that lies ahead in terms of organisational change. These schemes benefit all who seek a management or professional career. But they are doubly important for women whose options are often confounded by the need to balance child-bearing and rearing responsibilities, who may need to build personal esteem, and who may find it difficult to get clear unequivocal feedback.

Career life span

A worrying feature for careers generally and for the NHS in particular, given the long periods of initial training is the shortening of working life. There is a pronounced trend for early retirement at around age 50. This equates to a working life of around 30 years or of return on investment in development of say 20 years with, say, 10 years at peak level. This must have serious cost and resource implications for the NHS as a whole. For women employees the consequences are very serious. Given the biological facts, women's careers may slow down or stop for some years. Often they return and are at their peak performance in their forties, ready to spend another twenty years at work. However, with a trend for retirement at the age of fifty, often there is a reluctance to provide the necessary training for the post-40 women. This increases the pressure on women to achieve during their child-bearing years.

For those women who return with career expectations in their forties there may be dissatisfaction and disillusion so that they too leave at 50 having failed to achieve their objectives or to make their fullest contribution to the service. In other sectors women in their forties and fifties are increasingly sought after for key senior roles. The NHS should review its policies. Alternatively, women will certainly broaden their career options to look beyond the service so that, yet again, the NHS may not get full benefit.

Coming to terms with, and planning to achieve within, a realistic career life span is a major hurdle where women face different and greater pressures than men.

Building a new work culture

The final obstacle for women considered here is probably the most subtle and yet the most significant. It concerns the building of good relations at work with colleagues from a multiplicity of backgrounds, values and beliefs. An ethos of 'care' is often assumed to be a uniting value in the NHS but allusion has already been made to issues of power and status between the various professional groups. To this must be added camaraderie and culture built up through long years of training and the different life experiences of women and men. In the management team, this can result in misunderstandings and inaccurate interpretations of words and behaviour. This is a particular danger where one gender or the other is strongly in the majority because this generally results in a high level of understanding and agreement with 'the way we do things around here'. In these situations it requires real sensitivity to check out the understanding of the minority, whether women or men.

In most senior management situations it is still the case that women are entering a strongly male domain and this is also the situation in the NHS. The best solution is to create an open environment where such issues can be discussed and resolved. This can be handled through frank exchanges about how one thinks and feels about particular situations and issues. It is good to do this at the time or shortly after when all parties have good recall. Much has been written about miscommunication due to gender-related cues (see, for example, Deborah Tanner's *You Just Don't Understand*) but checking out has another benefit: it can help the whole team to tap into the experience and views of each member of the group.

If there is just one obstacle that the senior team can work to remove, this should be it. Good, open and effective communication between women and men, together with understanding, will pave the way for the eradication of all other obstacles. It will help create the new culture so much needed for success in the future.

References and further reading

NHS Executive (Women's Unit), London:
   Creative Career Paths 1 : Top Managers.
   Creative Career Paths 2 : Managers who have left the NHS.
   Creative Career Paths 3 : Managers in 15 NHS Organisations.
   Creative Career Paths 4 : Senior Nurses.
   Creative Career Paths 5 : Summary of Findings/Agenda for Action.
   Women Managers in the NHS: A Celebration of Success.
Tanner, Deborah (1991) *You Just Don't Understand: Women and Men in Conversation*, Virago, London.

PART SEVEN

MANAGING HEALTHY ORGANISATIONS

Tackling Violence at Work

Helen Kogan

Introduction

Recent figures from the latest British Crime Survey found that healthcare workers are three times more at risk from work-related violence than the general population. Furthermore, the latest household survey by the Health and Safety Executive in November 1997 found that nurses could be at a five times higher risk and a 1996 study by the National Audit Office into health and safety in NHS acute hospital trusts found that 14 per cent of the recorded accidents involved physical assault. The knock-on effects of these attacks are costly to both the victims and their employees. A violent incident can demoralise staff, undermine the drive to create an efficient working environment and incur long term sickness absence if it is not handled properly at the time. However, while it might be hopeful to say that violence can be totally eradicated within healthcare environments, there are preventive measures that can be taken to minimise the opportunities for staff to be attacked.

Indeed, the Health and Safety Commission (HSC), which encourages trusts to adopt control measures and to include violence within their risk assessment procedures under general health and safety practice, has recently produced user-friendly guidance. Frank Davies, Chairman of the HSC, urged trusts to disregard the short-term costs of putting such strategies in place at the launch of *Violence and Aggression to Staff in Health Services* by pointing to the long-term effects of the problem:

> Whilst these measures do have minor cost implications, this needs to be offset by the high costs of failing to act. A high level of violence to staff affects not only the staff exposed to the risks. Employers face costs in terms of reduced efficiency, sickness

absence and a bad 'image'. In relation to these costs, the expense of effective prevention measures is small.'

This chapter looks at some of the excellent advice provided by the guidance.

Legal obligation

Health and safety law applies to risks from violence as much as it does to other risks at work. Box 7.1.1 identifies the key points:

Box 7.1.1

Legal requirements

Health and Safety at Work etc Act 1974
Employers must:

- Protect the health and safety at work of their employees.
- Protect the health and safety of others who might be affected by the way they go about their work.

Management of Health and Safety at Work Regulations 1992
Employers must:

- Assess the risks to the health and safety of their employees.
- Identify the precautions needed.
- Make arrangements for the effective management of precautions.
- Appoint competent people to advise them on health and safety.
- Provide information and training to employees.

The Reporting of Injuries, Diseases and Dangerous Occurrences Regulations 1995
Employers must report cases in which employees have been off work for three days or more following an assault that has resulted in physical injury.

The Safety Representatives and Safety Committees Regulations 1977 and the Health and Safety (Consultation with Employees) Regulations 1996
Employers must consult with safety representatives and employees on health and safety matters.

Source: HSE, Violence and Aggression to Staff in Health Services, 1997

The recent fining of Swindon and Marlborough NHS Trust to the tune of £4,000 for breach of health and safety laws is a sharp reminder to management that there is a legal obligation to protect staff against violence. The Health and Safety Executive (HSE) found that the Trust had failed to implement a policy to protect its staff from exposure to violence and its Chief Executive resigned as a result.

The legal emphasis is clearly on risk assessment following the duties placed on employers by the Management of Health and Safety Regulations 1992. It is the employers' obligation to remove the risk at source and, if unable to do so completely, to introduce preventive strategies to control the risk. The definition of violence at work is given by the HSE as being: 'Any incident in which an employee is abused, threatened or assaulted in circumstances arising out of the course of his or her employment.'

Risk assessment

How you will assess the risk of violence will depend on the nature of the workplace. In a multiactivity workplace different departments will need individual assessments and the HSE suggests a five-step approach to this.

Look for hazards.

Consider the elements, which contribute to the risk of violence and the effect that they have on each other. For example:

- Look at records of incidents.
- Talk to local managers employees and representatives.
- Identify potential assailants.
- Consider particular activities which might present a high risk of violence such as refusing an appointment, administering medication or delivering unwelcome information.

The Royal College of Nursing points to an incident involving one of its members who was attacked by a patient's family after their request for someone to sit with their sick relative was refused on the grounds of staff shortages. While it may not always be possible to totally predict the circumstances that will predispose an employee to being attacked, situations where there are not enough staff to cover duties is an obvious flashpoint and should be assessed as such.

Who might be harmed and how?

- There is a need to identify all groups of employees including temporary staff, healthcare assistants and ancillary staff. Porters and domestics are generally overlooked but are just as much at risk as clinical staff.

- The level of staff training affects their vulnerability to assaults and the HSE advises that you consider this during your risk assessment.

UNISON reports that one of their members, a nursing assistant, Mrs June Knowles, underwent a patient attack which has left her unable to work. She describes her attack and its long-term effects.

It was about 10.15 at night and I was working on an acute ward sorting out medications. A new patient got me by the throat and shook me. For those few seconds you lose control and feel totally powerless. Luckily another member of staff came to my rescue and I was released. From then on I suffered pain and stiffness in my neck and an x-ray revealed the discs in my neck were out of alignment. I had been at the hospital 28 years but I wanted to carry on working until I decided to retire but I have had to leave my job because I cannot lift or carry out other duties.

Evaluate the risks

Are existing precautions adequate, or are more needed? For example, if the carrying of drugs creates risks make other delivery arrangements.
Other suggestions from the HSE include changing:

- the jobs people do;
- the circumstances in which they work;
- the way jobs are done;
- the way in which information is given to employees and the way it is communicated.

It also asks if there are confidential support systems for employees to encourage a return to work, if there is adequate training directed at relevant employees and if management involvement in drawing up procedures and policy is secured.

Indeed, a recent Royal College of Nursing (RCN) survey found that these types of support systems are frequently lacking. It suggests that incidents are underreported and assaults are sometimes regarded as 'normal'. For example, nurses rationalised offensive behaviour by interpreting it as an 'expression of pain' suffered or simply viewed it as part of the job. The College also found that it was underreported because its members did not have confidence in the ability of managers to tackle the issue effectively.

Many trusts are beginning to tackle this lack of confidence by explicitly stating their commitment to protecting staff. For example, Addenbrooke's NHS Trust has an equal opportunities policy that encourages staff to 'raise concerns if they consider they have suffered harassment by patients, service users or other members of the public.' Milton Keynes General NHS Trust includes the following statement in its Harassment at Work Policy:

> Milton Keynes General NHS Trust is committed to the elimination of all forms of harassment in the workplace. The Trust recognises that the nature of any sort of harassment causes staff to feel intimidated and creates a less effective working environment. The Trust views all complaints of harassment very seriously and will investigate and then take formal action as appropriate.

Record your findings

The main findings of the risk assessment must be recorded and might include:

- the hazards identified, potential assailants and high-risk areas;
- the staff groups exposed to risks;
- the existing preventive measures;
- evaluation of the remaining risks;
- any additional preventive or control measures identified.

Review and revise the assessment

This should be undertaken as part of the day-to-day management of health and safety. Furthermore, information should be made available to those responsible for policy and procedure. The HSE suggest that health and safety managers, boards and senior management need information on:

- significant risks;
- business plans for major capital and revenue investments, as justified by risk assessment;
- training requirements and their cost implications;
- accident and incident statistics;
- any serious incidents.

Preventive measures

Having completed the risk assessment, an effective policy needs to be created in order to prevent violent attacks. A positive health and safety culture is most likely if employees are involved. The development and implementation of control measures should involve consideration of:

- the workplace – physical aspects of the premise such as lighting, layout, noise and the provision of information to patients;

- working patterns and practice — factual information should be recorded about the need for precautions in patient records, care plans and other information systems. Community and primary care workers are particularly at risk and their practice should be assessed to reduced risk;
- staffing — staffing levels should be set to ensure enough staff to cope with foreseeable violence;
- training — training should be offered to all staff to help them work safely. Senior managers also need to know how to recognise the problems and to manage them;
- security — several types of systems can be considered including alarm, communication and monitoring systems. Good links with the police are also useful;
- response strategies — managers need to ensure that there are procedures in place to respond to incidents and that they match the level of risk. Debriefing strategies help employees and emphasise that the incidents are being taken seriously.

If an incident happens, despite implementing all the preventive measures suggested, prompt action by the trust is advised. This should take the form of bringing staff together to discuss what has happened and to debrief them. The HSE suggests that this debriefing can take two forms

1. technical, to find out what happened;
2. emotional, to ensure that those involved get the support that they require.

The involvement of management at this point is a good indicator that violent incidents are taken seriously. It might be that confidential counselling is also required for the victim and witnesses of the incident and this should be organised through the occupational health department.

Investigating the causes of violent incidents is an important element of providing an effective preventative system. Those carrying out the investigation need to be competent and to look at systemic problems rather than at individual errors. A review process should be established which is set out in Box 7.1.2:

> **Box 7.1.2**
>
> **Review**
>
> Policies, procedures and performance should be continually reviewed. All control systems deteriorate over time and may become inappropriate as a result of change. Examples of items the review should cover include:
>
> - Compliance with the violence policy and procedures.
> - Achievement of objectives set in plans.
> - Levels of staffing required.
> - Training of staff.
> - Analysis of records.
> - Whether accommodation design is appropriate.
> - The maintenance and performance of security systems.
>
> Review enables judgements to be made about the adequacy of performance, overall policy, specific procedures, required staffing levels and training requirements. Effective review also ensures necessary changes are implemented.
>
> *Source: HSE, Violence and Aggression to Staff in Health Services, 1997*

While this article has confined itself to acute trust settings, risks to healthcare workers operating in the community are also extremely high. The British Medical Association provides guidance to its members undertaking home visits, as do other employee organisations. It is an unfortunate reality that violence has become part of a healthcare employee's lot. It is not a situation, of course, that is specific to healthcare. Other employee groups have had to deal with an increasing number of attacks, particularly in the emergency services and in public sectors. However, there are effective ways of minimising the risk to employees if management is prepared to take the lead and introduce a proactive policy. An effective policy against violence will not provide personal benefits to employees by offering a form of protection against attack, but will lead to organisational gains in minimising the costly effects of such incidents.

Infection Control Management in Healthcare

Jennifer East, Director,
Infection Management Ltd

Hospital-acquired infection; although difficult to quantify accurately, remains an important problem and is responsible for substantial costs associated with the delivery of healthcare. In 1981, Meers *et al.* published the results of the first national prevalence survey of infection in hospital which showed that 9.2 per cent of 18,163 patients had acquired an infection during their hospital stay. This survey has been repeated and preliminary results show that a similar percentage of patients still acquire infection in hospital. The costs associated with a 5 per cent level of infection throughout the NHS was estimated, in 1986, to be in the region of £111 million or 950,000 lost bed days. It has also been shown in research carried out by Haley *et al.* (1985), that with an effective infection control programme at least one-third of those infections can be prevented. More recent research has identified that, with the changes in healthcare delivery, approximately 20 per cent of hospital-acquired infections are now first diagnosed and treated in the community. With patients becoming more vocal and aware of their right to a high standard of healthcare provision, complaints and litigation associated with the acquisition of infection in hospital are also on the increase and set to rise further in the foreseeable future.

Actions to prevent the spread of infection in populations have been taken for thousands of years with varying success. People with communicable diseases were incarcerated in pest houses and many forms of fumigation have been used. In particular, disinfection of the environment has been attempted with many products, including vinegar, sometimes successfully and sometimes not. During the Crimean War men were eight times more likely to die with sickness and wound infections in hospital than by being killed in battle. When Florence Nightingale introduced basic cleanliness and statistical information on the risks of dirt and infection, the health of the soldiers was greatly improved. Since Koch discovered in 1876 that a particular organism caused a specific disease, anthrax, public health and hospital staff have developed methods to prevent many of the diseases that were subsequently identified, mainly through improving sanitation and hygiene both in the hospital and the community.

The first nurse to join a microbiologist and form the first infection control team was appointed in 1959 by Dr Brendan Moore, Director of the Public Health Laboratory in Exeter, in response to a major outbreak of infection among patients and staff. This collaboration was very successful and so began an effective arrangement in hospitals and the community concerning the control of infection. Since that time the speciality has expanded and there is now at least one infection control nurse in nearly every acute hospital in the UK. This speciality is now spreading to psychiatric hospitals, nursing homes, community hospitals and the public health arena.

In recent years it has been recognised that there is a need to provide guidance on the management of the public health function, as outlined in the Acheson Report (1988), and the control of hospital infection, as set out in the Cooke Report (1988, 1995). The first Cooke Report was published in direct response to the findings of the inquiries into two outbreaks of infection at the Stanley Royd and Stafford hospitals which killed a number of patients. The first was an outbreak of salmonella food poisoning and the second of Legionnaire's disease. In both cases it was found that an effective infection control team and programme were not in place or not sufficiently supported by the hospital management to respond adequately to these major incidents.

In 1993 the combined working party of the Association of Medical Microbiologists, Hospital Infection Society, Infection Control Nurses Association and the Public Health Laboratory Service published the document *Standards in Infection Control in Hospitals*. The working party identified five core standards related to the areas of infection control practice which have a critical impact on the successful management of the programme. These include the management structure and responsibilities in infection control, development and implementation of policies and procedures, the provision of microbiological services, infection surveillance programmes and educational provision for all grades and types of staff. These standards have been implemented to varying degrees within the Health Service. However, they are an effective base on which to develop a programme which will meet the requirements of accreditation systems such as the King's Fund

Organisational Audit. Infection control services are unusual within healthcare in that an effective programme will have an impact on all aspects of hospital and community services.

Managerial responsibility

The ultimate responsibility for an effective service remains with the chief executive of each provider unit. They must ensure that there are sufficient personnel with clearly defined responsibilities, adequate lines of communication and other resources to facilitate the effective prevention, detection and control of infection. In hospitals and many community organisations this will entail the setting up of an Infection control committee and infection control team responsible for day- to-day activity and will include the provision of swift lines of communication to the management team of the facility. The need to resource this service adequately is underlined by the increasing threat posed to the hospitals by outbreaks of resistant organisms (e.g. multi-resistant *Staphylococcus aureus*, MRSA and multi-resistant tuberculosis, MRTB), together with outbreaks of diarrhoea and vomiting caused by virus.

Policy framework

The infection control team will usually initiate the development of policies and procedures. These should be ratified by the infection control committee, dated on implementation, and should undergo a documented review at least biannually. The team usually carries out the research and drafting of policies and then educates the healthcare staff on the new procedures or changes in guidance. Each healthcare provider unit will have a basic set of policies and procedures to which will be added additional measures relevant to particular aspects of care and practice.

Microbiology services

It is of critical importance to an effective infection control service to have a high-quality diagnostic provision from a microbiology laboratory. To ensure effective management of infections it essential that the team should have direct daily access to the laboratory staff to enable a swift investigation and response to identified infections which may impair the delivery of healthcare. Glenister *et al.* (1991) found that the most effective and efficient method of identifying hospital-acquired infection, in both time and cost, was that which utilised a combination of follow-up of positive microbiology laboratory reports by reviewing patient case notes and consulting with nursing staff to identify patients with infection. This method is called a ward liaison and laboratory surveillance system. However, the work of the infection control team must be seen as a separate and distinct function beyond that of the diagnostic service. It should therefore be adequately budgeted for and separately funded.

Surveillance programmes

Until recently the providers of healthcare have seen little need to support or develop effective surveillance programmes. However, such surveillance is now becoming an increasingly important quality indicator required by the purchasers. This has required infection control teams and committees to review current policies and develop new ones to cover this aspect of management of an effective programme. To be successful it requires support from other departments within the organisation, in particular IT and Clinical Audit. Again, to guarantee that this function is developed effectively it is necessary for it to be considered when reviewing resource implications and setting budgets. Frequently these functions are seen as necessary but not resourced, making it impossible for the team to provide a comprehensive infection control service.

Staff education

A comprehensive and wide-ranging educational programme is also a critical element of an effective infection control service, ranging from induction and orientation programmes for all healthcare staff, to the presentation of research projects to national conferences. In order to provide a successful education programme, adequate resources are required, including a budget for teaching materials such as films and videos, slides and books and for the photocopying of articles and research papers.

Legal liabilities

The activities of the infection control programme can also have a major impact on many other aspects of a healthcare organisation's legal responsibilities, which generally depend on the application of general common law principles and some statute law. Under the Occupiers Liability Act 1957, hospitals must provide safe premises for staff, patients and visitors. If patients are admitted to wards where there is an identified outbreak of infection the hospital authorities may be found liable for the death or permanent injury suffered by a patient if they acquire that infection. Recent litigation awards associated with the acquisition of infection have ranged from £10,000 to £50,000 and these are likely only to rise in the future. Clinical staff therefore have a duty to report suspected infections and the infection control team is responsible to the Chief Executive for taking the appropriate steps to prevent the spread of the infection.

There is a further duty on the organisation to prevent staff employed by the hospital from transmitting serious infection to others. If it became known to the hospital authorities that a member of staff was a carrier of a high-risk organism such as hepatitis B, then they must make appropriate arrangements to ensure there is no risk of spread of infection to other staff or patients, possibly even going as far as terminating the individual's employment. Although these restrictions are not necessary for carriers of less virulent organisms such as *Staphylococcus aureus* which are often carried by otherwise healthy individuals, special precautions are required when these organisms cause outbreaks of infection. The costs associated with the control of outbreaks of infection in hospitals have been estimated at anywhere between £10,000 to more than £100,000. In the case of preventable infections such as tuberculosis and hepatitis B, it is necessary to ensure that the healthcare staff are appropriately protected with immunisations and, where necessary, reviewed by the occupational health team if they are exposed to these organisms at work.

A patient could not possibly be blamed for introducing or spreading an infection in hospital. In such an instance it is necessary for the authorities to take all reasonable precautions to prevent the spread of infection including, where necessary, the provision of suitable isolation facilities. Similarly, a claim against the organisation in respect of acquisition of infection could only be upheld if the hospital had known about it and had failed to take appropriate action. A hospital can and has been held legally liable when a patient is discharged with specific infectious disease which is subsequently transmitted to another individual. In that case, the hospital was held to be negligent in discharging someone into the community who was likely to infect others and that the patient should have remained in its care until they were no longer infectious. When patients become infected due to breaks in aseptic techniques or hygiene the hospital may also be held responsible.

Healthcare organisations also have substantial responsibilities under the Health and Safety at Work Act 1974. This Act places responsibilities on the employer to provide and maintain plant and systems of work that are as far as is reasonably practicable safe and without risks to the health of employees. There is a responsibility of management to have advisors and safety officers, safety liaison officers and where staff require them safety committees. The Act also outlines the responsibilities of the employee to co-operate with the employer in complying with safe working practices. The Health and Safety Executive have recently taken considerable interest in hospitals' compliance with current Health and Safety Legislation, including the provision of effective infection control guidance, policies and practices. Another critical piece of legislation which has had an increasing impact on healthcare organisations is the Control of Substances Hazardous to Health Regulations 1988 and 1995. These regulations have been in force since October 1989 and introduced a framework for controlling the exposure of people to hazardous substances arising from work activity. In the recent updating of this legislation an additional emphasis has been given to the control of biological hazards as well as other toxic substances. The employer is responsible for assessing health risks created by the work and to identify and implement the appropriate measures to protect the health of the workforce and the employee is required to comply with these measures. These regulations are of particular relevance to infection control staff as they cover the use of chemicals for disinfection or sterilisation of equipment, disinfectants and cleaning materials used to ensure a safe environment, transport of specimens, protection of staff against infection such as hepatitis B or tuberculosis and the prevention of legionnella colonisation in water supplies. Fines associated with non-compliance with this legislation have been in the order of £10,000 to £15,000.

When putting appropriate controls in place the process of risk management can be utilised to great effect. There are two major areas to consider when reviewing infection control – the risks to the patient and the risks to the staff. In controlling these risks each can have an impact on the other and both are equally important. It is necessary to identify the risk exposures, what methods are suitable to control those risks, which is the best control method, the implementation of suitable controls and the evaluation and monitoring of improvements in risk reduction. It is essential that regular audits are carried out, that risks identified are addressed and that improved standards are maintained. Where identified risks cannot be resolved locally then these must be notified to managers responsible for risk management and safety within the organisation and where necessary remedial action should be taken. As part of the process it will also be useful to review relevant incident/accident reports which may highlight particular areas of risk. As part of the continuing review, these reports should also be monitored, to ensure a reduction in numbers associated with a reduction in risk exposure.

The full impact of hospital acquired infection is currently difficult to quantify. However, future research is likely to shed more light on this potentially preventable problem. The development of effective infection control, surveillance and audit will play an increasingly important role in the delivery of healthcare wherever it is provided.

It is the responsibility of everybody in healthcare to ensure that they are knowledgeable about all risk aspects of their work, what their personal risks are and the appropriate protective measures necessary to maintain their own, their colleagues' and their patients' safety.

References

Control of Substances Hazardous to Health Regulations. 1988 & 1995, London, HMSO.

Department of Health (1988) *Public Health In England* (The Acheson Report), London, HMSO.

Department of Health (1995) *Hospital Infection Control* (The Cooke Report) London, HMSO, HSG(95)10.

Glenister, H M *et al.* (1992) *A Study of Surveillance Methods for Detecting Hospital Infection*, PHLS, Colindale, London.

Haley, R W *et al.* (1985) 'The efficacy of infection surveillance and control programs in preventing nosocomial infections in US hospitals', *Am J Epidemiol*, 125: 182–205.

Health and Safety at Work Act 1974, London, HMSO.

The Infection Control Standards Working Party (1993) *Standards in Infection Control in Hospital*, London, HMSO (available from PHLS, Colindale, London).

Meers, PD *et al.* (1981) 'Report on the national survey of infection in hospitals 1980', *J Hosp Infect* (Supplement 2).

Occupiers Liability Act 1957, London, HMSO.

Steering Group of the Second National Prevalence Survey (1993) 'National prevalence survey of hospital acquired infections definitions. A preliminary report of the Steering Group of the Second National Prevalence Survey', *J Hosp Infect*, 24: 69–76.

7.3

Safer Patient Handling

Moira Tracy,
Health and Safety Adviser,
Victoria Infirmary NHS Trust

Fast changes

Things are moving fast in the area of patient handling. Some trusts now have successful policies which show that back pain from patient handling can be prevented. Healthcare establishments now have an opportunity to make large savings by:

- reducing sickness absence and ill-health retirement;
- avoiding rising insurance premiums;
- avoiding Health and Safety Executive enforcement;
- avoiding large costs of personal injury litigation.

On the other hand, organisations that do not embrace the changes will probably be deemed to break criminal law and will also find it hard to raise a defence against compensation claims. There are a few essential sources of guidance to keep you abreast which are (or will be) used in court.

- the most comprehensive will be the fourth edition of the *Guide to the Handling of Patients*;
- the Royal College of Nursing (RCN) has also published three booklets (see References) with the latest guidance and a Code of Practice;
- the Manual Handling Operations Regulations;
- the advice published by the Health Services Advisory Committee.

This chapter gives an overview of the main elements contained in these sources of guidance. The term 'back pain' is used throughout to refer to back, neck, shoulder and other musculo-skeletal disorders.

The law

- The Manual Handling Operations Regulations can be used in personal injury litigation as well as in criminal law. They state that the need for risky manual handling must be avoided, so far as is reasonably practicable. Where that is not 'reasonably practicable', the employer must do a risk assessment and take steps to reduce the risk 'to the lowest level reasonably practicable';
- 'Reasonably practicable' means to a level where the cost or effort further to reduce risk far outweighs the risk of injury to staff. Staff suing their employer could use to their advantage the EEC directive which led to our regulations: this directive does not have any wording like 'reasonably practicable' – its requirement is strict.

Examples from trusts that have a safer handling policy show that it is without doubt 'reasonably practicable' to implement such a policy. Therefore any healthcare organisation that does not strive towards such a policy is likely to be considered negligent and breaking the Regulations.

- The highest compensation awarded so far to a back-injured nurse is £345,000. Nurses are usually awarded £100,000 to £200,000 if they cannot work anymore, or £50,000 to £100,000 if they can resume work. Many claims are settled for £2,500 if Social Security benefit exceeds the likely compensation.
- The Health and Safety Executive (HSE) now have a programme of systematic inspections of the healthcare sector. They have served fines and improvement notices based on the Manual Handling Regulations. They regularly recommend that a safer handling policy is put in place;
- The positive side for employers is that if they follow the advice in the key texts referred to above, not only will HSE approve but it will be very difficult for an injured employee to prove negligence.

A safer handling policy

A safer handling policy states that a risk assessment must be made for handling tasks, and the risk must be reduced to the lowest level that is reasonably practicable. A patient's whole weight is never lifted manually. Patients are encouraged to assist in their own transfers. Appropriate handling equipment is used to reduce the risk from lifting and other handling tasks.

The policy does not prevent staff from giving a patient some support, or using pushing, pulling, upward or downward forces. But all tasks must be done with the equipment, environment and system of work that reduce the risk to the lowest level that is reasonably practicable.

When deciding what is reasonably practicable, the risks to the staff are assessed, taking into account the needs of the patient and any risk to the patient from the point of view of how elements of care are administered or withheld. The right balance must be found, where one party's benefit does not increase the other party's risk to unacceptable levels. An example is that when helping some patients to walk, nurses and physiotherapists run a high risk of injury if the patient falls unexpectedly. But if the patient has been assessed well and the carers position themselves properly, the risk is often acceptably small.

There should be almost no situations in someone's career where he or she needs to lift a patient manually. Emergency situations that can be foreseen should be assessed so that the most reasonable safe system can be planned for. It is only in the rarest emergencies that no one could have foreseen that staff may well find themselves risking their back to prevent a far greater risk to their patient.

Most often, what benefits the staff also benefits the patients. A safer handling policy means most patients are safer, more comfortable and can move independently more often.

Feasibility, cost and savings

An increasing number of organisations have a safer handling policy in place (often called 'minimal' or 'no-lifting policies'). Of the two who have reported numerical results, one has demonstrated a steady reduction in accidents down to half its initial level (Victoria Infirmary NHS Trust, Glasgow). Another reduced its sickness absence due to patient lifting by 84 per cent. This represented a saving of £400,000 in just one year (Wigan and Leigh NHS Trust). Others report qualitative improvements, for example 'nurses are less tired', 'there is less back pain', 'we wouldn't go back to the old ways' and 'patients like it'.

In order to achieve this result enough suitable handling equipment must be in place. If there are already a few hoists in bathrooms, the extra handling equipment needed is likely to cost 0.2 per cent to 0.3 per cent of the annual budget. Once in place, roughly 0.03 per cent of the annual budget will need to be allocated each year to replace equipment as it becomes old and for maintenance. These estimates are based on calculations once made for a large health authority and were confirmed by the experience of the Victoria Infirmary NHS Trust.

The equipment needs must be assessed locally, but some or many of the following are likely to be needed: height-adjustable baths, electric profiling beds, sling hoists, standing hoists, overhead hoists, sliding boards, sliding sheets, and small handling aids like rope ladders. Hoists bought nowadays should most often be the electric type to avoid any risk of cumulative strain with winching handles and for convenience.

The Disabled Living Foundation has produced a comprehensive guide to handling equipment.

Competent assistance

Every healthcare organisation should get one or more 'competent' persons to 'assist' it towards reducing risks (Management of Health and Safety Regulations). A 'Back Care Adviser' or 'Moving and Handling Co-ordinator' should report directly to one of the directors of the organisation in order to promote all the aspects discussed in this chapter. There is a network of Back Care Advisers called National Back Exchange, which provides an excellent way of keeping up to date in this fast-moving field.

Risk assessments

Risk assessments have to be done by law, and are extremely useful. By doing them big and small ways of reducing risks can be discovered. Decisions can be made as to where the priorities lie and how much money is needed to achieve aims. Documenting plans will be of assistance in dealing with the Health and Safety Executive if good standards cannot be achieved immediately. The RCN has produced a simple guide to risk assessments, with sample forms.

Reducing risks

The risk assessments should conclude with suitable ways of reducing risk. The main ones will be:

- Avoid the need for hazardous handling by changing the way the job is done;
- Provide handling equipment; improve the environment and furniture (see below);
- Give staff information on risks and on back care, instructions in care plans and training (see below);
- Spread the load between more people or over a longer time;
- Ensure adequate staffing levels;
- Ensure uniforms allow a good range of movement;
- Review job satisfaction and stress; there is evidence that these influence the levels of reported back pain.

Heavy lifting is not the only cause of back pain. Cumulative injury is caused by repeated, lighter tasks done in bent or otherwise awkward postures. So look at all factors to reduce risk.

Training

- Training is essential but is only one of the measures needed to reduce risk.
- Make sure that training is consistent with policy and with the equipment available in the wards.
- Complement classroom training with support from the instructor or from link people in the working area.
- Keep detailed, signed records of what each person has been taught: this is essential in claims for negligence.
- Impress on managers and supervisors that the training given to staff has little legal value unless it is enforced in the working area.
- The instructor must be competent and up to date. Nowadays a competent instructor cannot qualify after only a short course. Contact the RCN or National Back Exchange for details on the Interprofessional Curriculum – A Course for Back Care Advisors.

Equipment and environment

The risk assessments should determine handling equipment needs and any changes needed in the work environment.

- Bathrooms and toilets are often too small and sometimes hoists cannot get in: knock down walls if that is 'reasonably practicable'.
- Beds used by dependent patients must be height adjustable, and possibly be of the electric profiling type (which fold in several sections into a sitting position).
- Have a plan ready for patients whose weight is above the Safe Working Load of the equipment at hand.
- Select seats, wheelchairs, toilets; etc; which will help the patient to be independent and reduce the need for staff to bend or twist.
- In the community, there is less control over the environment, so risk assessments are essential and need to involve patients and all the parties involved in their care. Managers need to ensure that handling equipment is available very quickly – meanwhile, the patient may have to be nursed in bed.

Reporting back pain and incidents

Staff should report back pain, whether triggered by an accident or not. They should be encouraged to report all incidents, even those where they only felt minor pain. The back care adviser should use these reports to monitor practices and to encourage further improvements. For instance, one incident may trigger off a training or problem-solving session in the work area.

An incident report should also trigger extra care for the employee:

perhaps they need more advice, training, or for treatment to be arranged through the occupational health service. Incident reports are important to both staff and employer if the employee later decides to sue. By the time they sue, anything up to three years could have elapsed, so it is important that all the facts are written down shortly after the incident. The details that will be needed include:

- date, time, place, what happened;
- nature of injury and part of body injured;
- witness details and their statement of the facts;
- exact description of how the move was done and the equipment used: who was standing where, where were the hands, etc.;
- the moving and handling section of the care plan and a note of whether the move was done in accordance with the care plan or other instructions and whether handling equipment was available;
- name, date of birth, weight, capabilities, co-operation of the patient;
- any other tasks done that day that could have contributed to the injury;
- any space restrictions, floor hazards, etc., height of furniture, was bed height adjustable?
- the risk assessment for the area;
- evidence of any instructions or training given to the employee.

Review

An employer needs some way of reviewing whether their efforts towards safer patient handling are successful. Review should help to identify any remaining weak areas.

- Incident statistics and sickness absence provide some indications of progress, but note that staff could be injuring their backs without feeling any symptoms. They could later get insidious or acute back pain which could appear unrelated to their work if it started when they were at home.
- There should be a target number of staff trained on induction or refresher courses.
- Link people have a good knowledge of what is going on in their area – they should report back.
- Staff coming on refresher training provide good indications of what is happening in practice.
- It is possible to carry out an audit of the use of good movement and of equipment, and of patient care plans. Staff may 'cheat' if they know they are audited but this indicates at least whether they know the rules.
- Risk assessments need to be updated, equipment levels and future needs should be reviewed.

- As a result of the review, new objectives should be set.
- It is preferable to have the involvement of staff and managers at all levels in reviewing the current situation and setting new objectives.

Rehabilitation

The employer should help injured employees to get back to some form of work as soon as possible. There is evidence that people will make a faster recovery from back pain if they avoid long spells of absence. After six months' absence, an individual's likelihood of ever returning to work has fallen to about 50 per cent; after a year about 25 per cent; and after two years virtually nil (Pheasant, 1991). It is very much in an employer's interest to prevent long absence or ill-health retirement, as these give rise to the highest compensation claims.

When an employee has a back injury, they should get immediate advice from the occupational health unit and, if appropriate, a fast referral for physiotherapy or other treatment. Otherwise there is a risk that the employee's GP will have advised several weeks' bed rest, after which the employee waits several more weeks for a physiotherapy referral. This can lead to a long-term back pain problem.

The occupational health unit should discuss with the employee and their manager what form of work the employee could do, initially on a part-time basis. The back care adviser, physiotherapist or ergonomist may also be needed, to advise on risks in particular areas. The employee may need refresher training. Their normal work may have to be modified. If this means that they do not fulfil all their normal duties this should not matter, as if they were at home they would still be paid and someone would have to do their work for them anyway.

Pre-employment check

Healthcare organisations should have sound criteria for allowing or refusing employment to people who will have to handle patients. This is still a grey area, because it is almost impossible objectively to predict who might get a back injury. As many people have had back pain in their life and cope successfully with it, it would also not be right to reject everyone who has had back pain. The new Disability Discrimination Act also has to be taken into consideration: it seems that employers will not be able to refuse employment to people with disabilities unless they can demonstrate that the work cannot be made suitable to them. As there are yet no clear-cut answers, employers should concentrate on reducing risks at work so that the employment is suitable to most people.

References

Lloyd, P. *et al* (1996) *Guide to the Handling of Patients* 4th edn, National Back Pain Association, Teddington, in collaboration with the Royal College of Nursing.

Royal College of Nursing (1996) *RCN Code of Practice for Patient Handling*, London

Royal College of Nursing (1996) *Introducing a Safer Patient Handling Policy*, London

Royal College of Nursing (1996) *Manual Handling Assessments in Hospitals and the Community. An RCN Guide*

Manual Handling Operations Regulations 1992, HMSO, London

Health Services Advisory Committee, Health and Safety Commission (1992) *Guidance on Manual Handling of Loads in the Health Services*, HMSO, London.

Disability Discrimination Act 1995, HMSO, London.

Disabled Living Foundation (1994) *Handling People: Equipment, Advice and Information*, Disabled Living Foundation, London.

Management of Health and Safety at Work Regulations 1992

Pheasant, S. (1991) *Ergonomics, Work and Health*, Macmillan Press, London.

PART EIGHT

APPENDICES

Appendix I

Health Service Guidelines

HSG (97)1	The pay and conditions of service for general and senior managers
HSG (97)2; IASSL (97)2	Housing and community care: establishing a strategic framework
HSG (97)3	General Ophthalmic services I. Increase in NHS spectacle voucher values II. Changes to the forms and leaflets
HSG (97)4	Primary care dental services
HSG (97)5	PFI and market testing
HSG (97)6	NHS health and safety issues
HSG (97)8	Practice fund management and computer allowance
HSG (97)9	Workforce planning for general medical services: further guidance
HSG (97)10	Prescription irregularities and the Prescription Pricing Authority Fraud Investigation Unit
HSG (97)11	The welfare food scheme
HSG (97)12	Specific grant to Local Authorities in 1997/98 for the development of social care services for people with mental illness
HSG (97)13	Decisions of the Professional Conduct Committee of the General Medical Council
HSG (97)14	Purchasing effective treatment and care for drug misusers

HSG (97)15	Supplementary credit approvals to Local Authorities in 1997/98 for the development of social care services for people with a mental illness
HSG (97)16	I. Charges for drugs, appliances and wigs and fabric supports II. Prescription prepayment certificates III. Collection of charges IV. Statistical returns V. Forms and leaflets VI. Changes to the NHS low income scheme
HSG (97)17	Corporate governance in the NHS: controls assurance statements
HSG (97)18	Immigration and employment of overseas medical and dental students, doctors and dentists
HSG (97)19	Guidance notes on the processing, storage and issue of bone marrow and blood stem cells
HSG (97)20	Terms and conditions of service for the specialist registrar grade in public health medicine
HSG (97)21	General Dental Services: Peer Review and Clinical Audit in General Dental Practice
HSG (97)22	GP fundholding: revised list of goods and services
HSG (97)23	Ethics Committee Review of multi-centre research: establishment of multi-centre research ethics committee
HSG (97)24	Decisions of the NHS Tribunal
HSG (97)25	The National Health Service (Fundholding Practices) Amendment Regulations 1997
HSG (97)26	General Ophthalmic Services: increase to the NHS sight test fee for ophthalmic medical practitioners
HSG (97)27	Decisions of the Professional Conduct Committee of the General Medical Council
HSG (97)28	Central information collections from the NHS: business uses of information collected and details of control mechanisms
HSG (97)29	Treatment of service patients in NHS hospitals
HSG (97)30	The National Health Service

	(Fundholding Practices) Amendment Regulations 1997
HSG (97)31	Priority treatment for war pensioners
HSG (97)32	Responsibilities for meeting patient care costs associated with research and development in the NHS
HSG (97)33	Use of military helicopters by the NHS
HSG (97)34	The National Health Service (Fundholding Practices) Amendment No 2 Regulations
HSG (97)35	Decisions of the Professional Conduct Committee of the General Medical Council
HSG (97)36	Issue of alert letters about hospital and community medical and dental staff
HSG (97)37	Guidance to hospital managers and local authority social services departments on the Sex Offenders Act 1997
HSG (97)38	Investing in dentistry
HSG (97)39	The pay and conditions of service for general and senior managers
HSG (97)40	The year 2000 problem
HSG (97)41	Decisions of the Professional Conduct Committee of the General Medical Council
HSG (97)43	Patients who die in hospital
HSG (97)44	General Ophthalmic Services: increase to the NHS sight test fee for optometrists; increase in NHS domiciliary visiting fees from 1April 1997
HSG (97)45	Key features of a good diabetes service
HSG (97)46	Secretary of State's list for dental prescribing
HSG (97)47	Library and information services
HSG (97)48	General Ophthalmic Services: introduction of revised GOS forms clarification of GOS procedures
HSG (97)49	Cervical screening guidance for health authorities
HSG (97)50	General Dental Services Amendment 79: Statement of dental remuneration
HSG (97)900	Decisions of the Health Committee of the General Medical Council
HSG (97)901	Decisions of the Health Committee of the General Medical Council

HSG (97)902   Decisions of the Health Committee of the
General Medical Council

Source: Department of Health
Crown copyright is reproduced with the permission of the Controller of Her Majesty's Stationery office.

Appendix II

Executive Letters

EL (97)13; G:\HCDPH2\ PH\EL\FEB97	Public health responsibilities of the NHS
EL (97)14	Specialist workforce advisory group recommendations: higher specialist training numbers 1997/8
EL (97)17	Annual report of the Advisory Committee on Distinction Awards
EL (97)18	Implementing the reforms of specialist medical training
EL (97)19	Getting Trusts connected to NHSnet services
EL (97)20	Introduction of the augmented care period dataset
EL (97)21	1997 Departmental Report for the Department of Health
EL (97)22	Destruction of controlled drugs
EL (97)23	Terms and conditions of service for the specialist registrar grade in public health medicine
EL (97)24	General election guidance
EL (97)25	A working draft to develop a quality framework for HCHS medical and dental staffing
EL (97)26	Mental health (hospital guardianship and consent to treatment) amendment regulations 1997
EL (97)27	Personal medical services pilots and the NHS (Primary Care) Act 1997
EL (97)30	Devolution of responsibilities to education consortia
EL (97)31	National Specialist Commissioning Advisory Group (NSCAG) applications for designation and central purchasing
EL (97)32	Consent to treatment summary of legal rulings
EL (97)33	Changing the internal market
EL (97)34	Update to EL(96)13: security in the NHS
EL (97)35	Making available information about PFI projects
EL (97)36	Health Service Commissioner annual report for 1996–97 and selected cases report for October 1996 to March 1997
EL (97)37	GP commissioning groups
EL (97)38	Paediatric intensive care: a framework for the future

EL (97)39	NHS priorities and planning guidance 1998/99
EL (97)40	Patient's Charter: changes to monitoring arrangements for 1997/98
EL (97)41	SMAC statement on use of statins
EL (97)42	Access to secondary care services
EL (97)43	The Patient's Charter: privacy and dignity and the provision of single sex hospital accommodation
EL (97)44	National Lottery White Paper: healthy living centres
EL (97)46	Developing emergency services in the community: the final report
EL (97)47	Managing data quality improvements and data accreditation
EL (97)48	A code of practice in HCHS locum doctor appointment and employment
EL (97)49	Consulting the NHS on a set of provisional clinical indicators
EL (97)50	Local budget setting and financial management
EL (97)51	The use of HRGs in the 1998/99 business cycle
EL (97)52	Aseptic dispensing in NHS hospitals
EL (97)54	Payment of contractors for pharmaceutical services (phase 3); payments to dispensing doctors and to GPs for personal administration of medicines
EL (97)54	Payment of contractors for pharmaceutical services (phase 3): payments to dispensing doctors and payments to GPs for personal administration of medicines
EL (97)55	Corporate governance in the NHS: controls assurance statements
EL (97)56	NHS senior career development service
EL (97)57	Guidance on the use of the revised management standards in the NHS
EL (97)58	Education and training planning guidance
EL (97)59	The year 2000 problem
EL (97)60	Patient's Charter developing a new charter and changes to the immediate assessment in A&E standard

EL (97)61	NHS finance – additional money for patient care
EL (97)62; CI (97)24	Better services for vulnerable people
EL (97)63	Prescribing expenditure: guidance on allocations and budget setting for 1998–99
EL (97)64	Additional resources for the NHS 1997/98
EL (97)65	Health action zones – invitation to bid
EL (97)66	Improving outcomes in colorectal cancer: guidance on commissioning cancer services
EL (97)67	Cancer screening: quality assurance and management
EL (97)70	Tax avoidance
EL (97)71	Discount rates and the cost of capital
EL (97)72	Payment of contractors for pharmaceutical services (phase 3): payments to dispensing doctors and payments to non-dispensing GPs for personal administration of medicines
EL (97)73	Managing human resources in the NHS
EL (97)74	Family Health Service fraud: integrated programme of action
EL (97)75	Changes to the provisions of the Road Traffic Act
EL (97)76	Health service commissioner report: investigations completed April-September 1997
EL (97)77	Meeting patient care costs associated with research and development in the NHS: detailed guidance
EL (97)78	The management of doctors with problems
EL (97)79; CI (97)28	Substance misuse and young people
EL (97)80	National Drugs Strategy budget 1998/99 (aka Drug Action Team development funding)
EL (97)81	The new NHS white paper
EL (97)82	Corporate contracts and Common Information Core 1998/99 activity section
EL (97)83	Cervical screening programme: achieving quality standards in laboratories
EL (97)84	Appointments to the most senior posts in the NHS

Source: Department of Health
Crown copyright is reproduced with the permission of the Controller of Her Majesty's Stationery office.

NHS Trusts

England
Northern and Yorkshire

Airedale NHS Trust
Airedale General Hospital
Skipton Road
Steeton
Keighley
BD20 6TD
TEL: 01535 652511
FAX: 01535 651278

Bishop Auckland Hospitals NHS Trust
General Hospital
Cockton Hill Road
Bishop Auckland
Co. Durham
DL14 6AD
TEL: 01388 45400
FAX: 01388 454137

Bradford Community Health NHS
    Trust
Leeds Road Hospital
Maudsley Street
Bradford
BD3 9LH
TEL: 01274 494194
FAX: 01274 725652

Bradford Hospitals NHS Trust
Trust Headquarters
Corridor III
Bradford Royal Infirmary
Duckworth Lane
Bradford
BD9 6RJ
TEL: 01274 364787
FAX: 01274 364786

Calderdale Healthcare NHS Trust
Calderdale Health Authority
Royal Halifax Infirmary
Free School Lane
Halifax
HX1 2YP
TEL: 01422 357222
FAX: 01422 330509

Carlisle Hospitals NHS Trust
Cumberland Infirmary
Newtown Road
Carlisle
CA2 7HX
TEL: 01228 23444
FAX: 01228 814802

Cheviot & Wansbeck NHS Trust
Wansbeck General Hospital
Woodham Lane
Ashington
NE63 9JJ
TEL: 01670 521212
FAX: 01670 529927

City Hospitals Sunderland NHS Trust
Sunderland District General Hospital
Kayll Road
Sunderland
SR4 7TP
TEL: 0191 565 6256
FAX: 0191 514 0220

Cleveland Ambulance NHS Trust
Cleveland Ambulance Headquarters
Venture House
Marton Road
Middlesbrough
TS4 3TL
TEL: 01642 850888
FAX: 01642 855007

Community Health Care, North
    Durham NHS Trust
Earls House
Lanchester Road
Durham
DH1 5RD
TEL: 0191 333 6262
FAX: 0191 333 6363

Cumbria Ambulance Service NHS
    Trust
Ambulance Headquarters
Salkeld Hall
Infirmary Street
Carlisle,
Cumbria
CA2 7AN
TEL: 01228 596909
FAX: 01228 20382

Darlington Memorial Hospital NHS
    Trust
Memorial Hospital
Hollyhurst Road

Darlington
Co Durham
DL3 6HX
TEL: 01325 380100
FAX: 01325 743622

Dewsbury Health Care NHS Trust
Woodkirk House
Dewsbury District Hospital
Healds Road
Dewsbury
WF13 4HS
TEL: 01924 465105
FAX: 01924 816192

Durham County Ambulance Services
    NHS Trust
Ambulance Headquarters
Finchale Road
Framwellgate Moor
Durham
DH1 5JS
TEL: 0191 386 4488
FAX: 0191 383 1207

East Yorkshire Community
    Healthcare NHS Trust
Westwood Hospital
Beverley
HU17 8BU
TEL: 01482 886600
FAX: 01482 886541

East Yorkshire Hospitals NHS
    Trust
Castle Hill Hospital
Castle Road
Cottingham
East Yorkshire
HU16 5JQ
TEL: 01482 875875
FAX: 01482 876331

Freeman Group of Hospitals NHS
    Trust
Freeman Road
High Heaton
Newcastle Upon Tyne

NE7 7DN
TEL: 0191 284 3111
FAX: 0191 213 1968

Gateshead Healthcare NHS Trust
Whinney House
Durham Road
Low Fell
Gateshead
NE4 5AR
TEL: 0191 402 6000
FAX: 0191 402 6001

Gateshead Hospitals NHS Trust
Queen Elizabeth Hospital
Sheriff Hill
Gateshead
Tyne & Wear
NE9 6SX
TEL: 0191 487 8989
FAX: 0191 491 1823

Harrogate Health Care NHS Trust
Harrogate District Hospital
Lancaster Park Road
Harrogate
HG2 7SX
TEL: 01423 885959
FAX: 01423 523204

Hartlepool and East Durham NHS
  Trust
General Hospital
Holdforth Road
Hartlepool
Cleveland
TS24 9AH
TEL: 01429 266654
FAX: 01429 235389

Huddersfield Health Care Services
  NHS Trust
Acre House
64 Acre Street
Lindley
Huddersfield
HD3 3HE
TEL: 01484 422191
FAX: 01484 482278

Hull & Holderness Community
  Health NHS Trust
Victoria House
Park Street
Hull
HU2 8TD
TEL: 01482 223191
FAX: 01482 229668

Humberside Ambulance Services
  NHS Trust
Ambulance Headquarters
Springfield House
Springfield Way
Anlaby
HU10 6RZ
TEL: 01482 354277
FAX: 01482 658770

Leeds Community & Mental Health
  Services Teaching NHS Trust
The Mansion
Meanwood Park Hospital
Tongue Lane
Leeds
LS6 4QB
TEL: 0113 275 8721
FAX: 0113 274 5172

Newcastle City Health NHS Trust
Milrain Building
Newcastle General Hoospital
Westgate Road
Newcastle upon Tyne
NE4 6BE

North Durham Acute Hospitals NHS
  Trust
Dryburn Hospital
Durham
DH1 5TW
TEL: 0191 333 2333
FAX: 0191 333 2703

North Lakeland Healthcare NHS
  Trust
The Coppice
Garlands Hospital
Carlisle

CA1 3SX
TEL: 01228 31081
FAX: 01228 512240

North Tees Health NHS Trust
North Tees General Hospital
Hardwick
Stockton on Tees
Cleveland
TS19 8PE
TEL: 01642 617 617
FAX: 01642 624 089

North Tyneside Health Care NHS
    Trust
Finance Department
North Tyneside General Hospital
Rake Lane
North Shields
NE29 8NH
TEL: 0191 259 6660
FAX: 0191 293 2791

North Yorkshire Ambulance Service
    NHS Trust
Ambulance Headquarters
Fairfields
Shipton Road
York
YO3 6XW
TEL: 01904 628085
FAX: 01904 627049

Northallerton Health Services NHS
    Trust
16 South Parade
Northallerton
North Yorkshire
DL7 8SG
TEL: 01609 762515
FAX: 01609 777106

Northgate and Prudhoe NHS Trust
Northgate Hospital
Morpeth NE61 3BP
TEL: 01670 394000
FAX: 01670 394002

Northumberland Community Health
    NHS Trust
St George's Hospital
Morpeth
Northumberland
NE61 2NH
TEL: 01670 517006
FAX: 01670 510902

Northumberland Mental Health NHS
    Trust
St Georges Hospital
Morpeth
Northumberland
NE61 2NU
TEL: 01670 512121
FAX: 01670 511637

Northumbrian Ambulance NHS Trust
Ambulance Headquarters
Interlink House
Scotswood Road
Newcastle Upon Tyne
NE4 7BJ
TEL: 0191 273 1212
FAX: 0191 273 7070

Pinderfields and Pontefract Hospitals
    NHS Trust
Trust Headquarters
Pontefract General Infirmary
Friarwood Lane
Pontefract
WF8 1PL
TEL: 01977 600600
FAX: 01977 606777

Priority Healthcare Wearside NHS
    Trust
Cherry Knowle Hospital
Ryhope
Sunderland
SR2 0NB
TEL: 0191 565 6256
FAX: 0191 569 9455

Royal Hull Hospitals NHS Trust
Hull Royal Infirmary
Anlaby Road

Hull
HU3 2JZ
TEL: 01482 328541
FAX: 01482 674857

Royal Victoria Infirmary and
    Associated Hospitals NHS Trust
Queen Victoria Road
Newcastle upon Tyne
NE1 4LP
TEL: 0191 232 5131
FAX: 0191 261 2768

St James's and Seacroft University
    Hospitals NHS Trust
St James's University Hospital
Beckett Street
Leeds
LS9 7TF
TEL: 0113 243 3144
FAX: 0113 242 6496

Scarborough and North East
    Yorkshire Healthcare NHS Trust
Scarborough Hospital
Woodlands Drive
Scarborough
North Yorkshire
YO12 6QL
TEL: 01723 368111
FAX: 01723 377000

Scunthorpe and Goole Hospitals
    NHS Trust
Scunthorpe General Hospital
Cliff Gardens
Scunthorpe
DN15 7BH
TEL: 01724 282282
FAX: 01724 282427

Scunthorpe Community Health NHS
    Trust
Brumby Hospital
East Common Lane
Scunthorpe
DN16 1QQ
TEL: 01724 290065
FAX: 01724 271016

South Durham NHS Trust
Winterton Hospital
Sedgefield
Cleveland
TS21 3EJ
TEL: 01740 623777
FAX: 01740 624288

South Tees Acute Hospitals NHS
    Trust
Middlesbrough General Hospital
Ayresome Green Lane
Middlesbrough
Cleveland
TS5 5AZ
TEL: 01642 850850
FAX: 01642 854136

South Tees Community and Mental
    Health NHS Trust
Community Unit
West Lane Hospital
Acklam Road
Middlesbrough
Cleveland
TS5 4EE
TEL: 01642 813144
FAX: 01642 822717

South Tyneside Health Care NHS
    Trust
Harton Wing
South Tyneside District Health
    Unit
South Shields
Tyne and Wear
NE34 0PL
TEL: 0191 454 8888
FAX: 0191 427 9908

United Leeds Teaching Hospitals
    NHS Trust
Leeds General Infirmary
Great George Street
Leeds
LS1 3EX
TEL: 0113 243 2799
FAX: 0113 292 6336

Wakefield & Pontefract Community
   Health NHS Trust
Fernbank
3–5 St John's North
Wakefield
WF1 3QD
TEL: 01924 814814
FAX: 01924 814987

West Cumbria Health Care NHS
   Trust
West Cumberland Hospital
Hensingham
Whitehaven
Cumbria
CA28 8JG
TEL: 01946 693181
FAX: 01946 523100

West Yorkshire Metropolitan
   Ambulance Service NHS Trust
Threelands
Bradford Road
Birkenshaw
Bradford
BD11 2AH
TEL: 01274 707070
FAX: 01274 688727

York Health Services NHS Trust
Headquarters
Bootham Park
York
YO3 7BY
TEL: 01904 454063
FAX: 01904 454439

Trent

Barnsley Community & Priority
   Services NHS Trust
Trust Headquarters
Kendray Hospital
Doncaster Road
Barnsley
S70 3RD
TEL: 01226 730000
FAX: 01226 296782

Barnsley District General Hospital
   NHS Trust
Gawber Road
Barnsley
S75 2EP
TEL: 01226 730000
FAX: 01226 202859

Bassetlaw Hospital and Community
   Health Services NHS Trust
Barrowby House
Highland Grove
Worksop
Notts
S81 0JN
TEL: 01909 500990
FAX: 01909 480879

Central Nottinghamshire Healthcare
   NHS Trust
Trust Headquarters
Southwell Road
Mansfield
Notts
NG18 4HH
TEL: 01623 785050
FAX: 01623 634126

Central Sheffield University
   Hospitals NHS Trust
Royal Hallamshire Hospital
Glossop Road
Sheffield
S10 2JF
TEL: 0114 271 2051
FAX: 0114 271 3892

Chesterfield and North Derbyshire
   Royal Hospitals NHS Trust
NHS Trust
Calow
Chesterfield
Derbyshire
S44 5BL
TEL: 01246 277271
FAX: 01246 276955

Community Health Care Service
(North Derbyshire) NHS Trust
The Shrubberies
46 Newbold Road
Chesterfield
Derbyshire
S41 7PL
TEL: 01246 200131
FAX: 01246 551323

Community Health Services,
Southern Derbyshire NHS Trust
NHS Trust
Trust Headquarters, Babington
Hospital
Derby Road
Belper
Derbyshire
DE56 1WH
TEL: 01773 525099
FAX: 01773 820318

Community Health Sheffield NHS
Trust
Fulwood
Old Fulwood
Sheffield
S10 3TH
TEL: 01114 271 6700
FAX: 0114 271 6712

Derby City General Hospital NHS
Trust
Derby City Hospital
Uttoxeter Road
Derby
DE22 3NE
TEL: 01332 340131
FAX: 01332 290559

Derbyshire Ambulance Service NHS
Trust
Ambulance Headquarters
Kingsway
Derby
DE22 3XB
TEL: 01332 372441
FAX: 01332 46824

Derbyshire Royal Infirmary NHS
Trust
London Road
Derby
DE1 2QY
TEL: 01332 347141
FAX: 01332 295652

Doncaster Healthcare NHS Trust
St Catherine's Hospital
Tickhill Road
Balby
Doncaster
DN4 8QN
TEL: 01302 796400
FAX: 01302 796066

Doncaster Royal Infirmary &
The Montagu Hospital NHS
Trust
Armthorpe Road
Doncaster
DN2 5LT
TEL: 01302 366666
FAX: 01302 320098

Fosse Health NHS Trust
Trust Headquarters
Gipsy Lane
Humberstone
Leicester
LE5 0TD
TEL: 0116 462 0100
FAX: 0116 462 1222

Glenfield Hospital NHS Trust
Glenfield General Hospital
Groby Road
Leicester
LE3 9QP
TEL: 0116 872 1471
FAX: 0116 232 2377

Grantham and District Hospital NHS
Trust
Grantham and Kesteven General
Hospital
101 Manthorpe Road
Grantham

Lincolnshire
NG31 8DG
TEL: 01476 565232
FAX: 01476 593246

The King's Mill Centre for Health
   Care Services
NHS Trust
Mansfield Road
Sutton in Ashfield
NG17 4JL
TEL: 01623 22515
FAX: 01623 28834

Leicester General Hospital NHS Trust
Leicester General Hospital
Gwendolen Road
Leicester
LE5 4PW
TEL: 0116 492 0490
FAX: 0116 258 4666

Leicester Royal Infirmary NHS Trust
Leicester Royal Infirmary
Infirmary Square
Leicester
LE1 5WW
TEL: 0116 542 1414
FAX: 0116 582 5631

Leicestershire Ambulance and
   Paramedic Service NHS Trust
The Rosings
Forest Road
Narborough
Leicestershire
LE9 5EQ
TEL: 0116 752 0700
FAX: 0116 752 1311

Leicestershire Mental Health Service
   NHS Trust
Corporate Offices
Bridge Park Road
Thurmaston
Leicester
LE4 8PQ
TEL: 0116 692 3666
FAX: 0116 692 3953

Lincoln District Healthcare NHS
   Trust
Gervas House
Long Leys Road
Lincoln
LN1 1EF
TEL: 01522 546546
FAX: 01522 514920

Lincoln and Louth NHS Trust
County Hospital
Greetwell Road
Lincoln
LN2 5QY
TEL: 01522 512512
FAX: 01522 567727

Lincolnshire Ambulance & Health
   Transport Service NHS Trust
Cross o'Cliff Court
Bracebridge Heath
Lincoln
LN4 2HL
TEL: 01522 545171
FAX: 01522 534611

Mulberry NHS Trust
Holland Road
Spalding
Lincs
PE11 1UH
TEL: 01529 411000
FAX: 01529 411008

Northern General Hospital NHS
   Trust
Herries Road
Sheffield
S5 7AU
TEL: 0114 243 4343
FAX: 0114 256 0472

Nottingham City Hospital NHS Trust
Nottingham City Hospital
Hucknall Road
Nottingham
NG5 1PB
TEL: 01115 969 1169
FAX: 0115 962 8065

Nottingham Community Health
  NHS Trust
Linden House
261 Beechdale Road
Aspley
Nottingham
NG8 3EY
TEL: 0115 942 6000
FAX: 0115 942 8606

Nottingham Healthcare NHS Trsut
Duncan MacMillan House
Porchester Road
Nottingham
NG3 6AA
TEL: 0115 969 1300
FAX: 0115 969 3422

Nottinghamshire Ambulance Service
  NHS Trust
Beechdale Road
Nottingham
NG8 3LL
TEL: 0115 929 6151
FAX: 0115 929 9415

Pilgrim Health NHS Trust
Pilgrim Hospital
Sibsey Road
Boston
PE21 9QS
TEL: 01205 364801
FAX: 01205 354395

Queens Medical Centre Nottingham
  University Hospital NHS Trust
University Hospital
Queens Medical Centre
Derby Road
Nottingham
NG7 2UH
TEL: 0115 924 9924
FAX: 0115 970 9196

Rotherham General Hospitals NHS
  Trust
Rotherham District General Hospital
Moorgate Road
Oakwood

Rotherham
S60 2UD
TEL: 01709 820000
FAX: 01709 824000

Rotherham Priority Health Services
  NHS Trust
Doncaster Gate Hospital
Doncaster Gate
Rotherham
S65 1DW
TEL: 01709 820000
FAX: 01709 824890

Sheffield Childrens Hospital NHS
  Trust
Sheffield Childrens Hospital
Western Bank
Sheffield
S10 2TH
TEL: 0114 271 7000
FAX: 0114 272 3418

Southern Derbyshire Mental Health
  NHS Trust
Bramble House
Kingsway Hospital
Kingsway
Derby
DE22 3LZ
TEL: 01332 362221
FAX: 01332 624563

South Lincolnshire Community and
  Mental Health Services NHS Trust
Orchard House
Rauceby Hospital
Sleaford
Lincolnshire
NG34 8PP
TEL: 01529 416003
FAX: 01529 416092

South Yorkshire Metropolitan
  Ambulance and Paramedic Service
  NHS Trust
Ambulance Service Headquarters
Fairfield
Moorgate Road

Rotherham
S60 2BX
TEL: 01709 820520
FAX: 01709 827839

West Lindsey NHS Trust
Nat West Bank Chambers
2A Market Street
Gainsborough
DN21 2BA
TEL: 01427 811851
FAX: 01427 811646

Weston Park Hospital NHS Trust
Weston Park Hospital
Whitham Road
Sheffield
S10 2SJ
TEL: 0114 267 0222
FAX: 0114 268 4193

Anglia and Oxford

Addenbrookes NHS Trust
Addenbrookes Hospital
Hills Road
Cambridge
CB2 2QQ
TEL: 01223 245151
FAX: 01223 216520

Allington NHS Trust
Allington House
427 Woodbridge Road
Ipswich
Suffolk
IP4 4ER
TEL: 01473 275200
FAX: 01473 275275

Anglian Harbours NHS Trust
Northgate Hospital
Northgate Street
Great Yarmouth
Norfolk
NR30 1BU
TEL: 01493 337600
FAX: 01493 337809

Aylesbury Vale Community
  Healthcare NHS Trust
Manor House
Bierton Road
Aylesbury
Bucks
HP20 1EG
TEL: 01296 393363
FAX: 01296 392606

Bedfordshire and Shires Health Care
  NHS Trust
D Block
3 Kimbolton Road
Bedford
MK40 2NU
TEL: 01234 267444
FAX: 01234 795945

Bedford Hospitals NHS Trust
Bedford Hospital
Kempston Road
Bedford
MK42 9DJ
TEL: 01234 355122
FAX: 01234 218106

East Anglian Ambulance NHS
  Trust
Ambulance Headquarters
Hospital Lane
Hellesdon
Norwich
NR6 5NA
TEL: 01603 424255
FAX: 01603 418667

East Berkshire Community Health
  NHS Trust
East Berkshire Community Health
  Unit
King Edward VII Hospital
St Leonards Road
Windsor
Berks
SL4 3DP
TEL: 01753 860441
FAX: 01753 636014

East Berkshire NHS Trust
Church Hill House
Crowthorne Road
Bracknell
Berkshire
RG12 7EP
TEL: 01344 422722
FAX: 01344 867990

East Suffolk Local Health Services
   NHS Trust
Sampson House
PO Box 247
Foxhall Road
Ipswich
Suffolk
IP3 8PL
TEL: 01473 276584
FAX: 01473 276593

Heatherwood and Wexham Park
   Hospitals NHS Trust
Wexham Park Hospital
Wexham
Slough
Berkshire
SL2 4HL
TEL: 01753 633000
FAX: 01753 691343

Hinchingbrooke Health Care NHS
   Trust
Hinchingbrooke Hospital
Hinchingbrooke Park
Huntingdon
PE18 8NT
TEL: 01480 416416
FAX: 01480 416434

Horton General Hospital NHS
   Trust
Horton General Hospital
Oxford Road
Banbury
Oxfordshire
OX16 9AL
TEL: 01295 275500
FAX: 01295 229055

Ipswich Hospital NHS Trust
Ipswich Hospital
Ipswich
IP4 5PD
TEL: 01473 712233
FAX: 01473 702091

James Paget Hospital NHS Trust
Lowestoft Road
Gorleston
Great Yarmouth
Norfolk
NR31 6LA
TEL: 01493 452452
FAX: 01493 452819

Kettering General Hospital NHS Trust
Glebe House
Rothwell Road
Kettering
Northants
NN16 8UZ
TEL: 01536 492009
FAX: 01536 493767

King's Lynn and Wisbech Hospitals
   NHS Trust
Queen Elizabeth Hospital
Gayton Road
Kings Lynn
Norfolk
PE30 4ET
TEL: 01553 613613
FAX: 01553 613688

Lifespan Health Care Cambridge
   NHS Trust
Ida Darwin
Fulbourn
Cambridge
CB4 5EE
TEL: 01223 884043
FAX: 01223 884038

Luton and Dunstable Hospitals NHS
   Trust
Luton and Dunstable Hospital
Lewsey Road
Luton

Bedfordshire
LU4 0DZ
TEL: 01582 491122
FAX: 01582 598990

Mid Anglia Community Health NHS
    Trust
Thingoe House
Cotton Lane
Bury St Edmunds
Suffolk
IP33 1YJ
TEL: 01284 702544
FAX: 01284 703139

Milton Keynes Community Health
    NHS Trust
The Hospital Campus
Standing Way
Eaglestone
Milton Keynes
MK6 5NG
TEL: 01908 660033
FAX: 01908 694442

Milton Keynes General Hospitals
    NHS Trust
Milton Keynes General Hospital
Standing Way
Eaglestone
Milton Keynes
MK6 5LD
TEL: 01908 660033
FAX: 01908 669348

Norfolk and Norwich Health Care
    NHS Trust
Norfolk & Norwich Hospital
Brunswick Road
Norwich
NR1 3SR
TEL: 01603 286286
FAX: 01603 287547

Norfolk Mental Health Care NHS
    Trust
Drayton Old Lodge
146 Drayton High Road
Drayton

Norwich
NR8 6AN
TEL: 01603 421120
FAX: 01603 421140

North West Anglia Healthcare NHS
    Trust
53 Thorpe Road
Peterborough
PE3 6AN
TEL: 01733 318100
FAX: 01733 318139

Northampton Community
    Healthcare NHS Trust
Threeways
Princess Marina Hospital
Upton
Northampton
NN5 6UH
TEL: 01604 752323
FAX: 01604 544600

Northampton General Hospital NHS
    Trust
Resource Directorate/Finance
1st Floor
Billing Road
Northampton
NN1 5BD
TEL: 01604 545863
FAX: 01604 544960

Norwich Community Health
    Partnership NHS Trust
The Old Hall
Little Plumstead
Hospital Road
Norwich
NR13 5EW
TEL: 01603 711227
FAX: 01603 711483

Nuffield Orthopaedic NHS Trust
Windmill Road
Headington
Oxford OX3 7LD
TEL: 01865 741155
FAX: 01865 742348

Oxford Radcliffe NHS Trust
Level 3, John Radcliffe Hospital
Headley Way
Headington
Oxford
OX3 9DU
TEL: 01865 221817
FAX: 01865 741408

Oxfordshire Ambulance NHS Trust
Churchill Drive
Old Road
Headington
Oxford
OX3 7LH
TEL: 01865 740100
FAX: 01865 741974

Oxfordshire Community Health
    NHS Trust
Bourton House
18 Thorney Leys Park
Witney, Oxon
OX8 7GE
TEL: 01993 707605
FAX: 01993 707610

Oxfordshire Learning Disabilities
    NHS Trust
Slade House
Horspath Driftway
Headington
Oxford
OX3 7JH
TEL: 01865 747455
FAX: 01865 228182

Oxfordshire Mental Healthcare NHS
    Trust
Littlemore Hospital
Littlemore
Oxford
OX4 4XN
TEL: 01865 778911
FAX: 01865 223061

Papworth Hospital NHS Trust
Papworth Hospital
Papworth Everard

Cambridge
CB3 8RE
TEL: 01480 830541
FAX: 01480 831315

Peterborough Hospitals NHS
    Trust
Peterborough District Hospital
Thorpe Road
Peterborough
PE3 6DA
TEL: 01733 874962
FAX: 01733 558150

The Radcliffe Infirmary NHS
    Trust
Woodstock Road
Oxford
OX2 6HE
TEL: 01865 311188
FAX: 01865 224566

Rockingham Forest NHS Trust
St Mary's Hospital
London Road
Kettering
Northants
NN15 7PW
TEL: 01536 410141
FAX: 01536 493244

Royal Berkshire Ambulance Service
    NHS Trust
41 Barkham Road
Wokingham
Berkshire
RG41 2RE
TEL: 0118 779 1200
FAX: 0118 779 3923

Royal Berkshire & Battle Hospitals
    NHS Trust
Royal Berkshire Hospital
London Road
Reading
Berkshire
RG1 5AN
TEL: 0118 987 5111
FAX: 0118 987 8645

South Bedfordshire Community
  Healthcare NHS Trust
1 Union Street
Luton
Bedfordshire
LU1 3AN
TEL: 01582 485888
FAX: 01582 485667

South Buckinghamshire NHS Trust
Oakengrove
Shrubbery Road
High Wycombe
Buckinghamshire
HP13 6PS
TEL: 01494 526161
FAX: 01494 426114

Stoke Mandeville Hospital NHS
  Trust
Stoke Mandeville Hospital
Mandeville Road
Aylesbury
Buckinghamshire
HP21 8AL
TEL: 01296 315000
FAX: 01296 316256

Two Shires Ambulance NHS
  Trust
The Hunters
Buckingham Road
Deanshanger
Milton Keynes
MK19 6HL
TEL: 01908 264422
FAX: 01908 265014

West Berkshire Priority Care
  Services NHS Trust
Prospect Park Hospital
Honey End Lane
Tilehurst
Reading
RG30 4EG
TEL: 01734 586161
FAX: 01734 591135

West Suffolk Hospitals NHS Trust
Hardwick Lane
Bury St Edmunds
Suffolk
IP33 2QZ
TEL: 01284 713000
FAX: 01284 701993

North Thames

Barnet Community Healthcare NHS
  Trust
Trust Headquarters
Colindale Hospital
Colindale Avenue
London
NW9 5HG
TEL: 0181 200 1555
FAX: 0181 200 9499

Basildon and Thurrock General
  Hospitals NHS Trust
Basildon Hospital
Nethermayne
Basildon
Essex
SS16 5NL
TEL: 01268 533911
FAX: 01268 593757

Bedfordshire and Hertfordshire
  Ambulance Service NHS Trust
Bedfordshire Ambulance Service
Ambulance Headquarters
Hammond Road
Bedford
MK41 0RG
TEL: 01234 270099
FAX: 01234 270480

BHB Community Health Care NHS
  Trust
Trust Headquarters
St George's Hospital
117 Suttons Lane
Hornchurch
Essex
RM12 6RS

TEL: 01708 465000
FAX: 01708 465360

Camden & Islington Community
  Health Services NHS Trust
National Temperance Hospital
Vesey Strong Wing
Hampstead Road
London
NW1 2LT
TEL: 0171 530 3000
FAX: 0171 383 5579

Central Middlesex Hospital NHS
  Trust
Acton Lane
London
NW10 7NS
TEL: 0181 453 2195
FAX: 0181 453 2558

Chase Farm Hospitals NHS Trust
The Ridgeway
Enfield
Middlesex
EN2 8JL
TEL: 0181 366 6600
FAX: 0181 364 4833

Chelsea and Westminster Healthcare
  NHS Trust
Chelsea and Westminster Hospital
369 Fulham Road
London
SW10 9NH
TEL: 0181 748 8000
FAX: 0181 237 2888

City and Hackney Community
  Services NHS Trust
St Leonard's Hospital
Nuttall Street
London N1 5LZ
TEL: 0171 601 7740

Ealing Hospital NHS Trust
Ealing Hospital
Uxbridge Road
Southall

Middlesex
UB1 3HW
TEL: 0181 967 5656
FAX: 0181 967 5645

East Hertfordshire NHS Trust
Former Ambulance HQ
Ascots Lane
Welwyn Garden City
Hertfordshire
AL7 4HL
TEL: 01707 365254
FAX: 01707 368230

Enfield Community Care NHS
  Trust
Wenlock House
33 Easton Road
Enfield
Middlesex
EN1 1NJ
TEL: 0181 366 6600
FAX: 0181 366 9166

Essex Ambulance Service NHS Trust
Ambulance Headquarters
Broomfield
Chelmsford
Essex
CM1 7WS
TEL: 01245 443344
FAX: 01245 442920

Essex and Herts Community NHS
  Trust
Rutherford House
Haymeads Lane
Bishop's Stortford
CM23 5JH
TEL: 01279 655191
FAX: 01279 465873

Essex Rivers Healthcare NHS Trust
Trust Headquarters
Colchester General Hospital
Turner Road
Colchester
Essex
CO4 5JL

TEL: 01206 853535
FAX: 01206 854877

Forest Healthcare NHS Trust
Meadow House
740 Forest Road
Walthamstow
London E17 3HR
TEL: 0181 508 4077
FAX: 0181 535 6475

Hammersmith Hospitals NHS Trust
Hammersmith Hospital
Du Cane Road
London
W12 0HS
TEL: 0181 748 4666
FAX: 0181 740 3588

Harefield Hospital NHS Trust
Harefield Hospital
Harefield
Middlesex
UB9 6JH
TEL: 01895 823737
FAX: 01895 828821

Haringey Health Care NHS Trust
St Ann's Hospital
St Ann's Road
London
N15 3TH
TEL: 0181 442 6000
FAX: 0181 442 6567
Harrow and Hillingdon Healthcare
   Community NHS Trust
Malt House
285–301 Field End Road
Eastcote
Ruislip
HA4 9NJ

Havering Hospitals NHS Trust
Oldchurch Hospital
Romford
Essex
RM7 0BE
TEL: 01708 708038
FAX: 01708 754229

Hillingdon Hospital NHS Trust
Pield Field Heath Road
Uxbridge
Middlesex
UB8 3NN
TEL: 01895 279539
FAX: 01895 279946

Homerton Hospital NHS Trust
Management Offices
Homerton Row
Homerton
London
E9 6SR
TEL: 0181 919 5555
FAX: 0181 985 6376

Horizon NHS Trust
Harperbury Hospital
Harper Lane
Shenley
Radlett
Hertfordshire
WD7 9HQ
TEL: 01923 855912
FAX: 01923 855909

Hounslow and Spelthorne
   Community & Mental Health
   NHS Trust
Phoenix Court
531 Staines Road
Hounslow
Middlesex
TW4 5DP
TEL: 0181 565 2211
FAX: 0181 565 2249

Mid Essex Community and Mental
   Health NHS Trust
Trust Headquarters
Atlantic Square
Witham
Essex
CM8 2TL
TEL: 01376 393000
FAX: 01376 393001

Mid Essex Hospital NHS Trust
Broomfield Court
Pudding Wood Lane
Broomfield
Chelmsford
Essex
CM1 5WE
TEL: 01245 514449
FAX: 01245 514675

Mount Vernon and Watford
    Hospitals NHS Trust
H Block
Watford General Hospital
Vicarage Road
Watford WD1 8HB
TEL: 01923 244366
FAX: 01923 217440

New Possibilities NHS Trust
New Possibilities House
Turner Village
Turner Road
Colchester
Essex
CO4 5JP
TEL: 01206 844840
FAX: 01206 842301

Newham Community Health Services
    NHS Trust
Plaistow Hospital
Sydenham Building
Samson Street
London
E13 9EH
TEL: 0181 472 7001
FAX: 0181 470 2843

Newham Healthcare NHS Trust
1 Helena Road
Plaistow
London
E13 0DZ
TEL: 0181 472 1444
FAX: 0181 363 8330

North East Essex Mental Health
    NHS Trust

Severalls Hospital
Boxted Road
Colchester
Essex
CO4 5HG
TEL: 01206 852271
FAX: 01206 844435

North Hertfordshire NHS Trust
Lister Hospital
Coreys Mill Lane
Stevenage
Herts
SG1 4AB
TEL: 01438 314333
FAX: 01438 781146

North Middlesex Hospital NHS
    Trust
Sterling Way
Edmonton
London
N18 1QX
TEL: 0181 887 2000
FAX: 0181 887 4219

North West London Mental Health
    NHS Trust
IKEA Tower
255 North Circular Road
Brent Park
London
NW10 0JQ
TEL: 0181 830 0033
FAX: 0181 830 1372

Northwick Park and St Mark's NHS
    Trust
Northwick Park Hospital
Watford Road
Harrow
Middlesex
HA1 3UJ
TEL: 0181 864 3232
FAX: 0181 869 2009

Parkside Health NHS Trust
Paddington Community Hospital
Woodfield Road

London
W9 2BB
TEL: 0181 451 8000
FAX: 0181 451 8221

The Princess Alexandra Hospital
   NHS Trust
Princess Alexandra Hospital
Hamstel Road
Harlow
Essex
CM20 1QX
TEL: 01279 444455
FAX: 01279 8429371

Redbridge Health Care NHS Trust
Tantallon House, Goodmayes
   Hospital
Barley Lane
Goodmayes
Essex
IG3 8XJ
TEL: 0181 983 8000
FAX: 0181 970 8307

Riverside Community Health Care
   NHS Trust
5–7 Parsons Green
London
SW6 4UL
TEL: 0181 846 6767
FAX: 0181 846 7654

Riverside Mental Health NHS Trust
Commonwealth House
2–4 Chalkhill Road
London
W6 8DW
TEL: 0181 746 8954
FAX: 0181 746 8978

Royal Free Hampstead NHS Trust
Royal Free Hospital
Pond Street
Hampstead
London
NW3 2QG
TEL: 0171 794 0500
FAX: 0171 435 2861

Royal London Homoeopathic
   Hospital NHS Trust
Great Ormond Street
London
WC1N 3NR
TEL: 0171 837 8833
FAX: 0171 833 7229

Royal National Orthopaedic
   Hospital NHS Trust
Brockley Hill
Stanmore
Middlesex
HA7 4LP
TEL: 0181 954 2300
FAX: 0181 954 7249

St Albans and Hemel Hempstead
   NHS Trust
Financial Services
99 Waverley Road
St Albans
Hertfordshire
AL3 5TL
TEL: 01727 866122

St Mary's Hospital, Paddington NHS
   Trust
St Mary's Hospital
Praed Street
London
W2 1NY
TEL: 0171 725 6666
FAX: 0171 725 6200

Southend Community Care Services
   NHS Trust
Community House
Union Lane
Rochford
Essex
SS4 1RB
TEL: 01702 546354
FAX: 01702 546383

Southend Healthcare NHS Trust
Southend Hospital
Prittlewell Chase
Westcliff on Sea

Essex
SS0 0RY
TEL: 01702 435555
FAX: 01702 221300

Tavistock and Portman NHS Trust
Tavistock Centre
120 Belsize Park
London
NW3 5BA
TEL: 0171 435 7111
FAX: 0171 794 8741

Thameside Community Healthcare
    NHS Trust
Thurroch Community Hospital
Long Lane
Grays
Essex
RM13 2PX
TEL: 01375 390044
FAX: 01375 364400

Tower Hamlets Healthcare NHS Trust
Elizabeth Fry House
Mile End Hospital
Bancroft Road
London
E1 4DG
TEL: 0171 377 7920
FAX: 0171 377 7931

University College London
    Hospitals NHS Trust
10th Floor St. Martin's House
140 Tottenham Court Road
London
WC1P 9LN
TEL: 0171 380 4868
FAX: 0171 380 9728

Wellhouse NHS Trust
Edgware General Hospital
Burnt Oak Broadway
Edgware
Middlesex
HA8 0AD
TEL: 0181 952 2381
FAX: 0181 732 6807

West Hertfordshire Community
    Health NHS Trust
Head Office
99 Waverley Road
St Albans
Hertfordshire
AL3 5TL
TEL: 01727 811888
FAX: 01727 857900

The West London Healthcare NHS
    Trust
Uxbridge Road
Southall
Middlesex
UB1 3EU
TEL: 0181 574 2444
FAX: 0181 967 5002

West Middlesex University
    Hospitals NHS Trust
Twickenham Road
Isleworth
Middlesex
TW7 6AF
TEL: 0181 560 2121
FAX: 0181 565 2535

The Whittington Hospital NHS Trust
Highgate Hill
London
N19 5NF
TEL: 0171 288 5110
FAX: 0171 288 5985

Special health authorities

Great Ormond Street Hospital for
    Children NHS Trust
Great Ormond Street
London
WC1N 3JH
TEL: 0171 405 9200
FAX: 0171 829 8681

Moorfields Eye Hospital NHS Trust
162 City Road
London
EC1V 2PD

TEL: 0171 566 2491
FAX: 0171 566 2459

Royal Brompton Hospital NHS Trust
Sydney Street
London
SW3 6NP
TEL: 0171 351 8653
FAX: 0171 351 8290

The Royal Marsden NHS Trust
Fulham Road
London
SW3 6JJ
TEL: 0171 352 8171
FAX: 0171 823 3378

South Thames

Ashford Hospital NHS Trust
Ashford Hospital
London Road
Ashford
TW15 3AA
TEL: 01784 884204
FAX: 01784 255696

Bournewood Community and
  Mental Health NHS Trust
Bournewood House
Guildford Road
Chertsey
Surrey
KT16 0QA
TEL: 01932 872010
FAX: 01932 875346

Brighton Healthcare NHS Trust
Royal Sussex County Hospital
Eastern Road
Brighton
BN2 5BE
TEL: 01273 696955
FAX: 01273 626653

Bromley Hospitals NHS Trust
Farnborough Hospital
Farnborough Common

Orpington
Kent
BR6 8ND
TEL: 01689 815000
FAX: 01689 890552

The Canterbury & Thanet
  Community Healthcare NHS
  Trust
St Martin's Hospital
Littlebourne Road
Canterbury
Kent CT1 1AZ
TEL: 01227 459371
FAX: 01227 812268

Chichester Priority Care Services
  NHS Trust
9 College Lane
Chichester
West Sussex
PO19 4FX
TEL: 01243 787970
FAX: 01243 783965

Crawley Horsham NHS Trust
Crawley Hospital
West Green Drive
Crawley
West Sussex
RH11 7DH
TEL: 01293 600300
FAX: 01293 600360

Croydon Community NHS Trust
12–18 Lennard Road
Croydon, Surrey
CR9 2RS
TEL: 0181 680 2008
FAX: 0181 666 0495

Dartford & Gravesham NHS Trust
Joyce Green Hospital
Joyce Green Lane
Dartford
Kent
DA1 5PL
TEL: 01322 227242
FAX: 01322 283496

East Surrey Healthcare NHS Trust
Maple House
Canada Avenue
Redhill
Surrey
RH1 6HA
TEL: 01737 768511
FAX: 01737 769180

East Surrey Priority Care NHS
  Trust
Langley House
Church Lane
Oxted
Surrey
RH8 9LH
TEL: 01883 734000
FAX: 01883 714510

Eastbourne & County Healthcare
  NHS Trust
Woodhill
The Drive
Hellingly
Hailsham
East Sussex
BN27 4ER
TEL: 01323 440022
FAX: 01323 848987

Eastbourne Hospitals NHS Trust
District General Hospital
Kings Drive
Eastbourne
East Sussex
BN21 2UD
TEL: 01323 417400
FAX: 01323 413795

Epsom Health Care NHS Trust
Epsom General Hospital
Dorking Road
Epsom
Surrey
KT18 7EG
TEL: 01372 735735
FAX: 01372 735252

Frimley Park Hospital NHS Trust
Frimley Park Hospital
Portsmouth Road
Frimley, Camberley
Surrey
GU16 5UJ
TEL: 01276 604604
FAX: 01276 679173

Greenwich Healthcare NHS Trust
Memorial Hospital
Shooters Hill Road
London
SE18 3RZ
TEL: 0181 856 5511
FAX: 0181 312 6410

Guy's and St Thomas's NHS Trust
Guy's Hospital
St Thomas's Street
London
SE1 9RT
TEL: 0171 955 2783
FAX: 0171 945 4844

Hastings and Rother NHS Trust
St Anne's House
729 The Ridge
St Leonards on Sea
East Sussex
TN37 7QQ
TEL: 01424 754488
FAX: 01424 754263

Heathlands Mental Health NHS
  Trust
Heathlands House
The Ridgewood Centre
Old Bisley Road
Frimley
Camberley
Surrey
GU16 5QE
TEL: 01276 692919
FAX: 01276 605360

Kent Ambulance NHS Trust
Heath Road
Coxheath

Maidstone
Kent
ME17 4BG
TEL: 01622 747010
FAX: 01622 743565

Kent and Canterbury Hospitals NHS
    Trust
Kent & Canterbury Hospital
Ethelbert Road
Canterbury
CT1 3NG
TEL: 01227 766877
FAX: 01227 783017

Kent & Sussex Weald NHS Trust
Pembury Hospital
Pembury
Tunbridge Wells
Kent
TN2 4QJ
TEL: 01892 824267

Kingston and District Community
    NHS Trust
Woodroffe House
Tolworth Hospital
Red Lion Road
Surbiton
Surrey
KT6 4QU
TEL: 0181 390 0102
FAX: 0181 390 1236

Kingston Hospital NHS Trust
Kingston Hospital
Regent Wing
Glasworthy Road
Kingston upon Thames
Surrey
KT2 7QB
TEL: 0181 546 7711
FAX: 0181 547 2182

King's Healthcare NHS Trust
King's College Hospital
Denmark Hill
London
SE5 9RS

TEL: 0171 737 4000
FAX: 0171 346 3445

Lewisham and Guy's Mental Health
    NHS Trust
Leegate House
Burnt Ash Road
Lee Green
London
SE12 8RG
TEL: 0181 297 0707
FAX: 0181 297 8285

Lewisham Hospitals NHS Trust
Lewisham Hospital
Lewisham High Street
Lewisham
London
SE13 6LH
TEL: 0181 333 3000
FAX: 0181 333 3282

Lifecare NHS Trust
St Lawrence's Hospital
Coulsdon Road
Caterham
Surrey
CR3 5YA
TEL: 01883 346411
FAX: 01883 344564

Invicta Community Care NHS
    Trust
The Pagoda
Hermitage Lane
Maidstone
Kent
ME16 9PD
TEL: 01622 721818
FAX: 01622 751919

Mayday Health Care NHS Trust
Mayday Hospital
Mayday Road
Thornton Heath
Surrey
CR4 7YE
TEL: 0181 401 3000
FAX: 0181 401 3510

Medway NHS Trust
Residence 10
Medway Hospital
Windmill Road
Gillingham
Kent
ME4 4NY
TEL: 01634 830000
FAX: 01634 817367

Merton and Sutton Community NHS
    Trust
Trust Headquarters
Fountain Drive
Carshalton
Surrey
SM5 4NR
TEL: 0181 770 8000
FAX: 0181 643 5807

Mid-Kent Healthcare NHS Trust
The Maidstone Hospital
Hermitage Lane
Maidstone
Kent
ME16 9QQ
TEL: 01622 729000
FAX: 01622 721511

Mid-Sussex NHS Trust
The Princess Royal Hospital
Lewes Road
Haywards Heath
West Sussex
RH16 4EX
TEL: 01444 441881
FAX: 01444 441296

North Downs Community Health
    NHS Trust
Farnham Hospital
Hale Road
Farnham
Surrey
GU9 9QL
TEL: 01252 726666
FAX: 01252 717952

North Kent Healthcare NHS Trust
Trust Headquarters
Central Avenue
Sittingbourne
Kent
ME10 4NS
TEL: 01795 411411
FAX: 01795 478191

Optimum Health Services NHS Trust
Elizabeth Blackwell House
Wardells Grove
Avonley Road
London
SE14 5ER
TEL: 0171 635 5555
FAX: 0171 771 5115

Oxleas NHS Trust
Bexley Hospital
Old Bexley Lane
Bexley
Kent
DA5 2BW
TEL: 01322 526282
FAX: 01322 555491

Pathfinder NHS Trust
Springfield Hospital
61 Glenburnie Road
London
SW17 7DJ
TEL: 0181 672 9911
FAX: 0181 682 6869

Queen Mary's, Sidcup, NHS Trust
Queen Mary's Hospital
Sidcup
Kent
DA14 6LT
TEL: 0181 302 2678
FAX: 0181 308 3074

Queen Victoria Hospital NHS   .
    Trust
The Queen Victoria Hospital
Holtye Road
East Grinstead
West Sussex

RH19 3DZ
TEL: 01342 410210
FAX: 01342 317907

Ravensbourne Priority Health NHS
   Trust
Bassetts House
Broadwater Gardens
Farnborough
Orpington
Kent
BR6 7UA
TEL: 01689 853339
FAX: 01689 855662

Richmond, Twickenham and Roe-
   hampton Healthcare NHS Trust
Queen Mary University Hospital
Roehampton Lane
London
SW15 5PN
TEL: 0181 789 6611
FAX: 0181 789 1089

Surrey County NHS Trust
The Royal Surrey County Hospital
Egerton Road
Guildford
Surrey
GU2 5XX
TEL: 01483 571122
FAX: 01483 37747

Royal West Sussex NHS Trust
St Richard's Hospital
Spitalfield Lane
Chichester
West Sussex
PO19 4SE
TEL: 01243 788122
FAX: 01243 531269

St George's Hospital NHS Trust
St George's Hospital
Blackshaw Road
London
SW17 0QT
TEL: 0181 672 1255
FAX: 0181 725 3593

St Helier NHS Trust
St Helier Hospital
Wrythe Lane
Carshalton
Surrey
SM5 1AA
TEL: 0181 296 2000
FAX: 0181 641 4717

St Peters Hospital NHS Trust
Guildford Road
Chertsey
Surrey
KT16 0PZ
TEL: 01932 872000
FAX: 01932 698312

South Downs Health NHS Trust
Brighton General Hospital
Elm Grove
Brighton
East Sussex
BN2 3EW
TEL: 01273 696011
FAX: 01273 698312

South Kent Community Healthcare
   NHS Trust
Trust Headquarters
Ash Eton
Radnor Park West
Folkstone
Kent
CT19 5HL
TEL: 01303 222333
FAX: 01303 222334

South Kent Hospitals NHS Trust
William Harvey Hospital
Broomfield
Kennington Road
Willesborough
Ashford
Kent
TN24 0LZ
TEL: 01233 633331
FAX: 01233 616079

Surrey Ambulance Service NHS
    Trust
The Horseshoe
Bolters Lane
Banstead
Surrey
SM7 2AS
TEL: 01737 353333
FAX: 01737 370868

Surrey Heartlands NHS Trust
St Ebba's
Hook Road
Epsom
Surrey
KT19 8QJ
TEL: 01372 722212
FAX: 01372 725068

Sussex Ambulance Service NHS Trust
Ambulance Headquarters
40–42 Friars Walk
Lewes, East Sussex
BN7 2XW
TEL: 01273 489444
FAX: 01273 489445

Teddington Memorial Hospital NHS
    Trust
Hampton Road
Teddington
Middlesex
TW11 0JL
TEL: 0181 977 2212
FAX: 0181 977 1914

Thameslink Healthcare Services NHS
    Trust
Archery House
Bow Arrow Lane
Dartford
Kent
DA2 6PB
TEL: 01322 622219
FAX: 01322 622215

Thanet Health Care NHS Trust
Queen Elizabeth the Queen Motherl
    Hospital

St Peter's Road
Margate,
Kent
CT9 4AN
TEL: 01843 225544
FAX: 01843 220048

Wandsworth Community Health
    NHS Trust
Clare House
St George's Hospital
Blackshaw Road
London
SW17 0QT
TEL: 0181 700 0550
FAX: 0181 700 0593

Worthing Priority Care NHS
    Trust
Trust Headquarters
Arundel Road
Worthing
West Sussex
BN13 3EP
TEL: 01903 264121
FAX: 01903 691179

Worthing & Southlands Hospitals
    NHS Trust
Southlands Hospital
Upper Shoreham Road
Shoreham-by-Sea
West Sussex
BN43 6TQ
TEL: 01273 455622
FAX: 01273 446042

Special Health Authority

Bethlem and Maudsley NHS
    Trust
Bethlem Royal Hospital
Monks Orchard Road
Beckenham
Kent
BR3 3BX
TEL: 0181 776 4726
FAX: 0181 777 6039

South West

Andover District Community NHS
Trust
War Memorial Community Hospital
Charlton Road
Andover, Hants
SP10 3LB
TEL: 01264 358811
FAX: 01264 351424

Avalon, Somerset, NHS Trust
Avalon House
Broadway Park
Bridgewater
Somerset
TA6 5YA
TEL: 01278 446151
FAX: 01278 446147

Avon Ambulance Services NHS Trust
Ambulance Headquarters
Marybush Lane
Bristol
BS2 0AT
TEL: 0117 9277046
FAX: 0117 9251419

Bath and West Community NHS
Trust
Finance Department
St Martin's Hospital
Midford Road
Bath
BA2 5RP
TEL: 01225 834270
FAX: 01225 834291

Bath Mental Health Care NHS Trust
Bath NHS House
Newbridge Hill
Bath
BA1 3QE
TEL: 01225 313640
FAX: 01225 466223

Cornwall Healthcare NHS Trust
Porthpean Road
St Austell

Cornwall
PL26 6AD
TEL: 01726 291003
FAX: 01726 291080

Dorset Ambulance NHS Trust
Ambulance Headquarters
Ringwood Road
St Leonard's
Ringwood
BH24 2SP
TEL: 01202 896111
FAX: 01202 891978

Dorset Community NHS Trust
Grove House
Millers Close
Dorchester
Dorset
DT1 1SS
TEL: 01305 264479
FAX: 01305 264474

Dorset Healthcare NHS Trust
Trust Headquarters
11 Shelley Road
Boscombe
Bournemouth
BH1 4JQ
TEL: 01202 303400
FAX: 01202 309968

East Gloucestershire NHS Trust
Burlington House
Lypiatt Road
Cheltenham
Gloucestershire
GL50 2QN
TEL: 01242 221188
FAX: 01242 221214

East Somerset Hospital NHS Trust
Yeovil District Hospital
Higher Kingston
Yeovil
Somerset
BA21 4AT
TEL: 01935 75122
FAX: 01935 26850

East Wiltshire Health Care NHS
    Trust
Community Care Unit
St Margaret's Hospital
PO Box 415
Swindon
Wiltshire
SN3 4GB
TEL: 01793 425000
FAX: 01793 425005

Exeter and District Community
    Health Service NHS Trust
Newcourt House
Old Rydon Lane
Exeter
EX2 7JU
TEL: 01392 449700
FAX: 01392 445435

Frenchay Healthcare NHS Trust
Beckspool Road
Frenchay
Bristol
BS16 1ND
TEL: 0117 970 1070
FAX: 0117 975 3843

Gloucestershire Ambulance Service
    NHS Trust
Ambulance Headquarters
Horton Road
Gloucester
GL1 3PX
TEL: 01452 395050
FAX: 01452 383331

Gloucestershire Royal NHS Trust
Gloucestershire Royal Hospital
Great Western Road
Gloucester
GL1 3NN
TEL: 01452 528555
FAX: 01452 394555

Hampshire Ambulance Service NHS
    Trust
Highcroft
Romsey Road

Winchester
Hants
SO22 5DH
TEL: 01962 863511
FAX: 01962 842156

Isle of Wight Healthcare NHS
    Trust
Parkhurst Road
Newport
Isle of Wight
PO30 5TG
TEL: 01983 524081
FAX: 01983 534588

North Hampshire Hospitals NHS
    Trust
North Hampshire Hospital
Aldermaston Road
Basingstoke
Hampshire
RG24 9NA
TEL: 01256 313597
FAX: 01256 313098

Loddon NHS Trust
Parklands Hospital
Aldermaston Road
Basingstoke
Hants
RG24 9RH
TEL: 01256 314860
FAX: 01256 376584

Northern Devon Healthcare NHS
    Trust
Trust Headquarters
Riversvale
Litchdon Street
Barnstaple
North Devon
EX32 8ND
TEL: 01271 75851
FAX: 01271 25564

Phoenix NHS Trust
Brentry
Charlton Road
Westbury on Trym

Bristol
BS10 6JH
TEL: 0117 908 5000
FAX: 0117 950 5606

Plymouth Community Services NHS
    Trust
Mount Gould Hospital
Mount Gould Road
Plymouth
PL4 7QD
TEL: 01752 274407
FAX: 01752 272406

Plymouth Hospitals NHS Trust
Derriford Hospital
Derriford Road
Plymouth
PL6 8DH
TEL: 01752 777111
FAX: 01752 763041

The Poole Hospital NHS Trust
Poole General Hospital
Longfleet Road
Poole
Dorset
BH15 2JB
TEL: 01202 665511
FAX: 01202 442562

Portsmouth Health Care NHS
    Trust
St James' Hospital
Locksway Road
Portsmouth
Hants
PO4 8LD
TEL: 01705 822444
FAX: 01705 293012

Portsmouth Hospitals NHS Trust
De la Court House
St Mary's Hospital
Portsmouth
P63 6AD
TEL: 01705 286000
FAX: 01705 866413

Royal Bournemouth and
    Christchurch Hospitals NHS Trust
The Royal Bournemouth Hospital
Castle Lane East
Bournemouth
Dorset
BH7 7DW
TEL: 01202 303626
FAX: 01202 704077

The Royal Cornwall Hospitals NHS
    Trust
Treliske Hospital
Truro
Cornwall
TR1 3LJ
TEL: 01872 74242
FAX: 01872 40574

The Royal Devon & Exeter
    Healthcare NHS Trust
Royal Devon and Exeter Hospital
    (Wonford)
Barrack Road
Exeter
EX2 5DW
TEL: 01392 411611
FAX: 01392 403934

Royal National Hospital for
    Rheumatic Diseases NHS Trust
Upper Borough Walls
Bath
BA1 1RL
TEL: 01225 465941
FAX: 01225 421202

Royal United Hospital, Bath, NHS
    Trust
Royal United Hospital
Combe Park
Bath
BA1 3NG
TEL: 01225 428331
FAX: 01225 824395

Salisbury Health Care NHS Trust
Salisbury District Hospital
Salisbury

Wiltshire
SP2 8BJ
TEL: 01722 336262
FAX: 01722 339597

Severn NHS Trust
Rikenal
Montpellier
Gloucester
GL1 1LY
TEL: 01452 529421
FAX: 01452 383045

South Devon Healthcare NHS Trust
Hengrave House
Torbay Hospital
Lawes Bridge
Torquay
TQ2 7AA
TEL: 01803 614567
FAX: 01803 616334

Southampton Community Health
    Services NHS Trust
Central Health Clinic
East Park Terrace
Southampton
SO14 0YL
TEL: 01703 902500
FAX: 01703 902600

Southampton University Hospitals
    NHS Trust
Southampton General Hospital
Tremona Road
Shirley
Southampton
Hants
SO16 6UD
TEL: 01703 777222
FAX: 01703 794153

Southmead Health Services NHS Trust
Southmead Hospital
Westbury on Trym
Bristol
BS10 5NB
TEL: 0117 950 5050
FAX: 0117 959 0902

Swindon & Marlborough NHS Trust
Princess Margaret Hospital
Okus Road
Swindon
Wiltshire
SN1 4JR
TEL: 01793 536231
FAX: 01793 480817

Taunton & Somerset NHS Trust
Musgrove Park Hospital
Taunton
TA1 5DA
TEL: 01823 333444
FAX: 01823 336877

United Bristol Healthcare NHS Trust
Finance Department
PO Box 1053
Marlborough Street
Bristol
BS99 1YF
TEL: 0117 929 0666
FAX: 0117 925 2493

Westcountry Ambulance NHS Trust
Trust Headquarters
Powisland Drive
Plymouth
Devon PL6 6AB
TEL: 01752 767839
FAX: 01752 774788

West Dorset General Hospitals NHS
    Trust
West Dorset Hospital
Damers Road
Dorchester
Dorset
DT1 2JY
TEL: 01305 251150
FAX: 01305 254185

Weston Area Health NHS Trust
Weston General Hospital
Grange Road
Uphill
Weston Super Mare
Avon BS23 4TQ

TEL: 01934 636363
FAX: 01934 619275

Wiltshire Ambulance Service NHS
  Trust
Ambulance Service Headquarters
Malmesbury Road
Chippenham
Wiltshire
SN15 5LN
TEL: 01249 443939
FAX: 01249 443217

Wiltshire Healthcare NHS Trust
St Johns Hospital
Bradley Road
Trowbridge
Wiltshire
BA14 0QU
TEL: 01225 753610
FAX: 01225 777697

Winchester and Eastleigh Healthcare
  NHS Trust
Royal Hampshire County Hospital
Romsey Road
Winchester
SO22 5DG
TEL: 01962 824445
FAX: 01962 825396

West Midlands

Alexandra Healthcare NHS Trust
The Alexandra Hospital
Woodrow Drive
Redditch
B98 7UB
TEL: 01527 503030
FAX: 01527 517432

Birmingham Children's Hospital
  NHS Trust
The Children's Hospital
Ladywood Middleway
Ladywood
Birmingham
B16 8ET

TEL: 0121 454 4851
FAX: 0121 456 4697

Birmingham Heartlands and Solihull
  (Teaching) NHS Trust
Bordesley Green East
Birmingham
B9 5SS
TEL: 0121 766 6611
FAX: 0121 773 2842

Birmingham Women's Health Care
  NHS Trust
Birmingham Maternity Hospital
Queen Elizabeth Medical Centre
Edgbaston
Birmingham
B15 2TG
TEL: 0121 472 1377
FAX: 0121 627 2602

Black Country Mental Health NHS
  Trust
48 Lodge Road
West Bromwich
West Midlands
B70 8NY
TEL: 0121 553 7676
FAX: 0121 607 3571

Burton Hospitals NHS Trust
Burton Hospital
Belvedere Road
Burton on Trent
DE13 0RB
TEL: 01283 566333
FAX: 01283 566771

City Hospital NHS Trust
Dudley Road
Birmingham
B18 7QH
TEL: 0121 554 3801
FAX: 0121 551 6910

Coventry Healthcare NHS Trust
Parkside House
Quinton
Coventry

CV1 2NJ
TEL: 01203 553344
FAX: 01203 526800

Dudley Group of Hospitals NHS
  Trust
Wordsley Hospital
Wordsley
Stourbridge
West Midlands
DY8 5QX
TEL: 01384 456111
FAX: 01384 244395

Dudley Priority Health NHS Trust
Trust Headquarters
Ridge Hill
Brierley Hill Road
Stourbridge
DY8 5ST
TEL: 01384 457373
FAX: 01384 400217

First Community Health NHS Trust
Crooked Bridge Road
Stafford
ST16 3NE
TEL: 01785 222888
FAX: 01785 54432

The Foundation NHS Trust
St George's Hospital
Corporation Street
Stafford
ST16 3AG
TEL: 01785 257888
FAX: 01785 258969

The George Eliot Hospital NHS Trust
George Eliot Hospital
College Street
Nuneaton
Warwickshire
CV10 7DJ
TEL: 01203 351351
FAX: 01203 865058

Good Hope Hospital NHS Trust
Rectory Road

Sutton Coldfield
West Midlands
B75 7RR
TEL: 0121 378 2211
FAX: 0121 311 1074

Hereford and Worcester Ambulance
  Service NHS Trust
Ambulance Headquarters
Bransford
Worcester
WR6 5JD
TEL: 01886 834200
FAX: 01886 834210

Hereford Hospitals NHS Trust
County Hospital
Union Walk
Hereford
HR1 2ER
TEL: 01432 355444
FAX: 01432 354310

Herefordshire Community Health
  NHS Trust
Belmont Abbey
Belmont
Hereford
HR2 9RP
TEL: 01432 344344
FAX: 01432 363900

Kidderminster Healthcare NHS
  Trust
Kidderminster General Hospital
Bewdley Road
Kidderminster
DY11 6RJ
TEL: 01562 823424
FAX: 01562 825685

Mid Staffordshire General NHS
  Trust
Stafford District General Hospital
Weston Road
Stafford
ST16 3SA
TEL: 01785 257731
FAX: 01785 245211

Northern Birmingham Community
  Health NHS Trust
Waterlinks House
Richard Street
Birmingham
B7 4AA
TEL: 0121 359 5566
FAX: 0121 603 5567

Northern Birmingham Mental Health
  NHS Trust
71 Fentham Road
Erdington
Birmingham
B23 6AL
TEL: 0121 623 5500
FAX: 0121 623 5770

North Staffordshire Hospital NHS
  Trust
The Limes
Hartshill Road
Hartshill
Stoke on Trent
ST4 7PS
TEL: 01782 718003
FAX: 01782 718671

North Staffordshire Combined
  Healthcare NHS Trust
Bucknall Hospital
Eaves Lane
Bucknall
Stoke on Trent
ST2 8LD
TEL: 01782 273510
FAX: 01782 213682

North Warwickshire NHS Trust
139 Earls Road
Nuneaton
CV11 5HP
TEL: 01203 642200
FAX: 01203 351434

Premier Health NHS Trust
Trust HQ
St Michael's Hospital
Trent Valley Road

Lichfield
Staffordshire
WS13 6EF
TEL: 01543 441400
FAX: 01543 441430

The Princess Royal Hospital NHS
  Trust
The Princess Royal Hospital
Apley Castle
Telford
Shropshire
TF6 6TF
TEL: 01952 641222
FAX: 01952 243405

Robert Jones & Agnes Hunt
  Orthopaedic & District Hospital
  NHS Trust
Oswestry
Shropshire
SY10 7AG
TEL: 01691 655311
FAX: 01691 652613

The Royal Orthopaedic Hospital
  NHS Trust
Woodlands
Northfields
Birmingham
B31 2AP
TEL: 0121 685 4000
FAX: 0121 627 8211

Royal Shrewsbury Hospitals NHS
  Trust
Royal Shrewsbury Hospital
North
Mytton Oak Road
Shrewsbury
SY3 8XQ
TEL: 01743 261000
FAX: 01743 261006

The Royal Wolverhampton
  Hospitals NHS Trust
Trust Management Offices
Hollybush House
New Cross Hospital

Wolverhampton
WV10 0QP
TEL: 01902 642909
FAX: 01902 643173

Rugby NHS Trust
Brookfields
Hospital of St Cross
Barby Road
Rugby
CV22 5PX
TEL: 01788 572831
FAX: 01788 545151

Sandwell Healthcare NHS Trust
Finance Department
PO Box 3803
Lewisham Street
West Bromwich
B71 4JE
TEL: 0121 553 1831
FAX: 0121 607 3410

Shropshire Community Health
   Service NHS Trust
Trust Headquarters
Cross Houses
Shrewsbury
SY5 6JN
TEL: 01743 761242
FAX: 01743 761601

Shropshire Mental Health NHS Trust
The Royal Shrewsbury Hospital
Shelton
Bicton Heath
Shrewsbury
SY3 8DN
TEL: 01743 261230
FAX: 01743 261119

Solihull Healthcare NHS Trust
20 Union Road
Solihull
West Midlands
B91 3EF
TEL: 0121 711 7171
FAX: 0121 711 7212

South Birmingham Mental Health
   NHS Trust
PO Box 3805, Moneyhall Hospital
Moneyhall Lane
Kings Norton
Birmingham
B30 3QF
TEL: 0121 627 1627
FAX: 0121 627 8302

South Warwickshire General
   Hospital NHS Trust
Warwick Hospital
Lakin Road
Warwick
CV34 5BW
TEL: 01926 495321
FAX: 01926 403715

South Warwickshire Health Care
   NHS Trust
Community Health Offices
Alcester Road
Stratford upon Avon
CV37 6PW
TEL: 01789 269264
FAX: 01789 267799

South Warwickshire Mental Health
   Services NHS Trust
St Michael's Hospital
St Michael's Road
Warwick
CV34 5QW
TEL: 01926 496241
FAX: 01926 406700

Southern Birmingham Community
   Health NHS Trust
PO Box 3824, West Heath Hospital
Rednal Road
West Heath
Birmingham
B38 8FD
TEL: 0121 627 1627
FAX: 0121 627 8297

Staffordshire Ambulance Service
   NHS Trust

Ambulance Service Headquarters
70 Stone Road
Stafford
ST16 2RS
TEL: 01785 253521
FAX: 01785 246238

University Hospital Birmingham
   NHS Trust
Selly Oak Hospital
PO Box 881
Selly Oak
Birmingham
B29 6JS
TEL: 0121 627 1627
FAX: 0121 627 8613

Walsall Community Health NHS
   Trust
Upland House
5 Lichfield Road
Walsall
WS4 2HT
TEL: 01922 721007
FAX: 01922 656040

Walsall Hospitals NHS Trust
Manor Hospital
Moat Road
Walsall
West Midlands
WS2 9PS
TEL: 01922 656264
FAX: 01922 656621

Walsgrave Hospitals NHS Trust
Walsgrave Hospital
Clifford Bridge Road
Walsgrave
Coventry
CV2 2DX
TEL: 01203 538914
FAX: 01203 538899

Warwickshire Ambulance Service
   NHS Trust
Ambulance HQ
50 Holly Walk
Leamington Spa

CV32 4HY
TEL: 01926 881331
FAX: 01926 451162

West Midlands Ambulance Service
   NHS Trust
4th Floor, Falcon House
6 The Minories
Dudley
DY2 8NP
TEL: 01384 215555
FAX: 01384 215559

Wolverhampton Health Care NHS
   Trust
Cleveland/Leasowes
10/12 Tettenhall Road
Wolverhampton
WV1 4SA
TEL: 01902 310641
FAX: 01902 716834

Worcester Royal Infirmary NHS
   Trust
Newtown Branch
Newtown Road
Worcester
WR5 1JG
TEL: 01905 763333
FAX: 01905 767389

North West

Aintree Hospitals NHS Trust
Aintree House
Fazakerley Hospital
Longmoor Lane
Liverpool
L9 7AL
TEL: 0151 525 3622
FAX: 0151 525 6086

Blackburn, Hyndburn & Ribble
   Valley Health Care NHS Trust
Queens Park Hospital
Haslingden Road
Blackburn
BB2 3HH

TEL: 01254 263555
FAX: 01254 294805

Blackpool Victoria Hospital NHS
    Trust
Furness Drive
Poulton-le-Fylde
Lancashire
FY6 8ST
TEL: 01253 303041
FAX: 01253 303050

Blackpool, Wyre and Fylde
    Community Health Services NHS
    Trust
Wesham Park Hospital
Derby Road
Wesham
Preston
PR4 3AL
TEL: 01253 303244
FAX: 01253 303197

Bolton Hospitals NHS Trust
1st Floor
43 Churchgate
Bolton
BL1 1JF
TEL: 01204 390390
FAX: 01204 390794

Burnley Health Care NHS Trust
Burnley General Hospital
Casterton Avenue
Burnley
Lancashire
BB10 2PQ
TEL: 01282 474546
FAX: 01282 474444

Bury Health Care NHS Trust
Roch House
Fairfield General Hospital
Rochdale Old Road
Bury
BL9 7TD
TEL: 0161 764 6081
FAX: 0161 705 3875

Calderstones NHS Trust
Mitton Road
Whalley
Clitheroe
Lancashire
BB7 9PE
TEL: 01254 822121
FAX: 01254 823023

Cardiothoracic Centre Liverpool
    NHS Trust
Thomas Drive
Liverpool
L14 3LB
TEL: 0151 228 1616
FAX: 0151 220 8573

Central Manchester Healthcare NHS
    Trust
2nd Floor, Cobbett House
Manchester Royal Infirmary
Oxford Road
Manchester
M13 9WL
TEL: 0161 276 1234
FAX: 0161 273 6211

Cheshire Healthcare NHS Trust
Trust Headquarters
Barony Road
Nantwich
Cheshire
CW5 5QU
TEL: 01270 415300
FAX: 01270 610464

Chester & Halton Community NHS
    Trust
Victoria House
Holloway
Runcorn
Cheshire
WA7 4TH
TEL: 01928 790404
FAX: 01928 591153

Chorley and South Ribble NHS Trust
Chorley District Hospital
Preston Road

Chorley
PR7 1PP
TEL: 01257 261222
FAX: 01257 245366

Christie Hospital NHS Trust
Wilmstow Road
Withington
Manchester
M20 9BX
TEL: 0161 446 3000
FAX: 0161 446 3977

Clatterbridge Centre for Oncology
  NHS Trust
Clatterbridge Hospital
Clatterbridge Road
Bebington
Wirral
Merseyside
L63 4JY
TEL: 0151 334 1155
FAX: 0151 334 0882

CommuniCare NHS Trust
Trust Headquarters
Queens Park Hospital
Hollingdon Road
Blackburn BB2 3HH
TEL: 01254 356800
FAX: 01254 356823

Community Healthcare Bolton NHS
  Trust
St Peter's House
Silverwell Street
Bolton
BL1 1PP
TEL: 01204 77000
FAX: 01204 77004

The Countess of Chester Hospital
  NHS Trust
Countess of Chester Health Park
Liverpool Road
Chester
CH2 1UL
TEL: 01244 365000
FAX: 01244 365292

East Cheshire NHS Trust
Macclesfield District General
  Hospital
Westpark Branch
Prestbury Road
Macclesfield
Cheshire
SK10 3BL
TEL: 01625 661580
FAX: 01625 661644

Furness Hospitals NHS Trust
Furness General Hospital
Dalton Lane
Barrow in Furness
Cumbria
LA14 4LF
TEL: 01229 870870
FAX: 01229 871182

Greater Manchester Ambulance
  Service NHS Trust
Ambulance Service Headquarters
Bury Old Road
Whitefield
Manchester
M45 6AQ
TEL: 0161 231 7921
FAX: 0161 223 1351

Guild Community Healthcare NHS
  Trust
Moor Park House
46 Garstang Road
Preston
PR1 1NA
TEL: 01772 562656
FAX: 01772 200220

Halton General Hospital NHS
  Trust
Halton General Hospital
Runcorn
Cheshire
WA7 2DA
TEL: 01928 714567
FAX: 01928 791058

Lancashire Ambulance Service NHS
  Trust
Ambulance Service Headquarters
Broughton House
449–451 Garstang Road
Broughton
Nr Preston
PR3 5LN
TEL: 01772 862666
FAX: 01772 773098

Lancaster Acute Hospitals NHS Trust
Trust Headquarters
PO Box 98
Royal Lancaster Infirmary
Lancaster
LA1 4GG
TEL: 01524 583573
FAX: 01524 583586

Lancaster Priority Services NHS Trust
Lancaster Moor Hospital
Quernmore Road
Lancaster
LA1 3SL
TEL: 01524 586656
FAX: 01524 586479

Liverpool Women's Hospital NHS
  Trust
Crown Street
Liverpool
L8 7SS
TEL: 0151 708 9988
FAX: 0151 702 4028

London Ambulance Service NHS
  Trust
Ambulance Headquarters
220 Waterloo Road
London
SE1 8SD
TEL: 0171 928 0333
FAX: 0171 735 9557

Manchester Children's Hospitals
  NHS Trust
Royal Manchester Children's
  Hospital

Hospital Road
Pendlebury
Manchester
M27 1HA
TEL: 0161 727 2990
FAX: 0161 727 2456

Mancunian Community Health NHS
  Trust
Mauldeth House
Mauldeth Road West
Chorlton
Manchester
M21 7RL
TEL: 0161 958 4000
FAX: 0161 881 9366

Mental Health Services of Salford
  NHS Trust
Bury New Road
Prestwich
Manchester
M25 3BL
TEL: 0161 773 9121
FAX: 0161 772 3444

Mersey Regional Ambulance Service
  NHS Trust
Ambulance Headquarters
Elm House
Belmont Grove
Liverpool
L6 4EG
TEL: 0151 260 5220
FAX: 0151 206 7441

Mid Cheshire Hospitals NHS Trust
Leighton Hospital
Middlewich Road
Crewe
Cheshire
CW1 4QJ
TEL: 01270 255 141
FAX: 01270 587 696

North Manchester Healthcare NHS
  Trust
North Manchester General Hospital
Delaunays Road

Crumpsall
Manchester
M8 6RL
TEL: 0161 795 4567
FAX: 0161 720 2831

The North Mersey Community NHS
   Trust
Rathbone Hospital
Mill Lane
Liverpool
L13 4AW
TEL: 0151 250 3000
FAX: 0151 228 0486

The Oldham NHS Trust
District Headquarters
Westhulme Avenue
Oldham
OL1 2PN
TEL: 0161 624 0420
FAX: 0161 627 3130

Preston Acute Hospitals NHS Trust
Royal Preston Hospital
Sharoe Green Lane
Fulwood
Preston
PR2 4HT
TEL: 01772 716565
FAX: 01772 711559

Rochdale Healthcare NHS Trust
Birch Hill Hospital
Birch Road
Rochdale
OL12 9QB
TEL: 01706 377777
FAX: 01706 755130

Royal Liverpool and Broadgreen
   University Hospitals NHS Trust
Royal Liverpool University Hospital
Pembroke House
Prescot Street
Liverpool
L7 8XP
TEL: 0151 706 2000
FAX: 0151 706 5806

Royal Liverpool Children's Hospital
   NHS Trust
Alder Hey Children's Hospital
Eaton Road
Liverpool
L12 2AP
TEL: 0151 228 4811
FAX: 0151 228 0328

Salford Community Health Care
   NHS Trust
Joule House
49 The Crescent
Salford
M5 4NW
TEL: 0161 743 0466
FAX: 0161 743 0452

Salford Royal Hospitals NHS Trust
Hope Hospital
Stott Lane
Salford
Manchester
M6 8HD
TEL: 0161 789 7373
FAX: 0161 787 5974

St Helens and Knowsley Community
   Health NHS Trust
The Hollies
Cowley Hill Lane
St Helens
Merseyside
WA10 2AP
TEL: 01744 733722
FAX: 01744 453405

St Helen's & Knowsley Hospital
   NHS Trust
Whiston Hospital
Prescot
Merseyside
L35 5DR
TEL: 0151 426 1152
FAX: 0151 430 1150

South Cumbria Community and
   Mental Health NHS Trust
Community Health Offices

2 Fairfield Lane
Barrow in Furness
Cumbria
LA13 9AH
TEL: 01229 820552
FAX: 01229 823224

South Manchester University
    Hospitals NHS Trust
Trust Headquarters
Wythenshawe Hospital
Southmoor Road
Manchester
M23 9LT
TEL: 0161 998 7070
FAX: 0161 946 2037

Southport and Formby Community
    Health Services NHS Trust
Hesketh Centre
Albert Road
Southport
Merseyside
PR9 8BL
TEL: 01704 530940
FAX: 01704 530714

Southport and Formby NHS Trust
Finance & Supplies Department
PO Box 134
Southport
Merseyside
PR8 6PT
TEL: 01704 547471
FAX: 01704 543579

Stockport Acute Services NHS Trust
Hawthorn House
Stepping Hill Hospital
Poplar Grove
Stockport
SK2 7JE
TEL: 0161 419 1010
FAX: 0161 419 5003

Stockport Healthcare NHS Trust
Ash House
Stepping Hill Hospital
Poplar Grove

Stockport
SK2 7JE
TEL: 0161 419 5162
FAX: 0161 419 5169

Tameside and Glossop Acute
    Services NHS Trust
Tameside General Hospital
Fountain Street
Ashton Under Lyne
OL6 9RW
TEL: 0161 331 6470
FAX: 0161 331 6472

Tameside and Glossop Community
    & Priority Services NHS Trust
Tameside General Hospital
Fountain Street
Ashton Under Lyne
Ol6 9RW
TEL: 0161 331 5151
FAX: 0161 331 5007

Trafford Healthcare NHS Trust
Trust Headquarters
Trafford General Hospital
Moorside Road, Daryhulme
Urmston
Manchester
M41 5SL
TEL: 0161 746 2304
FAX: 0161 746 7214

The Walton Centre for Neurology
    and Neurosurgery NHS Trust
Rice Lane
Liverpool
L9 1AE
TEL: 0151 525 3611
FAX: 0151 529 4638

Warrington Community Healthcare
    NHS Trust
Winwick Hospital
Winwick
Warrington
WA2 8RR
TEL: 01925 655221
FAX: 01925 235089

Warrington Hospital NHS Trust
Warrington District General
  Hospital
Lovely Lane
Warrington
Cheshire
WA5 1QG
TEL: 01925 635911
FAX: 01925 662099

West Lancashire NHS Trust
Ormskirk & District General
  Hospital
Wigan Road
Ormskirk
L39 2AZ
TEL: 01695 577111
FAX: 01695 583933

Westmoreland Hospital NHS
  Trust
Westmoreland General Hospital
Burton Road
Kendal
Cumbria
LA9 7RG
TEL: 01539 732288
FAX: 01539 740852

Wigan & Leigh Health Services NHS
  Trust
The Elms
Royal Albert and Edward Infirmary
Wignan Lane
Wigan
WN1 2NN
TEL: 01942 773761
FAX: 01942 7737703

Wirral and West Cheshire
  Community NHS Trust
Victoria Central Hospital
Mill Lane
Wallasey
Liverpool
L44 5UF
TEL: 0151 604 7282
FAX: 0151 691 0306

The Wirral Hospital NHS Trust
Willow House
Finance Department
Clatterbridge Hopsital
Bebington Road
Merseyside
L63 4SJ
TEL: 0151 334 4000
FAX: 0151 604 7450

Worcestershire Community
  Healthcare NHS Trust
Isaac Maddox House
Shrub Hill Road
Worcester
WR4 9RW
TEL: 01905 681 511
FAX: 01905 681 515

Wrightington Hospital NHS
  Trust
Wrightington Hospital
Hall Lane
Appley Bridge
Wigan
Lancashire
WN6 9EP
TEL: 01257 252211
FAX: 01257 253809

Northern Ireland

Altnagelvin Hospitals HSS Trust
Altnagelvin Area Hospital
Glenshane Road
Londonderry
BT47 1SB
TEL: 01504 45171
FAX: 01504 611222

Armagh and Dungannon HSS
  Trust
Gosford Place
The Mall
Armagh
BT61 9AR
TEL: 01861 522262
FAX: 01861 522544

Belfast City Hospital HSS Trust
51 Lisburn Road
Belfast
BT9 7AB
TEL: 01232 329241
FAX: 01232 326614

Causeway HSS Trust
8E Coleraine Road
Ballymoney
BT53 6BP
TEL: 012656 66600
FAX: 012656 66630

Craigavon Area Hospital Group HSS
   Trust
68 Lurgan Road
Portadown
Craigavon
BT63 5QQ
TEL: 01762 334444
FAX: 01762 350068

Craigavon and Banbridge
   Community HSS Trust
Bannvale House
Moyallen Road
Gilford
BT63 5JX
TEL: 01762 831983
FAX: 01762 831993

Down Lisburn HSS Trust
Lisburn Health Centre
25 Linenhall Street
Lisburn
BT28 1BH
TEL: 01846 501309
FAX: 01846 501210

Foyle HSS Trust
Riverview House
Abercorn Road
Londonderry
BT48 6SA
TEL: 01504 266111
FAX: 01504 260806

Green Park HSS Trust
20 Stockman's Lane
Belfast
BT9 7JB
TEL: 01232 669501
FAX: 01232 382008

Homefirst Community HSS Trust
The Cottage
5 Greenmount Avenue
Ballymena
Co Antrim
BT43 6DA
TEL: 01266 633700
FAX: 01266 633733

Mater Infirmorum Hospital HSS
   Trust
45–51 Crumlin Road
Belfast
BT14 6AB
TEL: 01232 741211
FAX: 01232 741342

Newry and Mourne HSS Trust
5 Downshire Place
Newry
BT34 1DZ
TEL: 01693 60505
FAX: 01693 69064

North and West Belfast HSS
   Trust
Glendinning House
6 Murray Street
Belfast
BT1 6DP
TEL: 01232 327156
FAX: 01232 249109

North Down and Ards Community
   HSS Trust
23–25 Regent Street
Newtownards
BT23 4AD
TEL: 01247 816666
FAX: 01247 820140

Northern Ireland Ambulance Service
   HSS Trust
Ambulance Service Headquarters
12/22 Linenhall Street
Belfast BT2 8BS
TEL: 01232 246113
FAX: 01232 553655

Royal Group of Hospitals and Dental
   Hospital HSS Trust
274 Grosvenor Road
Belfast
BT12 6BP
TEL: 01232 240503
FAX: 01232 240899

South and East Belfast HSS Trust
Trust Headquarters
Knockbracken Healthcare Park
Saintfield Road
Belfast
BT8 8BH
TEL: 01232 790673
FAX: 01232 796632

Sperrin Lakeland HSS Trust
Trust Headquarters
Strathdene House
Tyrone and Fermanagh Hospital
Omagh
Co Tyrone
BT79 0NS
TEL: 01662 244127
FAX: 01662 244570

Ulster Comunity and Hospitals
   Trust
Health and Care Centre
39 Regent Street
Newtownards
Co Down
BT23 4AD
TEL: 01247 816666
FAX: 01247 820140

United Hospitals HSS Trust
Antrim Area Hospital
45 Bush Road
Antrim

BT41 2RL
TEL: 01849 424000
FAX: 01849 424654

Scotland

Aberdeen Royal Hospitals NHS
   Trust
Foresterhill House
Ashgrove Road West
Aberdeen
AB9 1ZB
TEL: 01224 681818
FAX: 01224 840597

Angus NHS Trust
Whitehills Hospital
Forfar
Angus
DD8 3DY
TEL: 01307 464551
FAX: 01307 465129

Argyll & Bute Unit NHS Trust
Trust Headquarters
Aros
Lochgilphead
Argyll
PA31 8LB
TEL: 01546 606600
FAX: 01546 606622

Ayrshire & Arran Community
   Healthcare NHS Trust
1a Hunters Avenue
Ayr
KA8 9DW
TEL: 01292 281821
FAX: 01292 610213

Borders Community Health Services
   NHS Trust
Headquarters
Huntlyburn House
Melrose
TD6 9BP
TEL: 01896 828282
FAX: 01896 822887

Borders General Hospital NHS Trust
Borders General Hospital
Near Melrose
TD6 9BS
TEL: 01896 754333
FAX: 01896 662291

Caithness & Sutherland NHS Trust
Caithness General Hospital
Wick
Caithness
KW1 5LA
TEL: 01955 605050
FAX: 01955 604606

Central Scotland Healthcare NHS
    Trust
Trust Headquarters
Royal Scottish National Hospital
Old Denny Road
Larbert
FK5 4SD
TEL: 01324 570700
FAX: 01324 563552

Dumfries & Galloway Acute &
    Maternity Hospitals NHS Trust
Dumfries & Galloway Royal
    Infirmary
Bankend Road
Dumfries
DG1 4AP
TEL: 01387 246246
FAX: 01387 241639

Dumfries & Galloway Community
    Health NHS Trust
Campbell House
Crichton Royal Hospital
Glencaple Road
Dumfries
DG1 4TG
TEL: 01387 255301
FAX: 01387 244101

Dundee Healthcare NHS Trust
Liff Hospital
Dundee
DD2 5NF

TEL: 01382 42300
FAX: 01382 581329

Dundee Teaching Hospitals NHS
    Trust
Ninewells Hospital
Dundee
DD1 9SY
TEL: 01382 660111
FAX: 01382 660445

East & Midlothian NHS Trust
Edenhall Hospital
Pinkie Burn
Musselburgh
EH21 7TZ
TEL: 0131 536 8000
FAX: 0131 536 8153

Edinburgh Healthcare NHS Trust
Astley Ainslie Hospital
133 Grange Loan
Edinburgh
EH9 2HL
TEL: 0131 537 9000
FAX: 0131 537 9500

Edinburgh Sick Children's NHS Trust
Royal Hospital for Sick Children
Sciennes Road
Edinburgh
EH9 1LF
TEL: 0131 536 0000
FAX: 0131 536 0001

Falkirk & District Royal Infirmary
    NHS Trust
Falkirk & District Royal Infirmary
Major's Loan
Falkirk
FK1 5QE
TEL: 01324 624000
FAX: 01324 612340

Fife Healthcare NHS Trust
Cameron House
Cameron Bridge
Leven
KY8 5RG

TEL: 01592 712812
FAX: 01592 712762

Glasgow Dental Hospital & School
    NHS Trust
378 Sauchiehall Street
Glasgow
G2 3JZ
TEL: 0141 211 9600
FAX: 0141 211 9800
FAX: 0141 311 2798 (School)

Glasgow Royal Infirmary University
    NHS Trust
Glasgow Royal Infirmary
84 Castle Street
Glasgow
G4 0SF
TEL: 0141 211 4000
FAX: 0141 211 4889

Grampian Healthcare NHS Trust
Westholme
Woodend General Hospital
Eday Road
Aberdeen
AB2 6LR
TEL: 01224 663131
FAX: 01224 840790

Greater Glasgow Community &
    Mental Health Services NHS
    Trust
Trust Headquarters
Gartnavel Royal Hospital
1055 Great Western Road
Glasgow
G12 0XH
TEL: 0141 211 3600
FAX: 0141 211 0306

Hairmyres & Stonehouse Hospitals
    NHS Trust
Hairmyres Hospital
East Kilbride
G75 8RG
TEL: 013552 20292
FAX: 013552 34064

Highland Communities NHS Trust
Royal Northern Infirmary
Ness Walk
Inverness
IV2 5SF
TEL: 01463 242860
FAX: 01463 713844

Inverclyde Royal NHS Trust
Inverclyde Royal Hospital
Larkfield Road
Greenock
PA16 0XN
TEL: 01475 633777
FAX: 01475 636753

Kirkcaldy Acute Hospitals NHS
    Trust
Victoria Hospital
Hayfield Road
Kirkcaldy
KY2 5AH
TEL: 01592 643355
FAX: 01592 647041

Lanarkshire Healthcare NHS Trust
Unit Office
Strathclyde Hospital
Airbles Road
Motherwell
ML1 3B2
TEL: 01698 230500
FAX: 01698 275674

Law Hospital NHS Trust
Law Hospital
Carluke
ML8 5ER
TEL: 01698 361100
FAX: 01698 376671

Lomond Healthcare NHS Trust
Vale of Leven District General
    Hospital
Alexandria
Dunbartonshire
G83 0UA
TEL: 01389 754121
FAX: 01389 755948

Monklands & Bellshill Hospital NHS
  Trust
Monklands District General Hospital
Monkscourt Avenue
Airdrie
ML6 0JS
TEL: 01236 748748
FAX: 01236 760015

Moray Health Services NHS Trust
Maryhill House
317 High Street
Elgin
Moray
IV30 1AJ
TEL: 01343 543131
FAX: 01343 540834

North Ayrshire & Arran NHS Trust
Crosshouse Hospital
Kilmarnock
KA2 0BE
TEL: 01563 521133
FAX: 01563 572496

Perth & Kinross Healthcare NHS
  Trust
Trust Headquarters
Taymount Terrace
Perth
PH1 1NX
TEL: 01738 623311
FAX: 01738 473278

Queen Margaret Hospital NHS Trust
Queen Margaret Hospital
Whitefield Road
Dunfermline
KY12 0SU
TEL: 01383 623623
FAX: 01383 624156

Raigmore Hospital NHS Trust
Raigmore Hospital
Old Perth Road
Inverness
IV2 3UJ
TEL: 01463 704000
FAX: 01463 711322

Renfewshire Healthcare NHS Trust
Trust Headquarters
Dykebar Hospital
Grahamston Road
Paisley
PA2 7DE
TEL: 0141 884 5122
FAX: 0141 884 5425

Royal Alexandra Hospital NHS Trust
Royal Alexandra Hospital
Corsebar Road
Paisley
PA2 9PN
TEL: 0141 887 9111
FAX: 0141 887 6701

Royal Infirmary of Edinburgh NHS
  Trust
Royal Infirmary of Edinburgh
1 Lauriston Place
Edinburgh
EH3 9YW
TEL: 0131 536 1000
FAX: 0131 536 3002

Scottish Ambulance Service NHS
  Trust
National Headquarters
Tipperlinn Road
Edinburgh
EH10 5UU
TEL: 0131 447 7711
FAX: 0131 447 4789

South Ayrshire Hospitals NHS Trust
The Ayr Hospital
Daimelington Road
Ayr
KA6 6DX
TEL: 01292 610555
FAX: 01292 288952

Southern General Hospital NHS
  Trust
Southern General Hospital
1345 Govan Road
Glasgow
G51 4TF

TEL: 0141 201 1100
FAX: 0141 201 2999

Stirling Royal Infirmary NHS Trust
Stirling Royal Infirmary
Livilands
Stirling
FK8 2AU
TEL: 01786 434000
FAX: 01786 450588

Stobhill NHS Trust
Stobhill General Hospital
133 Balomock Road
Glasgow
G21 3UW
TEL: 0141 201 3000
FAX: 0141 201 3887

The Victoria Infirmary NHS Trust
Queen's Park House
Langside Road
Glasgow
G42 9TT
TEL: 0141 201 6000
FAX: 0141 201 5825

West Glasgow Hospitals University
   NHS Trust
Administration Building
Western Infirmary
Dumbarton Road
Glasgow
G11 6NT
TEL: 0141 211 2000
FAX: 0141 211 1920

West Lothian NHS Trust
St John's Hospital at Howden
Livingston
West Lothian
EH54 6PP
TEL: 01506 491666
FAX: 01506 416484

Western General Hospitals NHS
   Trust
Western General Hospital
Crewe Road South

Edinburgh
EH4 2XU
TEL: 0131 537 1000
FAX: 0131 537 1001

The Yorkhill NHS Trust
Royal Hospital for Sick Children
Yorkhill
Glasgow
G3 8SJ
TEL: 0141 201 0000
FAX: 0141 201 0836

Wales

Bridgend and District NHS Trust
Nurses Home Offices
Bridgend General Hospital
Quarella Road
Bridgend
Mid Glamorgan
CF31 1YE
TEL: 01656 752752
FAX: 01656 665377

Cardiff Community Healthcare NHS
   Trust
'Trenewydd'
Fairwater Road
Llandaff
Cardiff
CF5 2LD
TEL: 01222 552212
FAX: 01222 578032

Carmarthen and District NHS Trust
West Wales General Hospital
Glangwili
Carmarthen
Dyfed
SA31 2AF
TEL: 01267 235151
FAX: 01267 237662

Ceredigion and Mid Wales NHS
   Trust
Bronglais General Hospital
Caradog Road
Aberystwyth

Dyfed
SY23 1ER
TEL: 01970 623131
FAX: 01970 635922

Derwen NHS Trust
St David's Hospital
Carmarthen
Dyfed
SA31 3HB
TEL: 01267 237481
FAX: 01267 221895

East Glamorgan NHS Trust
East Glamorgan General Hospital
Church Village
Pontypridd
Mid Glamorgan
CF38 1AB
TEL: 01443 218218
FAX: 01443 217213

Glan Hafren NHS Trust
Royal Gwent Hospital
Cardiff Road
Newport
Gwent
NP9 2UB
TEL: 01633 234234
FAX: 01633 221217

Glan Clwyd District General
    Hospital NHS Trust
Ysbyty Glan Clwyd
Bodelwyddan
Rhyl
Clwyd
LL18 5UJ
TEL: 01745 583910
FAX: 01745 583143

Glan-y-Môr NHS Trust
21 Orchard Street
Swansea
SA1 5BE
TEL: 01792 651501
FAX: 01792 517018

Gofal Cymuned Clwydian
    Community Care NHS Trust
Catherine Gladstone House
Hawarden Way
Deeside
Clwyd
CH5 2EP
TEL: 01244 538883
FAX: 01244 538884

Gwent Community Health NHS
    Trust
Grange House
Llanfrechfa Grange Hospital
Cwmbran
Gwent
NP44 8YN
TEL: 01633 838523
FAX: 01633 643817

Gwynedd Community Health NHS
    Trust
Bryn-y-Neuadd Hospital
Llanfairfechan
Gwynedd
LL33 0HH
TEL: 01248 682682
FAX: 01248 681832

Gwynedd Hospitals NHS Trust
Ysbyty Gwynedd
Penrhos Garnedd
Bangor
Gwynedd
LL57 2PW
TEL: 01248 384384
FAX: 01248 370629

Llandough Hospital and Community
    NHS Trust
Llandough Hospital
Penlan Road
Llandough
Penarth
South Glamorgan
CF64 2XX
TEL: 01222 711711
FAX: 01222 12843

Llanelli Dinefwr NHS Trust
Prince Philip General Hospital
Bryngwynmawr
Dafen
Llanelli
Dyfed
SA14 8QF
TEL: 01554 756567
FAX: 01554 772271

Morriston Hospital NHS Trust
Morriston Hospital
Morriston
Swansea
SA6 6NL
TEL: 01792 702222
FAX: 01792 703632

Nevill Hall & District NHS Trust
Nevill Hall Hospital
Abergavenny
Gwent
NP7 7EG
TEL: 01873 852091
FAX: 01873 859168

North Glamorgan NHS Trust
Prince Charles Hospital
Merthyr Tydfil
Mid Glamorgan
CF47 9DT
TEL: 01685 721721
FAX: 01685 388001

Pembrokeshire NHS Trust
Withybush General Hospital
Fishguard Road
Haverfordwest
Dyfed
SA61 2PZ
TEL: 01437 774000
FAX: 01437 774300

Powys Health Care NHS Trust
Unit Offices
Felindre
Bronllys Hospital
Bronllys
Brecon

Powys
LD3 0LS
TEL: 01874 711661
FAX: 01874 711828

Rhondda Health Care NHS
Trust
Llwynypia Hospital
Llwynypia
Rhondda
CF40 2LX
TEL: 01443 440440
FAX: 01443 431611

Swansea NHS Trust
Singleton Hospital
Sketty
Swansea
SA2 0QA
TEL: 01792 205666
FAX: 01792 208647

University Hospital of Wales
Healthcare NHS Trust
Heath Park
Cardiff
CF4 4XW
TEL: 01222 747747
FAX: 01222 742968

University Dental Hospital NHS
Trust
Heath Park
Cardiff
CF4 4XY
TEL: 01222 742422
FAX: 01222 743838

Velindre NHS Trust
Velindre Hospital
Velindre Road
Whitchurch
Cardiff
CF4 7XL
TEL: 01222 615888
FAX: 01222 522694

Welsh Ambulance Service NHS
  Trust
Trust Headquarters
HM Stanley Hospital
St Asaph
LL17 0WA
TEL: 01745 585106
FAX: 01745 584101

Wrexham Maelor Hospital NHS
  Trust
Wrexham Maelor General
  Hospital
Croesnewydd Road
Wrexham
Clwyd
LL13 7TD
TEL: 01978 291100
FAX: 01978 310326

Appendix IV

Health Authorities

England
Anglia and Oxford

Bedfordshire Health Authority
Charter House
Alma Street
Luton
LU1 2PL
TEL: 01582 744800

Berkshire Health Authority
Pendragon House
57–59 Bath Road
Reading
RG30 2BA
TEL: 0118 950 3094

Buckinghamshire Health Authority
Verney House
Gatehouse Close
Aylesbury
HP19 3ET
TEL: 01296 310000

Cambridge and Huntingdon Health
    Authority
Fulbourn Hospital
Cambridge
CB1 5EF
TEL: 01223 475000

East Norfolk Health Authority
St Andrew's House
Northside
St Andrew's Business Park
Thorpe St Andrew
Norwich
NR7 0HT
TEL: 01603 300600

North West Anglia Health Authority
St John's
Thorpe Road
Peterborough
PE3 6JG
TEL: 01733 882288

Northamptonshire Health Authority
Highfield
Cliftonville Road
Northampton
NN1 5DN
TEL: 01604 615000

Oxfordshire Health Authority
John Radcliffe Hospital
Headley Way
Headington

Oxford
OX3 9DU
TEL: 01865 741741

Suffolk Health Authority
PO Box 55
Foxhall Road
Ipswich
IP3 8NN
TEL: 01473 323323

North West

Bury & Rochdale Health Authority
21 Silver Street
Bury
BL9 0EN
TEL: 0161 762 3100

East Lancashire Health Authority
31/33 Kenyon Road
Lomeshaye Estate
Nelson
BB9 5SZ
TEL: 01282 619909

Liverpool Health Authority
Hamilton House
Pall Mall
Liverpool
L3 6AL
TEL: 0151 236 4747

Manchester Health Authority
Gateway House
Piccadilly South
Manchester
M60 7LP
TEL: 0161 237 2000

Morecambe Bay Health Authority
Tenterfield
Brigsteer Road
Kendal
LA9 5EA
TEL: 01539 735565

North Cheshire Health Authority
Lister Road
Astmoor
Runcorn
WA7 1TW
TEL: 01928 593000

North West Lancashire Health
    Authority
Wesham Park Hospital
Derby Road
Wesham
Preston
PR4 3AL
TEL: 01253 306305

St Helens & Knowsley Health
    Authority
Cowley Hill Lane
St Helens
WA10 2AP
TEL: 01744 733722

Salford & Trafford Health Authority
Peel House
Albert Street
Eccles
M30 0NJ
TEL: 0161 931 2000

Sefton Health Authority
3rd Floor
Burlington House
Crosby Road North
Waterloo
Liverpool
L22 0QP
TEL: 0151 920 5056

South Cheshire Health Authority
1829 Building
Countess of Chester Health Park
Chester
CU2 1UL
TEL: 01244 650300

South Lancashire Health Authority
Grove House
Langton Brow

The Green
Eccleston
PR7 7PD
TEL: 01257 452222

Stockport Health Authority
Springwood
Poplar Grove
Stockport
SK7 5BY
TEL: 0161 410 4600

West Pennine Health Authority
Westhulme Avenue
Oldham
OL1 2PN
TEL: 0161 455 5700

Wigan & Bolton Health Authority
Bryan House
61 Standishgate
Wigan
WN1 1AH
TEL: 01204 390000

Wirral Health Authority
St Catherine's Hospital
1st Floor
Administration Block
Church Road
Tranmere
Wirral
L42 0LQ
TEL: 0151 651 0011

West Midlands

Birmingham Health Authority
1 Vernan Road
Edgbaston
Birmingham
B16 9SA
TEL: 0121 695 2222

Coventry Health Authority
Christchurch House
Greyfriars Lane
Coventry

CV1 2GQ
TEL: 01203 552225

Dudley Health Authority
12 Bull Street
Dudley
West Midlands
DY1 2DD
TEL: 01384 239376

Herefordshire Health Authority
Victoria House
Eign Street
Hereford
Herefordshire
HR4 0NA
TEL: 01432 262000

North Staffordshire Health Authority
District Offices
Heron House
Great Fenton Business Park
120 Grove Road
Stoke on Trent
Staffordshire
ST4 4LX
TEL: 01782 298000

Sandwell Health Authority
Kingston House
438 High Street
West Bromwich
West Midlands
B70 9LD
TEL: 0121 500 1500

Shropshire Health Authority
William Farr House
Shrewsbury
Shropshire
SY3 8XL
TEL: 01743 261300

Solihull Health Authority
19 Union Street
Solihull
West Midlands
B91 3DH
TEL: 0121 704 5191

South Staffordshire Health Authority
Mellor House
Corporation Street
Stafford
Staffordshire
ST16 3SR
TEL: 01785 252233

Walsall Health Authority
Lichfield House
27–31 Lichfield Street
Walsall
West Midlands
WS1 1TE
TEL: 01922 720255

Warwickshire Health Authority
Westgate House
Market Street
Warwick
Warwickshire
CV34 3DH
TEL: 01926 495074

Wolverhampton Health Authority
Coniston House
Chapel Ash
Wolverhampton
West Midlands
WV3 0XE
TEL: 01902 420202

Worcestershire Health Authority
Isaac Maddox House
Shrub Hill Road
Worcester
WR4 9RW
TEL: 01905 763333

Trent

Barnsley Health Authority
Hillder House
49/51 Gawber Road
Barnsley
S75 2PY
TEL: 01226 779922

Doncaster Health Authority
White Rose House
Ten Pound Walk
Doncaster
DN4 5DJ
TEL: 01302 320111

Leicestershire Health Authority
Gwendolen Road
Leicester
LE5 4QS
TEL: 0116 273 1173

Lincolnshire Health Authority
Cross O'Cliff
Bracebridge Heath
Lincoln
LN4 2HL
TEL: 01522 513355

North Derbyshire Health Authority
Scarsdale Hospital
Newbold Road
Chesterfield
S41 7PF
TEL: 01246 231255

North Nottinghamshire Health
   Authority
Ransom Hospital
1 Standard Court
Park Row
Nottingham
NG1 6GN
TEL: 01623 622515

Nottingham Health Authority
1 Standard Court
Park Row
Nottingham
NG1 6GN
TEL: 0115 912 3344

Rotherham Health Authority
220 Badsley Moor Lane
Rotherham
S65 1QU
TEL: 01709 382647

Sheffield Health Authority
Fulwood House
5 Old Fulwood Road
Sheffield
S10 3TG
TEL: 0114 271 1100

South Derbyshire Health Authority
Derwent Court
1 Stuart Street
Derby
DE1 2FZ
TEL: 01332 363971

South Humber Health Authority
Health Place
Wrawby Road
Brigg
DN20 8GS
TEL: 01652 659659

Northern and Yorkshire

Bradford Health Authority
New Mill
Victoria Road
Saltaire
Shipley
West Yorkshire
BD18 3LD
TEL: 01274 366007

County Durham Health Authority
Appleton House
Lanchester Road
Durham
Co Durham
DH1 5XZ
TEL: 0191 333 3233

East Riding Health Authority
Grange Park Lane
Willerby
Hull
North Humberside
HU10 6DT
TEL: 01482 650700

Leeds Health Authority
Blenheim House
West One
Duncombe Street
Leeds
Yorkshire
LS1 4PL
TEL: 0113 295 2000

Newcastle and North Tyneside
   Health Authority
Benfield Road
Walkergate
Newcastle upon Tyne
Tyne & Wear
NE6 4PF
TEL: 0191 219 6000

North Cumbria Health Authority
Wavell Drive
Rosehill Business Park
Carlisle
Cumbria
CA1 2SE
TEL: 01288 603612

North Yorkshire Health Authority
Resource Centre
Rydedale House
60 Piccadilly
York
North Yorkshire
YO1 1PE
TEL: 01904 825110

Northumberland Health Authority
East Cottingwood
Morpeth
Northumberland
NE61 2PD
TEL: 01670 514331

Gateshead and South Tyne Health
   Commission
Horsley Hill Road
South Shields
Tyne & Wear
NE33 3BN
TEL: 0191 401 4500

Sunderland Health Authority
Durham Road
Sunderland
Tyne & Wear
SR3 4AF
TEL: 0191 565 6256

Tees Health Authority
Poole Hospital
Stokesley Road
Nunthorpe
Middlesbrough
Cleveland
TS7 0NJ
TEL: 01642 320000

Wakefield Health Authority
White Rose House
West Parade
Wakefield
West Yorkshire
WF1 1LT
TEL: 01924 814400

South Thames

Bexley and Greenwich Health
    Authority
221 Erith Road
Bexleyheath
Kent DA7 6HA
TEL: 0181 298 6000

Bromley Health Authority
Global House
10 Station Approach
Hayes
Bromley
Kent BR2 7EH
TEL: 0181 462 2211

Croydon Health Authority
Knollys House
17 Addiscombe Road
Croydon
CR9 6HS
TEL: 0181 315 8315

East Kent Health Authority
Protea House
New Bridge
Marine Parade
Dover
CT17 9BW
TEL: 01304 227227

East Surrey Health Authority
Health Commission Offices
West Park Road
Horton Lane
Epsom
Surrey
KT19 8PB
TEL: 01372 731111

East Sussex Health Authority
250 Willington Road
Eastbourne
East Sussex
BN20 9AL
TEL: 01323 520000

Kingston and Richmond Health
    Authority
17 Upper Brighton Road
Surbiton
Surrey
KT6 6LH
TEL: 0181 390 1111

Lambeth, Southwark and Lewisham
    Health Authority
Wilson Hospital
Crammer Road
Mitcham
Surrey
CR4 4TP
TEL: 0171 716 7000

Merton, Sutton and Wandsworth
    Health Authority
Wilson Hospital
Cranmer Road
Mitcham
Surrey
CR4 4TP
TEL: 0181 648 3021

West Kent Health Authority
Preston Hall
Aylesford
Kent
ME20 7NJ
TEL: 01622 710161

West Surrey Health Authority
The Ridgewood Centre
Old Bisley Road
Frimley
Camberley
Surrey
GU16 5QE
TEL: 01276 671718

West Sussex Health Authority
The Causeway
Worthing
West Sussex
BN12 6BN
TEL: 01903 708400

North Thames

Barking and Havering Health
Authority
The Clock House
East Street
Barking
Essex
IG11 8EY
TEL: 0181 532 6201

Barnet Health Authority
Hyde House
The Hyde
Edgware Raod
London
NW9 6QQ
TEL: 0181 201 4701

Brent and Harrow Health Authority
Grace House
Harrovian Business Village
Bessborough Road
Harrow
Middlesex

HA1 3EX
TEL: 0181 422 6644

Camden and Islington Health
Authority
Hobson House
155 Gower Street
London
WC1E 6BH
TEL: 0171 383 4888

Ealing, Hammersmith and Hounslow
Health Authority
1 Armstrong Way
Southall
Middlesex
UB2 4SA
TEL: 0181 893 0303

East and North Hertfordshire Health
Authority
Charter House
Park Way
Welwyn Garden City
Herts
AL8 6JL
TEL: 01707 390864

East London Health Authority
81–91 Commrcial Road
London
E1 1RD
TEL: 0171 655 6666

Enfield and Haringey Health
Authority
Alexander Place
Lower Park Road
New Southgate
London
N11 1ST
TEL: 0181 361 7272

Hillingdon Health Authority
Kirk House
97–109 High Street
Yiewsley
West Drayton
Middlesex

UB7 7HJ
TEL: 01895 452000

Kensington, Chelsea and
    Westminster Health Authority
50 Eastbourne Terrace
London
W2 6LX
TEL: 0171 725 3333

North Essex Health Authority
Collingwood Road
Witham
Essex
CM8 2TT
TEL: 01376 516515

Redbridge and Waltham Forest
    Health Authority
Beckets House
2–14 Ilford Hill
Ilford
Essex
IG1 2QX
TEL: 0181 478 5151

South Essex Health Authority
Arcadia House
Warley Business Park
Brentwood
Essex
CM13 3AT
TEL: 01277 632127

West Hertfordshire Health
    Authority
Tenman House
63–77 Victoria Street
St Albans
Herts
AL1 3ER
TEL: 01727 792800

South and West

Avon Health Authority
King Square House
King Square

Bristol
BS2 8EE
TEL: 0117 976 6600

Cornwall and Isles of Scilly Health
    Authority
Tregonissey Road
St Austell
PL25 4QN
TEL: 01726 777777

Dorset Health Authority
Victoria House
Princes Road
Ferndown
BH22 9JR
TEL: 01202 893000

Gloucestershire Health Authority
Victoria Warehouse
The Docks
Gloucester
GL1 2EL
TEL: 01452 3000222

Isle of Wight Health Authority
Whitecroft
Sandy Lane
Newport
Isle of Wight
PO30 3ED
TEL: 01983 535455

North and East Devon Health
    Authority
Dean Clarke House
Southernhay East
Exeter
EX1 1PQ
TEL: 01392 406192

North and Mid Hampshire Health
    Authority
Harness House
Aldermaston Road
RG24 9NB
TEL: 01256 332288

Portsmouth and South East
Hampshire Health Authority
Finchdean House
Milton Road
Portsmouth
PO3 6DL
TEL: 01705 838340

Somerset Health Authority
Wellsprings Road
Taunton
TA2 7PQ
TEL: 01823 333491

South and West Devon Health
Authority
The Lescaze Offices
Shinners Bridge
Dartington
Devon
TQ9 6JE
TEL: 01803 866665

Southampton and South West
Hampshire Health Authority
Oakley Road
Southampton
SO16 4GX
TEL: 01703 725400

Wiltshire Health Authority
Southgate House
Pans Lane
Devizes
SN10 5EQ
TEL: 01380 728899

Northern Ireland

Eastern Health and Social Services
Board (EHSSB)
Champion House
12–22 Linenhall Street
Belfast
BT2 8BS
TEL: 01232 321313

Northern Health and Social Services
Board (NHSSB)
County Hall
182 Galgorm Road
Ballymena
BT42 1QB
TEL: 01266 662083

Southern Health and Social Services
Board (SHSSB)
Tower Hill
Armagh
BT61 9DR
TEL: 01861 410041

Western Health and Social Services
Board (WHSSB)
15 Gransha Park
Clooney Road
Londonderry
BT47 1TG
TEL: 01504 860086

Scotland

Argyll and Clyde Health Board
Ross House
Paisley
PA2 7BN
TEL: 0141 842 7200

Ayrshire and Arran Health Board
Boswell House
7–10 Arthur Street
Ayr
KA7 1QJ
TEL: 01298 611040

Borders Health Board
Huntlyburn House
Melrose
TD6 9DB
TEL: 08196 825500

Dumfries and Galloway Health Board
Grierson House
The Crichton
Bankhead Road

Dumfries
DG1 2ZG
TEL: 01387 246246

Fife Health Board
Springfield House
Cupar
Fife
KY15 5UP
TEL: 01334 656200

Forth Valley Health Board
33 Spittal Street
Stirling
FK8 1DX
TEL: 01786 463031

Grampian Health Board
Summerfield House
2 Eday Road
Aberdeen
AB9 8Q
TEL: 01224 663456

Greater Glasgow Health Board
Dalian House
PO Box 15329
350 St Vincent Street
Glasgow
G3 8YZ
TEL: 0141 201 4444

Highland Health Board
Beechwood Park
Inverness
IV2 3HG
TEL: 01463 239851

Lanarkshire Health Board
14 Beckford Street
Hamilton
ML3 0TA
TEL: 01698 281313

Lothian Health Board
148 The Pleasance
Edinburgh
EH8 9RS
TEL: 0131 536 9000

Orkney Health Board
Gordon House
New Scapa Road
Kirkwall
KW15 1BQ
TEL: 01856 885400

Shetland Health Board
Gilbert Bain Hospital
Lerwick
ZE1 0RB
TEL: 01595 696767

Tayside Health Board
PO Box 75
Luna Place
Dundee Technology Park
Dundee
DD2 1TP
TEL: 01382 561818

Western Isles Health Board
37 South Beach Street
Stornoway
PA87 2BN
TEL: 01851 702997

Health Education Board for Scotland
Woodburn House
Caanan Lane
Edinburgh
EH10 4SG
TEL: 0131 447 8044

Common Services Agency
Trinity Park House
South Trinity Road
Edinburgh
EH5 3SE
TEL: 0131 552 6355

Wales

Bro Taf Health Authority
6th Floor
Churchill House
Churchill Way
Cardiff

CF1 4TW
TEL: 01222 226216

Dyfed Powys Health Authority
St David's Hospital
Carmarthen
Dyfed SA31 3HB
TEL: 01267 234501

Gwent Health Authority
Mamhilad House
Mamhilad
Pontypool
Gwent
NP4 0YP
TEL: 01495 765065

Iechyd Morgannwg Health
41 High Street
Swansea
SA1 1LT
TEL: 01792 458066

North Wales Health Authority
Preswylfa
Hendy Road
Mold
Clwyd CH7 1PZ
TEL: 01352 700227

APPENDIX V

Useful Addresses

Abingdon Consultancy
80 Baker Road
Abingdon
Oxfordshire
OX14 5LJ
TEL: 01235 522480

Acumen Solutions
Concept House
271 High Street
Berkhamsted
Hertfordshire HP4 1AA
TEL: 01442 876633

The Amalfi Partnership
15 Durham Road
East Finchley
London N2 9DP
TEL: 0181 444 7178

Applied Research & Technologies
BT Laboratories
Martlesham Heath
Ipswich
Suffolk IP5 3RE

Glaxo Wellcome UK Ltd
Stockley Park West
Uxbridge
Middlesex UB11 1BT
TEL: 0181 990 9000
FAX: 0181 990 4321

The Help for Health Trust
Highcroft
Romsey Road
Winchester
Hampshire SO22 5D11
TEL: 01962 849100

Infection Management Ltd
81 Ox Lane
Harpenden
Hertfordshire
AL5 4PH
TEL: 01582 763331
FAX: 01582 763331

The Institute of Health Services
    Management (IHSM)
7-10 Chandos Street
London W1M 9DE
TEL: 0171 460 7654
FAX: 0171 460 7655

The Institute of Health
    Services Management
    Scottish Council
Mews Cottage
Bellevue Lane
Ayr KA7 2DA
TEL: 01292 280814
FAX: 01292 280814

London International Healthcare
11 Grove Road
Northwood
Middlesex HA 2AP
TEL: 01923 825634

NAHSPRO (National Association of
    Health Service Public Relations
    Officers)
Mid Staffordshire General
    Hospitals
Weston Road
Stafford
ST16 3SA
TEL: 01785 230485

NEXUS
Alexandra House
Alexandra Terrace
Guildford
Surrey GU! 3DA
TEL: 01483 306912
FAX: 01483 306125

Roffey Park Management Institute
Forest Road
Horsham
West Sussex
RH12 4TD
TEL: 01293 851644
FAX: 01293 851565

Index of Adverisers